LONDON'S
ODDITIES

Vicky Wilson

London's Oddities

Written by Vicky Wilson
Photography by Andrew Kershman & Susi Koch
Edited by Abigail Willis
Book design by Susi Koch & Lesley Gilmour

Second edition published in 2025 by
Metro Publications Ltd
London, United Kingdom
www.metropublications.com

Metro® is a registered trade mark of Associated Newspapers Limited. The METRO mark is under licence from Associated Newspapers Limited.

Printed and bound in China. This book is produced using paper from registered sustainable and managed sources.

ISBN 978-1-902910-83-3

MIX
Paper | Supporting
responsible forestry
FSC
www.fsc.org FSC® C016973

LONDON'S
ODDITIES

Acknowledgements

Many people have suggested London oddities to me, many of which are included in these pages. In addition, thanks to Tom Neville, Nancy Wilson and Dermot Wilson for accompanying me on often hectic trips around London – and to Tom for his always insightful comments on the resulting text. Thanks also to Andrew Kershman and Susi Koch of Metro Publications for suggesting this project to me and together with Lesley Gilmour for bringing it to life in print.

About the Author

Vicky Wilson is a writer and editor specialising in architecture and the arts and is the author of the Metro Publications guidebooks London's Houses, Walking Oxford and Walking Bristol. A former resident of a narrow boat moored in North London, she is now based in Bristol.

For anyone wanting more information, I would recommend the following websites:

bollardsoflondon.blogspot.co.uk
british-history.ac.uk/survey-london
c20society.org.uk
carolineld.blogspot.co.uk
cinematreasures.org
coalholesoflondon.wordpress.com
diamondgeezer.blogspot.co.uk
ghostsigns.co.uk
hatads.org.uk
hidden-london.com
historic-uk.com
historicengland.org.uk
ianvisits.co.uk
knowledgeoflondon.com
londoncanals.co.uk
londongardensonline.org.uk

londonhistorians.wordpress.com
londonist.com
londonremembers.com
londonsociety.org.uk
londonunveiled.com
medieval-london.blogspot.co.uk
memoirsofametrogirl.com
municipaldreams.wordpress.com
secret-london.co.uk
spitalfieldslife.com
stinkpipes.blogspot.co.uk
subbrit.org.uk
tiredoflondontiredoflife.com
underground-history.co.uk
victorianweb.org

"Look deep . . . and then you will
understand everything better."
Albert Einstein

St Antholin's spire, Round Hill

Foreword

Walking through most parts of London produces puzzles – entire buildings or bits of street furniture, monuments or memorials that seem out of place, out of time or simply inexplicable. Sometimes we are intrigued enough to explore their stories; sometimes they become so familiar we cease to notice their strangeness.

This book contains elements of the London streetscape that have piqued my own curiosity to the point where I have wanted to find out why they are as they are. Often that initial question has led to discoveries of other surprising artefacts, or to an appreciation of the quirks of the history and present regulation of the city. My findings are collected here as 'oddities' – though the word has many nuances. Some things would be odd under any circumstances, such as a pumping station in the form of an Egyptian temple or a stone bomb dedicated to the defenders of airstrikes. Some are the work of notably odd people, whether Horace Walpole's Strawberry Hill or the churches of Nicholas Hawksmoor. Some are odd by being relocated in new contexts, such as a Wren spire grounded in a 1960s housing estate or a South Seas whalebone in a suburban street. Some seem odd now because of the way the world has changed around them, such as the pioneering social housing experiments of the mid-19th and early 20th century, which put to shame London's current attempts to house its citizens. Some are odd through having survived redundancy and others through having been ingeniously repurposed.

Of course, one person's oddity is another person's norm, and not everything that is odd is interesting. For that reason I have included only those oddities that engaged me enough to make me want to research, revisit and write about them. This is a personal selection and other people, no doubt, would have come up with very different lists. On the whole, I have omitted items within museums, with the justification that part of a museum's purpose is to collect oddities; art, which by its very nature often sets out to explore an alternative vision of the world; the many pubs, restaurants or other commercial venues that trade on oddity to attract punters; and places whose oddity is accessible to the public only rarely. As you might expect, though, some oddities are just too interesting to exclude and exceptions to all of these rules appear in these pages.

London in the 21st century is changing so fast that significant landmarks – let alone mere curiosities – can be uprooted or destroyed in moments. Everything mentioned within these pages existed at the time of writing – though some, such as a Black Cat advertising sign on Dingley Road, disappeared between one draft and another. Others, such as the London Stone and Broadwick Street pump, were removed for safekeeping when the first edition was published but have now been reinstalled.

There are many excellent books and websites about London, but I would especially like to thank the ever-alert crew at Londonist.com for uncovering a seemingly never-ending stream of oddities within the capital. I am also grateful to the many London bloggers – as well as to websites specialising in everything from bollards to cinema design – for enriching my understanding of the streets that surround me.

Contents

Redefining
the City

1.1 Roman Walls
1.2 Great Fire of London

Roman wall at the Barbican Estate, see page 14

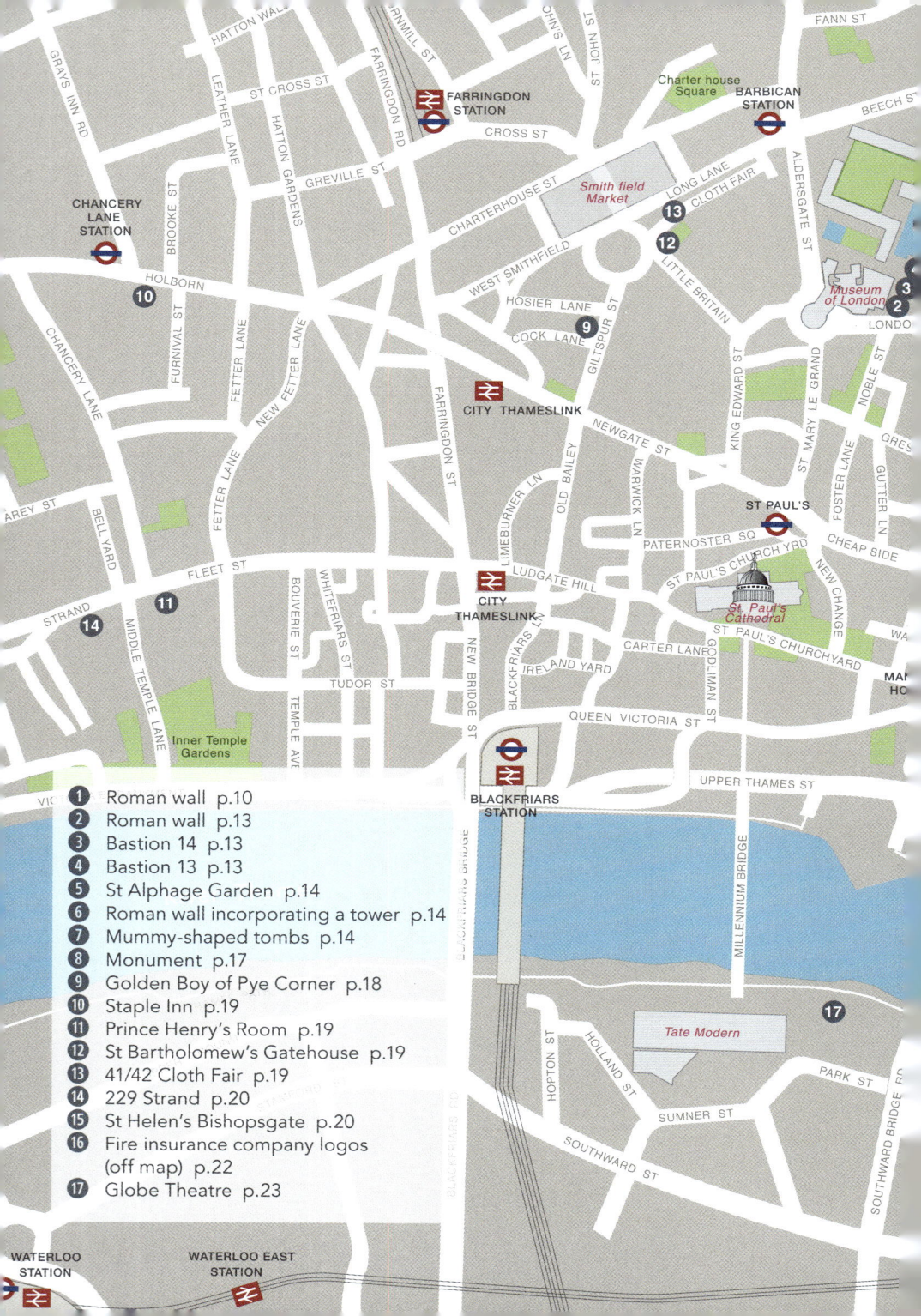

HATTON WALL
ST CROSS ST
GRAYS INN RD
LEATHER LANE
HATTON GARDENS
GREVILLE ST
FARRINGDON RD
JRNMILL ST
JOHN'S LN
ST JOHN ST
FANN ST
BEECH ST

FARRINGDON STATION
CROSS ST
Charter house Square
BARBICAN STATION

CHANCERY LANE STATION
HOLBORN
BROOKE ST
CHARTERHOUSE ST
Smith field Market
Long Lane
Cloth Fair
ALDERSGATE ST

13

WEST SMITHFIELD
12
LITTLE BRITAIN
Museum of London
3
2
LONDO

10
FURNIVAL ST
FETTER LANE
NEW FETTER LANE
HOSIER LANE
COCK LANE
GILTSPUR ST
9
KING EDWARD ST
ST MARY LE GRAND
FOSTER LANE
NOBLE ST
GUTTER LN
GRES

CHANCERY LANE
FETTER LANE
FARRINGDON ST
CITY THAMESLINK
NEWGATE ST
WARWICK LN
ST PAUL'S
PATERNOSTER SQ
CHEAP SIDE

LIMEBURNER LN
OLD BAILEY
LUDGATE HILL
ST PAUL'S CHURCH YRD
NEW CHANGE

AREY ST
BELL YARD
STRAND
14
11
FLEET ST
BOUVERIE ST
WHITEFRIARS ST
CITY THAMESLINK
St. Paul's Cathedral
ST PAUL'S CHURCHYARD
WA

MIDDLE TEMPLE LANE
TUDOR ST
TEMPLE AVE
NEW BRIDGE ST
BLACKFRIARS LN
IRELAND YARD
CARTER LANE
GODLIMAN ST
MAN HO

QUEEN VICTORIA ST

Inner Temple Gardens
UPPER THAMES ST

BLACKFRIARS STATION

MILLENNIUM BRIDGE
Tate Modern
17

HOPTON ST
HOLLAND ST
PARK ST
SOUTHWARK BRIDGE RD

SUMNER ST
SOUTHWARK ST

WATERLOO STATION
WATERLOO EAST STATION

1 Roman wall p.10
2 Roman wall p.13
3 Bastion 14 p.13
4 Bastion 13 p.13
5 St Alphage Garden p.14
6 Roman wall incorporating a tower p.14
7 Mummy-shaped tombs p.14
8 Monument p.17
9 Golden Boy of Pye Corner p.18
10 Staple Inn p.19
11 Prince Henry's Room p.19
12 St Bartholomew's Gatehouse p.19
13 41/42 Cloth Fair p.19
14 229 Strand p.20
15 St Helen's Bishopsgate p.20
16 Fire insurance company logos (off map) p.22
17 Globe Theatre p.23

Redefining the City

Bun hill Fields

CHISWELL ST

Barbican Centre

SILK ST

ROPEMAKER ST

MOOR LANE

MOORGATE STATION

WILSON ST

SUN STREET PASSA

BRUSHFIELD ST

16 →

WOOD ST

FORE ST

ST ALPHAGE GDN

5

ELDON ST

FINSBURY CIRCUS

LIVERPOOL ST

LIVERPOOL STREET STATION

BISHOPSGATE

MIDDLESEX ST

LONDON WALL

BASINGHALL AVE

ALDERMANBURY

BASINGHALL ST

COLEMAN ST

MOORGATE

THROGMORTON AVE

OLD BROAD ST

WORMWOOD ST

HOUNDSDITCH

BEVIS MARKS

ALDGATE

KING ST

OLD JEWRY

PRINCE'S ST

LOTHBURY

THREADNEEDLE ST

BISHOPSGATE

15

ST MARY AVE

ALDGATE HIGH ST

POULTRY

BANK

CORNHILL

LEADENHALL ST

JEWRY ST

MINORIES

QUEEN ST

QUEEN VICTORIA ST

WALBROOK

ST SWITHIN'S LN

KING WILLIAM ST

LOMBARD ST

GRACECHURCH ST

LIME ST

FENCHURCH ST

FENCHURCH STREET STATION

CRUTCHED FRIARS

CROSSWALL

CANNON ST

COLLEGE ST

CANNON STREET STATION

CANNON ST

MONUMENT

8

PUDDING LN

MINCING LANE

MARK LANE

GREAT TOWER ST

SEETHING LN

PEPYS ST

1

TOWER HILL

TO GAT

LOWER THAMES ST

BYWARD ST

TOWER HILL

Trinity Square Gardens

SOUTHWARK BRIDGE

LONDON BRIDGE

Tower of London

River Thames

PARK ST

STONEY ST

MONTAGUE CL

HMS Belfast

TOWER BRIDGE

TOOLEY ST

HAY'S LANE

LONDON BRIDGE STATION

LONDON BRIDGE ST

RD ST

Scoop City Hall

Potters Fields Park

1.1 Roman Walls

Walking around London today, you can't help but be confounded by the scale of new development. Clusters of cranes perform an automaton dance against a backdrop of ever-changing skies; hoardings depicting ostentatious new buildings with ridiculous names bar access to pavements and obscure familiar features from public view. Destroyed by the Great Fire in the mid-17th century and severely damaged by the Blitz 300 years later, the City of London has been rebuilt again and again. So perhaps it is not surprising that so little of Roman London – Londinium – survives in any accessible form.

Established in 43CE, Londinium was for almost 500 years an important port and substantial settlement of between 30,000 and 60,000 people, about one-tenth the size of Rome. It reached its zenith in the 2nd century before declining 300 years later as the Romans abandoned Britain to the Anglo-Saxons. Occupying roughly the same area as the City of London today, it was protected by the river to the south and by a defensive 3-mile-long wall on its landward side, stretching in a rough semi-circle from the Tower of London to Blackfriars in a series of straight sections that linked Aldgate, Bishopsgate, Cripplegate, Newgate and Ludgate. Built at some point between 190 and 225CE, the wall constituted a substantial construction project, if minor in scale compared to the 73 miles of Hadrian's Wall, erected to impress the emperor on a visit in 122CE and to defend his dominion's northern perimeter from the barbarians beyond.

The ground level of Londinium was up to 7 metres below the level of the current City, yet fragments of the wall still break the surface in surprising places. One of the oddest sections of this ❶ **Roman wall**, in its juxtaposition of old and new, can be found in the courtyard of the Grange City Hotel in Cooper's Row near Tower Hill. Walk through the bar or under the porte cochère and you find yourself confronted by a substantial and obviously ancient stretch of brick and stone. One end pokes into a tiled recess cluttered with flimsy aluminium chairs and tables; a row of fussy ornamental trees in pots only serves to strengthen the contrast between the robust, purposeful and enduring defensive wall and the frivolous superfluity and ephemerality of its new surroundings.

About 6 metres high and 2.5 metres thick, London's Roman wall consisted of a sandstone plinth supporting a rubble-and-mortar core faced and capped with Kentish ragstone and interspersed at intervals with horizontal courses of tile bonding. At Cooper's Row the lower half of the visible structure is Roman and you can see both the ragstone and double courses of tiles. On the other side, accessed through a gap, you can clearly identify the sloped base of the plinth. Above the Roman section of the wall, reached via a double staircase on the inner or hotel side, is a medieval sentry walk with loopholes that offered the archers within a wide field of fire but those without only a narrow opening to aim at. The arrangement is unprecedented on other stretches of wall, possibly indicating that special defensive measures were introduced in the area around the Tower.

We know that Londinium contained a three-storey basilica fronting a generous 2-hectare forum as well as baths, an amphitheatre and a Mithraeum or temple to Mithras, the head of a mystery religion open only to initiates. Ironically much of this – as well as the wall itself – would not have been unearthed were it not for subsequent demolition and development or bomb damage from WW2.

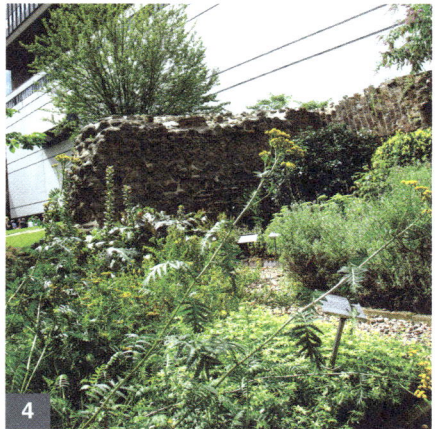

A fragment of the base of an arch of the basilica discovered during the construction of Leadenhall Market at the end of the 19th century now sits in the basement of hairdresser Nicholson & Griffin on Gracechurch Street. The Mithraeum was found in the 1950s during the construction of Bucklersbury House in Queen Victoria Street; it was dug up and moved some 90 metres down the road, where it remained on show for half a century before being dug up again to make way for another wave of construction. Returned to near its original site, it can now be viewed in a purpose-built display space as part of Bloomberg's European headquarters at 12 Walbrook.

Also the subject of a dedicated display are fragments of Londinium's amphitheatre – the eastern entrance, segments of the curved arena wall and some timber drains – discovered under the Guildhall Art Gallery during its redevelopment in 1985 and now shown in situ. A gathering place where up to 10,000 spectators would watch events sponsored by wealthy individuals, the amphitheatre hosted wild animal hunts and gladiatorial combats, in which slaves fought to the death, as well as public executions. It makes today's sporting competitions look distinctly civilised.

Most of the other accessible remains of London's Roman wall are clustered around London Wall itself. Perhaps the most bizarre – and least visited – is an 11-metre-long fragment of ❷ **Roman wall** that now resides underground in London Wall car park, having been uncovered in 1953 during the car park's construction. Despite its age, the wall has a sturdiness and sophistication of detailing that contrasts with the crude, leaking tunnel that surrounds it. With the top of the sandstone plinth level with the car park floor, the visible section above has a triple course of tile bonding at its base, with triple and double courses above; the back and sides have lost their external ragstone

facing, exposing the rubble core. Walking the length of the echoing car park can be an unsettling experience, even if you are not hunting down the ghosts of Roman soldiers; to avoid a long tramp underground enter at Brewers' Hall Garden, just east of the point where the overbearing Alban Gate crosses the street.

Near the main car park entrance you can find two of the twenty or so bastions that once punctuated the wall. The ruins of ❸ **bastion 14**, now squatting in front of Richard Rogers' Wood Street office building and Alban Gate, were topped by a medieval tower and later faced internally with brick to serve as a house and then warehouse during the 19th century. Street surveys from the 1840s show the bastion completely integrated into the surrounding buildings, and its historical significance was not recognised until the area was bombed during WW2. Traces of the Roman foundations are still visible along with the brick lining and remains of a staircase.

❹ **Bastion 13** was incorporated as an apse into the Court Room of the Barber-Surgeons' Hall, built in the early 1600s before being destroyed by the Great Fire, rebuilt, and then destroyed again during the Blitz. An oddity in itself, the Barber-Surgeons' guild was an unlikely-sounding unification of the two professions dating from a 1540 Act of Parliament that stipulated that no surgeon could perform the duties of a barber and vice versa, but both could extract teeth. The red and white striped poles still advertising barbers' shops today recognise the amalgamation, with red denoting surgeons and white barbers. Among the ruins here you can distinguish recesses that once held fireplaces, slots for joists and bricks pocked to receive render. The interior of the bastion itself – where you can see the substantial Roman infrastructure along with the sloping brickwork that formed the grand apse – now shelters a physic garden of medicinal plants in commemoration of the garden created on the same site in 1597 by botanist and surgeon John Gerard.

Other remains of London's Roman wall can be found along Noble Street and in ❺ St Alphage Garden, where the Roman base is topped with red brick with a diaper pattern of twice-baked blackened bricks and crenellations added in the mid-15th century. But the most incongruous survivals are scattered through the Barbican Estate, a pioneering and unashamedly Brutalist housing development and cultural centre built in the 1960s and 1970s to repopulate an area that had become deserted outside business hours (following the destruction of WW2, the population of the parish of Cripplegate had sunk to less than 50). The Roman Cripplegate fort pre-dated the construction of the wall by about a century but the visible remains here are largely from the medieval period, when long stretches of wall were rebuilt, a defensive ditch was dug around the outside and a series of towers was added. From the 13th century some of the towers were appropriated as defences against the outside world by hermits from the nearby Church of St James in the Wall.

In a surreal conjunction of old and new, an extensive section of ❻ Roman wall incorporating a tower now stands at the edge of one of the estate's ornamental lakes, which itself marks the position of the medieval ditch; openings in the coarse stonework of the ancient structure offer glimpses of the sophisticated amalgam of brick, concrete and glazing that makes up the elevations of the 20th-century housing behind. Another tower, faced in roughly dressed stone with its rubble core visible where the circle is incomplete, has survived at about two-thirds of its original height, a sturdy sentry from a former age abandoned among the slender concrete posts and walkways of the new development.

The curious row of ❼ mummy-shaped tombs mounted on a plinth beside the lake date from the early 19th century.

Roman builders were pioneers in city planning as well as in the use of brick and concrete, so it is perhaps appropriate that the most visible remains of their efforts in London are now housed within a complex that launched a utopian approach to inner-city planning and made stunning use of the two materials. Designed by architects Chamberlin, Powell and Bon, the Barbican's mix of sculpted concrete towers, low-rise terraces, streets in the sky criss-crossing an extensive pedestrianised zone, urban landscaping and cultural facilities proved that Brutalism, with the correct levels of maintenance, did not inevitably generate social alienation (though the lack of signage can produce discombobulation).

The rate of new development in London today means the life cycle of City structures can be nearer to 20 than 2,000 years. Yet it is in part thanks to ongoing waves of destruction and renewal that the layers of Londinium's history have been uncovered. The remains may be fragmentary in comparison with Roman survivals in other major cities of the empire, but their rarity and unlikely settings make them special – as well as odd.

1. Roman wall,
   Grange City Hotel Courtyard,
   Cooper's Row, EC3N 2BQ
2. Roman wall, car park,
   23 London Wall, EC2V 5DY
3. Bastion 14, London Wall, EC2V 5DY
4. Bastion 13, London Wall, EC2V 5DY
5. St Alphage Garden, EC2Y 5EL
6. Cripplegate Tower,
   Barbican Estate, EC2Y 8BH
7. Tombs, Wallside,
   Barbican Estate, EC2Y 8DS

5

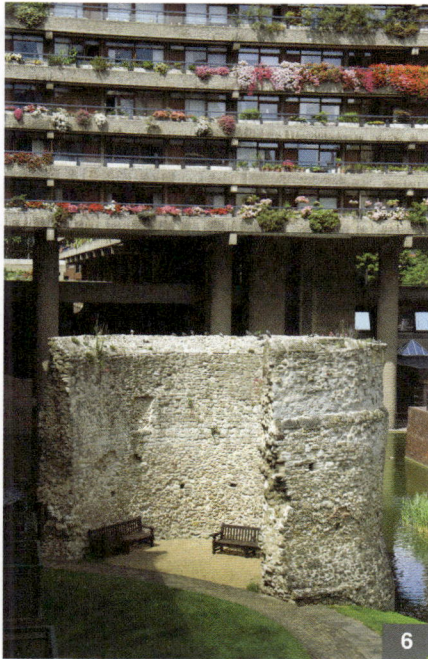

6

6

7

1.2 Great Fire of London

Every six-year-old in England seems to learn about the Great Fire of London, the conflagration that swept through the City's medieval streets between 2 and 5 September 1666, destroying the overcrowded alleys that lay within the Roman defensive wall, from the Tower of London in the east to Temple in the west, and from the river in the south to Moorgate in the north. Unsurprisingly, such a dramatic event has left a legacy of London oddities that range from memorials and survivals to planning decisions and protective legislation.

The fire began in the bakery of Thomas Farriner (or Farynor) on Pudding Lane near London Bridge one Sunday evening; its rapid progress through the overcrowded warren of streets was helped by Londoners' habit of extending their wood-framed properties with projecting upper storeys or jetties that almost touched across the narrow lanes. It was eventually to consume some 13,000 houses and more than 80 churches – not least because Lord Mayor Thomas Bloodworth initially insisted that 'a woman could piss it out' and so delayed ordering buildings to be demolished to create firebreaks. While the death toll has been claimed to be in single figures, it is likely that the intense heat meant few corpses were recovered and the deaths of the poor went largely unrecorded.

Christopher Wren and others submitted plans for rebuilding the City on a grid of grand avenues, circuses and squares, but difficulties in settling compensation claims and an economy depleted by the Anglo-Dutch wars meant new buildings largely followed pre-fire lines, albeit with wood replaced by stone and improvements in safety and hygiene. It was a missed opportunity for London to attain the baroque elegance of Paris or Stockholm, making the City of London itself something of an oddity – the sort of wholesale recreation in different materials pursued by some German cities following the destruction of WW2. Roman London was in fact built on a grid, but the narrowness of the streets and changes wrought in the medieval period make the pattern virtually imperceptible from the ground, so to walk through the tangle of courts and lanes around Smithfield Market or Fleet Street feels like revisiting an era when towns grew organically.

Memorials

The ❽ **Monument**, still the tallest freestanding stone column in the world, was commissioned by Charles II to commemorate the fire and promote his own role as saviour of the City. Mounted on a massive 12-metre-high pedestal and topped by a gilded urn of fire – itself an economy measure since the planned statue of the king proved too costly – its height of 61 metres marks the distance between its location in Monument Street and the Pudding Lane bakery where the fire began. Though denied his place at the summit, Charles does play a prominent role in the extraordinary allegorical relief created by Caius Gabriel Cibber for the pedestal, where he is depicted in full wig and cloak offering help to a semi-naked woman (representing the City) overcome by heat from the billowing flames. The royal pose, legs turned out and hand on hip, is identical to that of the statue in the centre of Soho Square, also by Cibber.

Even today, flanked by more recent skyscrapers such as the bullying Walkie Talkie and the slender Shard across the river, the Monument's eruption in the narrow streets is extraordinary. But there is another reason for its classification as an oddity. Designed by Christopher Wren and scientist Robert Hooke, who were soon to collaborate on Greenwich Observatory, the fluted column was conceived as a giant telescope, with a basement observation station below the hollow core and open top. Unfortunately vibrations from wind and traffic made it unfit for purpose.

Though baker Thomas Farriner had admitted the fire was started by sparks from his oven, conspiracy theories to explain the scale of the disaster abounded and in 1681 an inscription blaming 'Popish frenzy' for the devastation was added to the north side of the Monument's pedestal. The words were chiselled out in 1830, but the claim is repeated in the dedication below the ❾ **Golden Boy of Pye Corner**, a statue at first-floor level at the junction of Cock Lane and Giltspur Street, whose inscription also bizarrely attributes the cause of the fire to 'the sin of gluttony'. Though the wooden carving of a plump naked boy – his arms folded across his belly, perhaps indicating shame – is claimed to mark the spot where the fire stopped, historians believe it is more likely that he was originally a shop sign and the inscriptions were added later. In the late 19th century the statue was gilded, giving him unintended connotations of Buddhist idols or even greedy bankers (by coincidence, his face bears a striking resemblance to Thatcherite chancellor Nigel Lawson as a young man).

8. Monument, Monument St, EC3R 8AH
    www.themonument.info
9. Golden Boy of Pye Corner, corner of
    Cock Lane & Giltspur St, EC1A 9DD

Survivors

The near-wholesale destruction wrought by the fire automatically confers the status of oddities on the area's few surviving buildings. ⑩ **Staple Inn** in High Holborn, an undulating terrace of half-timbered buildings dating from 1585, probably offers the clearest picture of how London's medieval street façades might have looked. The five bays to the east were part of the original Inn of Chancery, which provided training for would-be lawyers as well as the premises where wool was weighed and taxed. The two slightly more elaborate bays to the west, with an extra half storey and small projections at each end, were a house.

Following new building regulations, several Great Fire survivors had their medieval timbers covered over for a couple of centuries or more – Staple Inn in fireproof plaster and ⑪ **Prince Henry's Room**, the gateway to the Inner Temple on Fleet Street, by an elaborate false front that was not removed until 1900. During the 18th century the building was a waxworks museum with intriguing exhibits including a recreation of the execution of Charles I and a clockwork model that kicked passers-by.

⑫ **St Bartholomew's Gatehouse**, a timber structure built in 1595 on top of what was once the southern entrance to the nave of the church in West Smithfield, is another rare survivor whose Tudor origins – including a shield with the coat of arms of original resident William Scudamore above the stone archway – were revealed only following bomb damage during WW1. Archive photographs from the early 20th century show an inconspicuous brick façade with signs for 'C. Burrell: Dealer in Pickled Tongues, Sweetbreads' and the strange combination of 'Booksellers & Tobacconists'. Seen from the street today, it looks like a simple two-storey building topped by a small attic gable but from the churchyard you can see that it steps back through its three floors.

⑬ **41/42 Cloth Fair**, built between 1597 and 1614 as part of a complex of eleven dwellings grouped around a square, survived thanks to the protection of the walls of St Bartholomew's priory. A walk through Cloth Court, the alley at the side of the building, conveys the claustrophobia of the narrow medieval streets much more evocatively than the pristine, over-restored façade on Cloth Fair itself. You can get

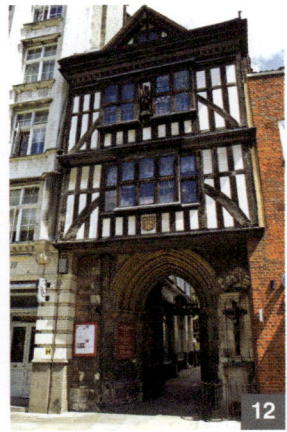

a good idea of the way medieval houses spread across the street (known today as exploiting air rights) from **14** **229 Strand**. Built in 1625, this building has two sets of jetties, with an overhang at first-floor level and a further projection for supporting its top two storeys.

Stone buildings such as the Guildhall, the Tower and some of the City's churches survived total destruction – as well as churches on the periphery where a 'miraculous' change of wind direction halted the fire's progress. Now dwarfed by 30 St Mary Axe (the Gherkin), the largest of the pre-fire churches in the City is **15** **St Helen's Bishopsgate**, which has the distinction of having survived the Great Fire and both World Wars before suffering damage in the 1992-93 IRA bombing campaign. It is also an oddity in being made up of two parallel churches set side by side after a nunnery was added to the existing building at the start of the 13th century: records from 1385 complain of the nuns 'winking and waving' at the lay congregation over the screens dividing the two structures. Within the nuns' quire you can still see the narrow door leading to the dormitory from which they would emerge to sing Matins at 3am as well as the 'squint' – a series of small stone arches through

which nuns too sick to attend services could glimpse the rituals.

Walking round the back of the church reveals layers of history, with Saxon masonry and Roman bricks reused from previous buildings intermingled with traces of medieval window arches and a fine row of gargoyles. One of the two doorways was given an elaborate classical frontispiece in 1633 and the other is an elegant pastiche created by Quinlan Terry as part of the 1990s restoration. There is also a plaque to Robert Hooke, co-designer of the Monument, who was buried here until the end of the 19th century when his remains were removed to the City of London Cemetery at Wanstead along with hundreds of other decaying bodies deemed to be a health hazard. A commemorative window to Hooke was destroyed in the IRA blast.

10. Staple Inn, High Holborn, WC1V 7PZ
11. Prince Henry's Room,
    17 Fleet St, EC4Y 1AA
12. St Bartholomew's Gatehouse,
    West Smithfield, EC1A 7BE
13. 41/42 Cloth Fair, EC1A 7JQ
14. 229 Strand, WC2R 1BA
15. St Helen's Bishopsgate, EC3A 6AT

15

Legacy

One of the results of the Great Fire was the development of property insurance, with each individual insurance company establishing its own fire brigade to minimise compensation claims. By 1690, ten per cent of houses were insured and properties displayed the companies' moulded **16** **lead, copper or terracotta logos** at first-floor level. You can still see some of these on houses today including a collection in Princelet Street in Shoreditch: notably for the Phoenix company, established in 1782 to provide protection to sugar bakers and refineries (the plaque depicts a silver-painted phoenix rising from the flames with the word 'protection' underneath); for the Sun company, founded at the start of the 18th century and still in operation today; for Salop, with its logo of three leopard heads, the arms of its home town of Shrewsbury; and for Hand-in-Hand, established in 1696 at Tom's Coffee House in St Martin's Lane, with a plaque depicting clasped hands topped by a crown. The figures beneath are the householders' policy numbers. Obviously the system was flawed, with rival companies ignoring burning buildings insured by others, so in 1833 the London Fire Engine Establishment was created, funded through contributions from the individual firms, to provide an organisation that would answer any call.

The Great Fire also saw the introduction of planning regulations, with Charles II declaring that 'no man whatsoever shall presume to erect any House or Building, great or small, but of Brick, or Stone, and if any man shall do the contrary, the next Magistrate shall forthwith cause it to be pulled down'. A similar ban on thatch persists to the present, with the result that over 300 years after the Great Fire, special permission had to be granted to reconstruct the **17 Globe Theatre** on Bankside with a thatched roof – the only example in central London.

16. Fire insurance company logos,
    Princelet St, E1 6QH
17. Globe Theatre, Bankside, SE1 9DT

17

Kirkaldy's Testing Works, see page 48

Infrastructure, Industry & Amenity

HIGHGATE

Hampstead
Heath

HOL

CRICKLEWOOD

Shoot Up Hill

KILBURN

SWISS COTTAGE

BELSIZE PARK

CHALK FARM

PRIMROSE HILL

CAMDEN TOWN

BARNS

38

London
Zoo

35

KING'S
CROSS

Regent's
Park

KENSAL

MAIDA VALE

LADBROKE

GROVE

Westway

Edgware Rd

PADDINGTON

MARYLEBONE

BLOOMSBURY

Oxford St

SOHO

4

WHITE CITY

NOTTING HILL

BAYSWATER

11

Bayswater Rd

MAYFAIR

Trafalgar
Square

3

28

Kensington
Park

Hyde Park

6

SHEPHERDS
BUSH

Green
Park

St James's
Park

Westminster
Bridge

19

KNIGHTSBRIDGE

Buckingham
Palace

HAMMERS

WESTMINSTER

Lambeth
Bridge

LAM

King's Rd

PIMLICO

17

Tate
Britain

VAUXHA

CHELSEA

FULHAM

Lambeth

Putney Lower
Common

Bishops

STOCKWELL

PUTNEY

Park

WANDSWORTH

Clapham
Common

26

20

24

39

27

Wandsworth

List of sites

1. Panyer Boy p.28
2. Stone boundary marker p.28
3. London Stone p.28
4. Tyburn Gate marker p.29
5. Tower Street sign p.30
6. Trafalgar Square standards p.30
7. Greenwich Observatory standards p.30

8. Greenwich Meridian p.31
9. Crossness Pumping Station (off map) p.33
10. Isle of Dogs Pumping Station p.35
11. 23–24 Leinster Gardens p.36
12. Gibson Square ventilation shaft p.36
13. Circus Place obelisk p.36
14. Greathead ventilation shaft p.36
15. 'Pineapple' ventilation shaft p.38
16. Paternoster Vents p.38
17. Eduardo Paolozzi ventilation shaft p.38
18. Plant enclosure & shaft, Culling Road p.38
19. Wellington Arch p.39
20. Weihurst Gardens (off map) p.40
21. Albany Road p.40
22. Kennington Cross p.40
23. Royal Courts of Justice p.40
24. Tooting Broadway (off map) p.40
25. Three Mills p.42
26. Wimbledon Windmill (off map) p.44
27. Brixton Windmill p.44
28. Bottle Kiln p.46
29. Kirkaldy's Testing Works p.48

30. London's 'Roman Baths' p.50
31. New Broad Street Baths p.52
32. Greenman Street Baths p.52
33. Finsbury Health Centre p.55
34. Bevin Court p.56
35. Penguin Pool at London Zoo p.56
36. Former Apollo p.59
37. Former Carlton p.59
38. Former Gaumont State p.59
39. Former Tooting Granada (off map) p.59
40. Former Granada (off map) p.62
41. Former Coronet (off map) p.62
42. Black Friar Public House p.63

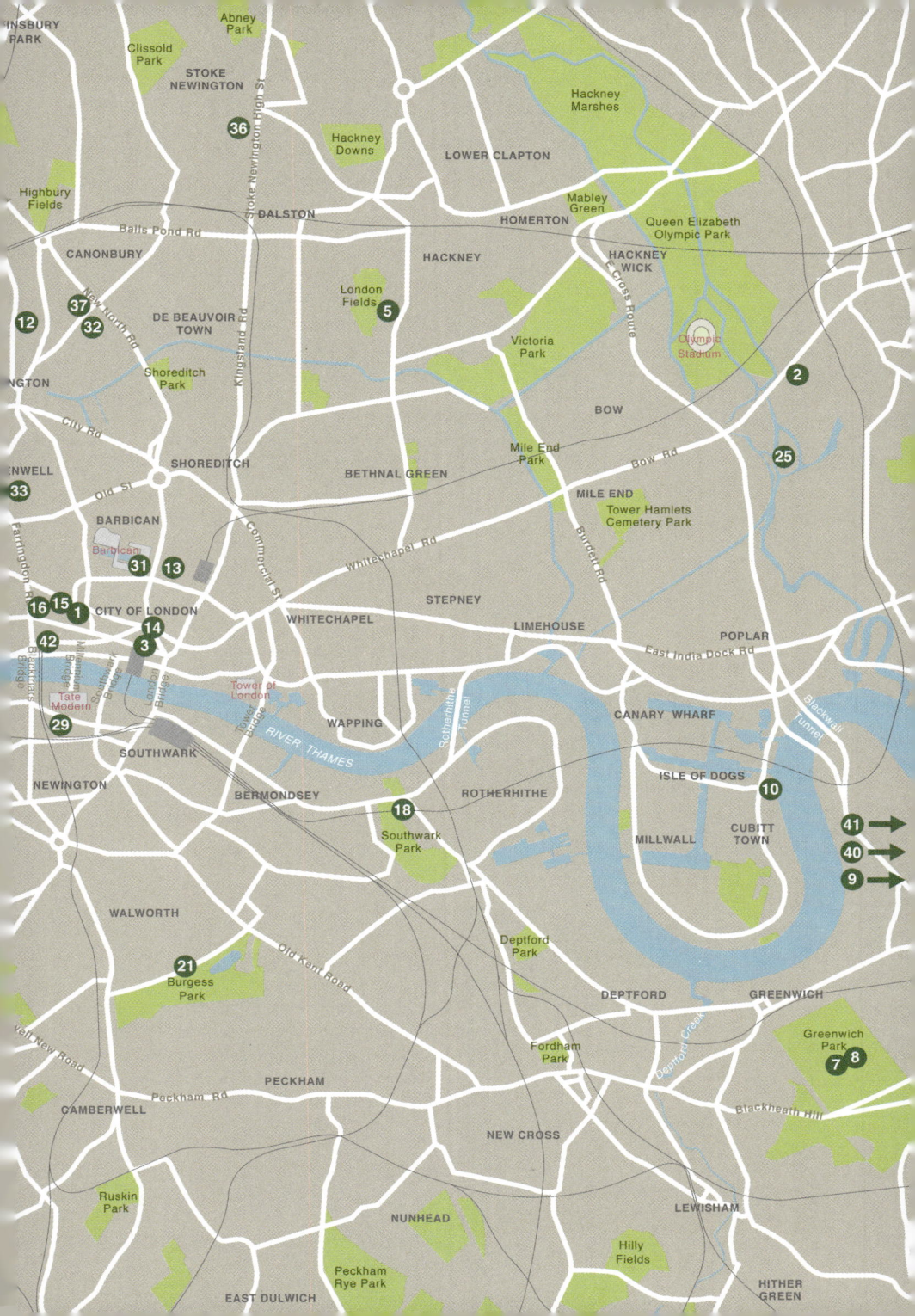

FINSBURY PARK
Abney Park
Clissold Park
STOKE NEWINGTON
36
Hackney Marshes
Hackney Downs
LOWER CLAPTON
Highbury Fields
Balls Pond Rd
DALSTON
HOMERTON
Mabley Green
Queen Elizabeth Olympic Park
HACKNEY WICK
CANONBURY
12
37
32
DE BEAUVOIR TOWN
London Fields
5
HACKNEY
Victoria Park
E.Cross Route
Olympic Stadium
2
New North Rd
Shoreditch Park
Kingsland Rd
BOW
City Rd
NWELL
33
SHOREDITCH
BETHNAL GREEN
Mile End Park
Bow Rd
25
Farringdon Rd
Old St
BARBICAN
Barbican
31
13
Commercial St
Whitechapel Rd
MILE END
Tower Hamlets Cemetery Park
Burdett Rd
16
15
1
CITY OF LONDON
14
3
STEPNEY
WHITECHAPEL
LIMEHOUSE
POPLAR
42
Blackfriars Bridge
Millennium Bridge
Southwark Bridge
London Bridge
Tower Bridge
Tower of London
East India Dock Rd
Blackwall Tunnel
29
Tate Modern
SOUTHWARK
WAPPING
RIVER THAMES
Rotherhithe Tunnel
CANARY WHARF
NEWINGTON
BERMONDSEY
ROTHERHITHE
ISLE OF DOGS
10
18
Southwark Park
MILLWALL
CUBITT TOWN
41
40
9
WALWORTH
21
Burgess Park
Old Kent Road
Deptford Park
DEPTFORD
GREENWICH
well New Road
PECKHAM
Peckham Rd
Fordham Park
Greenwich Park
7
8
CAMBERWELL
Ruskin Park
NUNHEAD
NEW CROSS
Blackheath Hill
LEWISHAM
Peckham Rye Park
Hilly Fields
EAST DULWICH
HITHER GREEN

2.1 Measures & Markers

London still has milestones, plaques and posts that mark historically significant distances and boundaries, but their claims should be treated with caution. For instance, the ❶ **Panyer Boy** in Panyer Alley near St Paul's Underground – a low-relief plaque dated 27 August 1688 that depicts a boy sitting on a basket – bears the inscription 'When Ye have sought the Citty Round / Yet still this is the highest Ground'. It may have seemed so in the 17th century, but modern surveying shows that of the two hills on which the Roman settlement of Londinium was founded, it is Cornhill rather than Ludgate Hill – the site of St Paul's and the plaque – that is marginally higher. Some sources claim the boy represents Bacchus and was a sign for the Panyer pub, destroyed in the Great Fire of 1666, in which case the image predates the inscription. Others suggest he is sitting on

a bread basket and was created as a sign for the bakers' market in nearby Bread Street.

A more unlikely claim – but which turns out to be true – is made on a ❷ **stone boundary marker** at the junction of the High Street and Rick Roberts Way in Stratford. This states that the estate of St Mary Rotherhithe – over four miles to the south on the other side of the Thames – 'extends 5 feet 3 inches northward of this stone'. Dating from 1731, the obelisk in fact delineates the boundary of land purchased in 1659 in trust for the poor of the parish – an excellent investment, to judge by the shiny apartment building beside which it now stands.

❸ **London Stone**, opposite Cannon Street station, is a marker whose history is still imbued with mystery. The relic is claimed by some to be part of a Roman milestone that once stood at the heart of the City and was the point from which all distances to the rest of Roman Britain were measured. Others believe it was an object of prehistoric Druidic worship and still others that it is a talismanic monument whose safeguarding ensures that London will continue to flourish.

The stone was obviously well known by the 12th century, when 'de Lundenstane' appeared as a surname for people living nearby. Shakespeare used it as the site for a rabble-rousing speech by 1450s revolutionary Jack Cade in *Henry VI, Part 2*: 'And here, sitting / upon London-stone, I charge and command that, of the / city's cost, the pissing-conduit run nothing but / claret wine this first year of our reign.' By Elizabethan times London Stone also acted as a tourist attraction: it is recorded by a French visitor in *Les Singularitez de Londres* as measuring the equivalent of 90 x 60 x 30 centimetres.

1

Today the stone's dimensions are only 53 x 43 x 30 centimetres and references from the 1670s to the 'remayning parte' of London Stone imply it may have been damaged during the Great Fire. In 1742 it was moved to the north side of the street beside Wren's St Swithin's church; in 1962, when the church's bomb-damaged remains were demolished, it was set into the wall of the building that replaced it, protected by a decorative iron grille that had been provided by the London Archeological Society in 1869. Until early 2016 the best way to see the stone was to peer behind the magazine rack in the WH Smith shop at 111 Cannon Street – a very odd way of catching a glimpse of a landmark that was once central to London's sense of itself. The stone's Cannon Street home was redeveloped in recent years and it briefly found refuge in the Museum of London. It has now returned to the site to grace the exterior of the new building.

Just as incongruous in its present setting is a ❹ stone inscribed 'half-a-mile from Tyburn Gate' that now stands on a tatty wooden plinth in the porch of the Hilton Metropole at the junction of Edgware Road and the Westway. Tyburn Gate, at what is now Marble Arch, was the site of the Tyburn gallows (see page 234), and the reminder of gruesome mass public hangings sits oddly within the bland anonymity of an international hotel. Probably erected between 1760 and 1829, at which point the gallows had been replaced by a toll gate, the stone was removed in 1886 to make way for new development and put into storage; in 1909 it was presented by the developers to the London County Council, which mounted it outside a bank on the site; when that in turn was demolished in 1930 the stone disappeared from public view before reappearing at the hotel entrance when it opened 60 years later.

London Stone was well enough known to form part of 17th-century addresses (as

LONDON STONE

in 'neere London stone'), but London's most distinctive address belongs to Apsley House on the south-east corner of Hyde Park. Built by Robert Adam in the 1770s and the former home of the Duke of Wellington, it was the first house after the Knightsbridge tollgate and so became known simply as Number One, London.

Londoners had to wait another century for the system that gave the city its postal districts. Introduced in 1856 by social reformer Rowland Hill, the inventor of a postage stamp that enabled the cost to be paid by the sender rather than the recipient, this divided the capital into ten areas: N, S, E, W, NE, NW, SE, SW, WC and EC. The success of the initiative was evaluated a decade later by novelist Anthony Trollope, who worked for the General Post Office (GPO) for some 30 years. Trollope found that the S and NE postcodes were underused: S was subsumed into SE or SW but the authorities balked at officially merging NE into E because of residents' snobbish disdain for East London. So initially letters addressed NE were simply piled up and sorted along with E district mail without anyone being told.

A reminder of the NE district remains in the ❺ **street sign for Tower Street** on the corner of Martello Terrace and Martello Street in Hackney (Tower Street changed its name to Martello Street in 1938). The only area outside Greater London with a London postcode is the village of Sewardstone, still designated by the postal services as E4, despite being 12 miles north of Trafalgar Square and administered by the Epping Forest district of Essex.

Since the late 13th century distances to London have been marked from the south of Trafalgar Square, where the statue of Charles I now stands (a plaque marks the spot). But Trafalgar Square is also the site of an odder set of measuring devices: the ❻ **Trafalgar Square standards**, against

which anyone could (and can) check the accuracy of their ruler or measuring tape. The standards were created by a commission chaired by astronomer and mathematician George Airy between 1838 and 1842 after the previous set was destroyed along with most of the Palace of Westminster in a fire caused by overloading the furnace with an old form of wooden receipts known as tally sticks.

Three new sets of standards were produced – one for the Guildhall, one for the ❼ **gate of the Royal Greenwich Observatory** below the Shepherd Gate clock (see page 103) and the third installed on the north side of Trafalgar Square in 1876. Relocated slightly following the pedestrianisation of the area in 2003, they consist of a brass plaque that shows the correct lengths of 1 foot, 2 feet and an imperial yard as well as plaques showing a chain (66 feet), a pole or perch (16.5 feet or a quarter of a chain) and 100 feet (moving west) as well as links (moving east; 100 links make a chain). The measurements on the main plaque are only accurate at 62 degrees Fahrenheit (the metal expands or contracts at higher or lower temperatures), so you probably need to bring along a thermometer too if you want to test their accuracy.

George Airy was also responsible for establishing another London standard: the prime or ❽ **Greenwich Meridian** at the Royal Greenwich Observatory, which separates the eastern and western hemispheres in the same way as the equator separates north from south. Its primacy was adopted in 1884 following a conference of delegates from 25 nations (the French abstained, and clung on to the primacy of the Paris Meridian for several decades). The line was formerly marked by a brass strip, now upgraded to stainless steel and supplemented at night with a green laser beam. Unbeknown to the many tourists who queue to stand with one foot in each of the eastern and western worlds, recent technology has shown that Airy's measuring technique was flawed. Since the 1990s, the official meridian has been designated as lying some 100 metres to the east of the tourist line.

1. Panyer Boy, corner of Cheapside & Panyer Alley, EC2V 6AA
2. Boundary marker, corner of High St & Rick Roberts Way, Stratford, E15 2FP
3. London Stone, Cannon St, EC4N
4. Tyburn Gate marker, 225 Edgware Rd, W2 1JU
5. Tower Street sign, Martello St, E8 3PE
6. Trafalgar Square standards, WC2N 5DN
7. Shepherd Gate standards, Greenwich Observatory, Blackheath Ave, SE10 8JX
8. Greenwich Meridian, Greenwich Observatory, Blackheath Ave, SE10 8JX
   www.rmg.co.uk/royal-observatory

2.2 Waste & Water

Crossness Pumping Station

The first thing you notice when you arrive at ⑨ **Crossness sewage works** is the stench – perhaps hardly surprising, since the site on Bazalgette Way in Abbey Wood has been processing London's human waste for 150 years. More extraordinary is the old pumping station itself, a group of solid Victorian industrial buildings housing machines of impressive scale and beauty. On open days this redundant temple to waste disposal is staffed by volunteers in bowler hats and frock coats (men who tend the machines) or long skirts and pinnies (women who serve Victoria sponges and cream teas), while visitors don hard hats that seem unreassuringly flimsy in relation to the vast engines that drive the pumps. But even odder in social terms is the story of London's sewage disposal, in which poor areas to the east became a dumping ground for the millions of gallons of waste produced each day by the city's wealthier inhabitants upriver.

Popularisation of the flush toilet following the Great Exhibition of 1851 may have improved personal hygiene, but it had dire consequences for London's sewerage system. Domestic WCs usually emptied into inadequate cesspits that overflowed into rainwater drains discharging into streams and ditches connected directly to the Thames. Soon the river was a vast open sewer – as well as a source of drinking water for the city's public pumps, resulting in deadly cholera outbreaks (see page 97). A particularly hot summer in 1858 gave rise to the Great Stink, during which the stench from the water flowing under the noses of MPs sitting in the Houses of Parliament galvanised them to allow the Metropolitan Board of Works (MBW) to borrow £3 million (about £200 million in today's money) to evolve a network that would 'prevent any part of the sewage within the Metropolis from passing into the River Thames in or near the Metropolis' – in other words, to move the problem elsewhere. The new system, designed by MBW engineer Joseph Bazalgette, consisted of 85 miles of connecting sewers that directed all waste into large tunnels below the newly created embankments on either side of the river (see page 84). The sewage then flowed under gravity to pumping stations at Abbey Mills on the north bank and Deptford in the south. At Deptford pumps lifted the waste to an overground covered pipe known as the Ridgeway, which can still be seen running to Crossness.

At Crossness four huge steam-driven engines bizarrely named after members of the royal family – Victoria, Prince Consort, Albert Edward and Alexandra – pumped waste into a covered reservoir with a capacity of 25 million gallons, where it was held until just after high tide before being released into the river to be washed out to sea. Since the engines had to operate continuously to cope with the influx of waste, the MBW built cottages with gardens for its workers literally on top of the reservoir – it is said they grew fine tomatoes – and even provided a school for their children. There was no attempt to treat the raw sewage: Bazalgette's mission was simply to get rid of it. In 1886, six sludge vessels were commissioned to dump the waste further out at sea, a practice that continued until 1998.

The main Crossness building was the work of architect Charles Henry Driver, who also designed its even grander, Byzantine counterpart at Abbey Mills (best viewed, alongside its streamlined and shiny 1997 replacement, from the north end of Lea

Valley Park). From the outside, Crossness resembles an Italian palazzo, built in gault brick with red brick and Portland stone arches and stringcourses. The main entrance, obscured by a later extension but still visible from inside the building, was ornamented with the coats-of-arms of the MBW and adjacent counties and the complex originally included a 60-metre chimney with polychrome decoration that could be seen for miles around. Each of the capitals on the stone columns supporting the window arches is unique; one on the south wall of the engine house is said to represent the head of Bazalgette himself.

Yet even this exterior does little to prepare the visitor for the engine-house interior, a masterpiece of ornamental cast ironwork aptly known as the 'cathedral on the marsh'. As in a baroque church, columns and capitals, arches and screens are all intricately moulded and gilded or decorated in glowing colours. The four largest surviving rotative beam engines in the world, with 13-metre-long rocking beams at first-floor level and pistons that descend through two floors to the basement, lurk at the corners. In the centre, flanked by two arcades of columns at ground-floor level, is a double-height octagon – like the crossing of a cathedral – that brings in light from the upper-floor windows. Its eight columns support screens

featuring the MBW monogram amid surprisingly delicate patterns of leaves, flowers and fruit – including figs, perhaps for their laxative qualities! Separating ground from first floor is a grating whose pattern echoes the rippling surface of water and allows heat from the engines to be vented through the roof.

Crossness was opened by the Prince of Wales in April 1865: after setting the immense wheel – 8.25 metres in diameter – in motion to start the engine, he sat down in the cavernous space to have lunch with 500 guests including the archbishops of Canterbury and York and other members of the royal family. The facility lasted for almost a century before being decommissioned in 1956 and was then used as storage and workshops until 1985; the engines, originally manufactured in Birmingham and transported to London by barge, were left untouched because moving them was deemed too costly. The Crossness Engine Trust then spent almost 20 years restoring the Prince Consort before repainting parts of the interior and moving on to the Victoria.

9. Crossness Pumping Station,
   Bazalgette Way, SE2 9AQ
   www.crossness.org.uk

Isle of Dogs Pumping Station

Like the new zinc-clad shed at Abbey Mills, today's water-treatment and pumping plants usually favour a modernist aesthetic of streamlined forms and industrial materials. But the 1988 facility on the aptly named Folly Wall, off Stewart Street in the Isle of Dogs, is a notably odd exception. Its purpose is simply to pump excess surface water into the Thames to prevent its low-lying surroundings from flooding, but its eclectic styling – a mix of Chinese temple, Egyptian tomb and jet engine that became a calling card for post-modernism – is saturated with meaning.

The Egyptian motifs, which include oversized columns flanking a small opening resembling the spirit door of a tomb, make allusion to the street furniture on Balzagette's Victoria Embankment (see page 84), itself perhaps a reference to pioneering pharaonic attempts to divert the waters of the Nile for irrigation. In his extensive explanation of the symbolism of his design (which can be found on his website), architect John Outram describes his Isle of Dogs building as a 'temple to storms', with its overhanging roof a 'raft' covering an 'ark' and its brick walls – sloping inwards at the top like those of a fortress – a 'mountain of nativity'. In this reading, the split pediment represents an eagle's wings and the circular fan a cave set within two mountains. The columns that dominate the entrance façade are giant trees and the blue bricks that flow across the façade represent water pouring into the river. Two other pumping stations were commissioned from leading architects at the same time, but Richard Rogers and Nicholas Grimshaw fulfilled the brief with utilitarian buildings – Rogers on Tidal Basin Road near Royal Victoria Dock with a series of cylinders and Grimshaw on Store Road in North Woolwich with a simple shed. Their rational responses only highlight the eccentricity of Outram's cosmic temple.

That the **10 Isle of Dogs pumping station** houses only machinery, visited once a week for maintenance, perhaps explains why all its bombast is on the outside. At Crossness, by contrast, the remote site mitigated against external grandstanding and it was the workers inside the cathedral on the marsh who were privy to pumping-station pomp and glory.

10. Isle of Dogs Pumping Station,
    Stewart St, E14 3ET

2.3 Ventilation

The need to ventilate London's network of tunnels – whether for road, rail or sewerage – has resulted in a range of bizarre structures that erupt into the urban landscape but play no active part within it. Some are disguised as art objects or classical monuments, others are wackily space age or simply utilitarian.

Road & Rail

For safety reasons, Transport for London keeps the location of many ventilation structures a secret, so the examples Londoners know of are like the tip of an iceberg. One of the oldest is at ⑪ **23-24 Leinster Gardens** in Bayswater, venting a stretch of the Metropolitan Railway, which when it opened in 1863 was the world's first underground. Part of what is now the District Line between Paddington and Bayswater runs through a cut-and-cover tunnel punctuated by open stretches that enabled trains to emerge to vent off smoke and steam. When two houses in the upmarket terrace were demolished to create a venting gap, engineers replaced them with a 1.5-metre-thick false front that exactly matched its neighbours down to the balconies, first-floor balustrading and planters. Look carefully and you can spot the fake façades by their blacked-out windows.

The same desire to protect genteel neighbourhoods from the crude requirements of infrastructure surfaced 150 years later with a ⑫ **shaft in Gibson Square** that vents the Victoria Line between King's Cross and Highbury & Islington. Designed during the line's construction in 1970 by Quinlan Terry, a 'New Classical' architect much admired by the Prince of Wales, the structure reduces the language of a Roman temple to a series of gestures, exemplified by the 'dome', which closer inspection reveals to be made of wire mesh. It's hard to beat as an example of clothing the utilitarian in fake grandeur and looks distinctly incongruous

within its everyday English context of park benches, rose gardens and lawns. It was commissioned after residents objected to the idea of a 15-metre concrete shaft, which would have looked more honestly out of place.

Other examples of shafts in classical guise include the squat ⑬ **obelisk in Circus Place**, just off Finsbury Circus in the City, installed in 1999 to provide ventilation for a London Underground gas tank. Standing 6.2 metres high, it was designed as series of modules that could be stacked without scaffolding in the course of a single day, with false joints to give it the appearance of being carved from solid stone – somewhat unconvincingly, especially as you can see wire mesh and daylight through the vents towards the top of each of its faces. A decorative medallion depicts architect George Dance the Younger, who laid out the Finsbury Estate in the late 1770s. Many sources say the shaft pays homage to Dance's more elegant obelisk of 1771 in St George's Circus in Southwark, though this was in fact designed by the architect's rival, Robert Mylne.

Another imposing shaft outside Bank station in nearby Cornhill commemorates ⑭ **James Henry Greathead** (1844–1896), a pioneering London Underground engineer who invented the circular shield used to bore tunnels under the Thames (see p.324). Though the shape of the plinth echoes that of the statue of Wellington opposite, its size and the vents at the sculpture's base reveal that this is more than

11

11

11

12

13

14

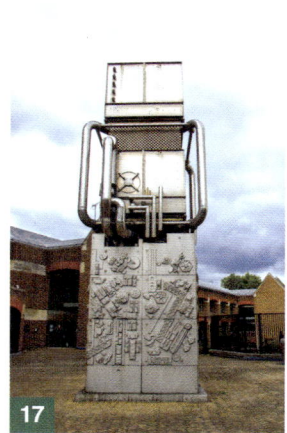

just a memorial. It seems appropriate that a tribute to an engineer should be useful as well as decorative.

Paternoster Square, near St Paul's in the City, has two ventilation shafts disguised as large-scale sculpture. Designed by William Whitfield as part of the square's controversial redevelopment in the late 1990s, the **15** 'pineapple' – a fluted column topped by a gilded urn and shooting flames, with vents beneath – could be a miniature version of the Monument transported several blocks west were it not that the classical elegance of its proportions is compromised by a massive base accommodating ventilation for an underground service road. Thomas Heatherwick's **16** **Paternoster Vents**, installed in 2002, is a dramatic and unapologetically modern piece of public art inexplicably tucked away in a little-visited courtyard. Squeezed uncomfortably into its setting, it cools an underground electricity station, with its fan-like wings engineered to maximise surface area.

The quirkiest example of a contemporary artist's take on the lowly ventilation shaft is probably **17** **Eduardo Paolozzi's 1982 design** for Pimlico Underground – a fitting commission for the station that serves Tate Britain. Standing forlornly in a small brick-paved piazza, the shaft looks like a robot that has lost its way to the future. Around its base is a series of panels with low reliefs depicting the sculptor's trademark cogs and wheels, clock faces and dials, spacemen and aeroplanes, mechanistic insects and butterflies. As a vision of the future it is by now long out of date, its clumsy cassette players superseded by sleek micro-technology. But its celebration of the machine is matched by a welcome refusal to hide the structure's true function.

Much larger in scale and still coolly futuristic in appearance are six sculptural shafts designed by architect Ian Ritchie in 2000 for the Jubilee Line extension between London Bridge and Canary Wharf. Probably the oddest is the **18** **plant enclosure and shaft** at Culling Road in Southwark, between Canada Water and Bermondsey stations. A series of discs stacked one above the other, increasing in diameter towards the top, the ventilation zone looks like a grounded flying saucer or perhaps a miniature version of Frank Lloyd Wright's Guggenheim Museum in New York. The basically rectangular plant enclosure is articulated with curves and bulges and both parts are clad in copper

panels in shades of blue-green. You can find Richie's completely different solutions to the same problem at Durand's Wharf and Downtown Road (between Canary Wharf and Canada Water) and Ben Smith Way near Bermondsey.

But the grandest – and perhaps best disguised – ventilation shaft is the monumental **19 Wellington Arch** at Hyde Park Corner, designed in 1826 by Decimus Burton to commemorate Britain's victory in the Napoleonic Wars and moved to its present location in 1885. Hollow inside, one pier formerly housed a small police station and the other a park-keeper's residence; in the early 1960s the northern pier was cleared to serve as a ventilation shaft for the new road tunnel running under Hyde Park Corner.

11. 23-24 Leinster Gardens, W2 3AN
12. Shaft, Gibson Square, N1 0RD
13. Obelisk, Circus Place, EC2M 5TN
14. James Greathead, Cornhill, EC3V 3ND
15. Column, Paternoster Square, EC4M 7DX
16. Paternoster vents, EC4M 7AQ
17. Paolozzi shaft, Pimlico Underground, Bessborough St, SW1V 2JA
18. Plant enclosure & shaft, Culling Rd, SE16 2TN
19. Wellington Arch, Hyde Park Corner, W1J 7JZ

Sewers & Toilets

Stench pipes, or stink pipes – slender cast-iron columns that release foul-smelling and potentially dangerous sewer gas far above the heads of passers-by – are among the least noticed features of London streets. It is easy to mistake them for lamp posts until you look up and realise they are much taller and lack any obvious purpose. Sometimes several line a road, indicating that a sewer runs below; sometimes they stand in isolation.

Commissioned following the Great Stink of summer 1858 (see page 33), during which hot weather and low water levels exacerbated the smell of human waste dumped in the Thames, London's new sewers were a major engineering feat and civic achievement. So it is unsurprising that Victorian engineers sought to dignify the humble stench pipe with classical detailing. You can find elegant examples in many streets in south London: **20 Weihurst Gardens** (near the junction with King's Lane) in Carshalton has a wonderful pipe with a moulded base, a collar halfway up, a sphere with four mouths to release the gases sitting on its capital and what looks like a weathervane at the top. **21 Albany Road** in Camberwell has a typical group of three pipes with fluted bases flanked by collars decorated with geometric and organic patterns.

Shafts ventilating public conveniences – often located in prominent positions at the junctions of main roads – tend to be more elaborate still. Examples include the resplendent ventilation shaft cum lamp post designed by Alexander Thomson in Lewisham (see page 83) and the column topped by a golden crown that ventilates the former gents' toilets at **22 Kennington Cross** (now home of appropriately named community arts project Artslav). Another grand shaft multitasking as a lamp post ventilates the public toilets opposite the **23 Royal Courts of Justice** in the Strand: air is extracted through simple vents in the base of an elaborate standard bearing five lamps on swirling branches. There is a similar standard just outside **24 Tooting Broadway Underground** – in this case, adding a third function beyond venting and lighting in the form of arrows directing travellers to London, Wimbledon, Wandsworth or Croydon.

20. Weihurst Gardens, SM1 4PQ
21. Albany Rd, SE17 2QQ
22. Kennington Cross, SE11 4EZ
23. Royal Courts of Justice, Strand, WC2R 1A
24. Tooting Broadway, Mitcham Rd, SW17 9PA

21

21

21

22

23

2.4 Industrial Remnants

Three Mills

㉕ Three Mills – a manmade island near Three Mills Lane in Bromley-by-Bow – has several claims to oddness, past and present. House Mill, deriving its power from the relatively insignificant River Lea yet said to be the world's largest tidal mill, has been used at various times not only to grind grain for both flour and gin but also to manufacture gunpowder. Surprisingly, it was in operation as late as 1941 and together with neighbouring Clock Mill stands as a rare survivor. More recently, these former industrial buildings have been home to enterprises as seemingly polarised as the East London Science School, a free school housed in Clock Mill, and 3 Mills Studios, which transformed a former distillery and warehouses into a production facility used for the first *Big Brother* TV series.

Listed in the Doomesday Book as early as 1086, these were the first recorded tidal mills in Britain. The present buildings date from a few centuries later: House Mill was built by Huguenot Daniel Bisson in 1776 and Clock Mill, which incorporates two oast houses, by MP and malt distiller Philip Metcalfe in the early 1800s, re-using the clock and bell from an earlier structure. From 1872 the site was dominated by gin manufacturer J & W Nicholson, which ran a mill and distillery until one of its warehouses was bombed during WW2: burning alcohol set the river aflame for three days. Clock Mill continued in operation for another decade and Nicholson used parts of the island for warehousing and storage until the 1970s. The mills operated by closing a sluice gate

at high tide to trap the water and then controlling its flow back downstream at a rate that would turn the wheels; at their most efficient, each tide could provide seven to eight hours of power. Grain delivered by cart or barge was hoisted in sacks to the top floor then fed by gravity through wooden chutes to the second-floor smutting and dressing area where it was cleaned to rid it of the ergot fungus (from which LSD is derived). Once prepared, it was fed down to the millstones on the first floor to be ground. All the power used in the process was free – a combination of water and gravity.

Within House Mill today (open for guided tours and run by the House Mill Trust) you can still see the hoist mechanism and grain stores, two of the oldest millstones and the metal damsel shaft, so called because of its incessant 'chattering'. The grinding process rocked the timber-framed building with such force that it had to be stabilised between tides by boys employed to climb up and insert pegs into the structure – you get a sense of the damage inflicted from the extensive bracing that holds the back of the building together. On the ground floor, suspended over the water, doors open to reveal the four massive water wheels, the largest 6 metres in diameter.

In an upstairs office are boxes marked 'Nicholson Gin' and an 18th-century gin bottle. But the most evocative area is the pattern room, its shelves and tables piled high with thousands of dusty wooden forms. These are replicas of every small section of equipment, once used as moulds to re-cast replacements for individual broken parts. All have been carefully labelled and catalogued – though to a casual observer it seems impossible that anyone could ever find the piece they might need should the wheels turn again, as the charity that runs the site hopes.

25. Three Mill Lane,
    Bromley-by-Bow, E3 3DU
    www.housemill.org.uk

London Windmills

26

The windmill once sited on Three Mills Island was dismantled in about 1840, but London still has windmills in St Mary's Lane, Upminster (dating from 1803), at the end of Windmill Road on Wimbledon Common, and at Blenheim Gardens, Brixton (both dating from 1817). At the time of writing, Upminster – an octagonal wooden smock mill on a brick base – was undergoing much-needed restoration and repair.

26 **Wimbledon windmill** – also a wooden smock mill – ceased operation in 1864 and its two-storey octagonal brick base was converted into apartments. It is here that Robert Baden-Powell wrote parts of *Scouting for Boys* in 1908 and more recently the building provided accommodation for Wimbledon Common rangers. With its tower and cap rising through its base like the body of a woman clothed in a crinoline, the juxtaposition of industrial remnant and domestic additions such as conventional front porches, ranges of chimneys and a rooftop balustrade is frankly bizarre. Part of the mill is still private accommodation and part has been a museum since 1975.

27 **Brixton windmill** is even more of an oddity, both in construction – a conical brick tower mill with two pairs of sails – and in having retained some of its machinery, which is again being used to grind flour. Built for miller John Ashby, it was owned by successive generations of his family for over a century until 1935 – though for 40 years it was used only as storage after new housing built following the arrival of the railways reduced wind impact and the Ashbys moved their business to a watermill in Mitcham. In 1902 they returned, installing a modular steam-driven mill within the Brixton tower. Flour was produced for Harrods and West End stores as well as an on-site shop and bakery.

Brixton windmill re-opened to visitors for brief periods in the 1960s and 1970s, having been fitted with new sails and parts sourced from a derelict mill in Lincolnshire. Following a further half century of vandalism and neglect, it was restored fully from 2010, its brickwork covered in black tar to protect it from rain and its white-painted sails or sweeps repaired. Formerly a brooding, forlorn presence in the corner of a suburban park, it is back in working order. Even more surprisingly, the modular mill of 1902, now powered by electricity, is supplied not only with organic wheat from East Anglia but with grain grown in South London – making flour that once again feeds local residents.

26. Wimbledon windmill,
    Windmill Rd, SW19 5NR
    www.wimbledonwindmill.org.uk
27. Brixton windmill,
    Blenheim Gardens, SW2 5EU
    www.brixtonwindmill.org

27

Bottle Kiln

At the south end of Walmer Road, Notting Hill, is a surprising survivor of the pottery industry established in the area in the 1830s and commemorated in Pottery Lane immediately to the south. A conical brick updraught kiln – known as a **28** **bottle kiln** because of its distinctive shape – is sandwiched incongruously between two small terraces of 20th-century mews houses opposite Avondale Park. Wander around the back into Hippodrome Mews – named after an unsuccessful racecourse set up nearby in 1837 – and you see that the kiln has been cleverly incorporated into one of the houses, its tapered funnel capped with glass to let in light. At 7.5 metres high and 6 metres in diameter, it must make a gloriously dramatic room.

What is now Avondale Park was owned from the mid-1820s by the Adams family. It was here that high-quality clay was dug from pits to be moulded into bricks and tiles fired in kilns like this one, built to a design used since medieval times. Records indicate that the Walmer Road kiln was rebuilt in 1879 by Charles Adams, whose company at the time specialised in tiles, drainpipes and flowerpots. A decade later the land known as Adams' Brickfield was bought by the parish and transformed into the present park.

In the first half of the 19th century, the area around the kiln was one of London's most notorious slums. In addition to the potteries, it had become a centre for pig-farming, with more than 3,000 pigs sharing hovels with the families who looked after them. The combination proved lethal: the disused clay pits soon filled with stinking stagnant water, slurry and sewage, with the largest, covering about an acre of Avondale Park, known as 'the Ocean'. The average local lifespan in the early 1800s was just 11 years 7 months compared with a London average of 37. While the pig-keepers were allegedly poor but honest, brick-makers had a reputation as 'notorious types' given to 'riotous living' and Pottery Lane and Walmer Road were nicknamed 'Cut-Throat Lane'. Charles Dickens described the area as 'a plague spot scarcely equalled for its insalubrity by any other in London… In these hovels, discontent, dirt, filth and misery are unsurpassed by anything known even in Ireland.'

Times have changed, of course, and today the little houses in Hippodrome Mews fetch well over £1 million.

28. Bottle kiln,
     Walmer Rd, W11 4ES

Kirkaldy's Testing Works

At 99 Southwark Street is a four-storey Italianate building with the unusual motto 'Facts Not Opinions' inscribed in the pediment over one of its entrances. Open the door and you find yourself in a dusty room filled with strange and intriguing machinery on a massive scale. This is the **㉙ Kirkaldy's Testing Works**, the former premises of a small family-run business with a far-reaching international reputation that was to revolutionise procedures for testing construction materials such as cast iron, steel and concrete.

Health and safety has become a 21st-century mantra, but it was not always the case. Back in the late 19th century, disasters such as the collapse of the Tay railway bridge, with the loss of more than 60 lives, could have been avoided if the properties of the new materials used in its construction had been better understood. Scottish engineer and draughtsman David Kirkaldy (1820–1897) recognised the problem and pioneered the independent and rigorous testing of materials and the definition and establishment of standards. His work in Southwark was continued until 1965 by two subsequent generations of his family.

Uncompromising and of a nervous disposition, Kirkaldy was not easy to deal with. In 1861 he left his engineering job in Glasgow and spent two years designing the machine that still, in all its baffling complexity, fills the ground floor of the Southwark Street building. He supervised its construction in Leeds over a period of 15 months, paying for the work in stages from his own pocket. Impatient at delays, he eventually had the still-unfinished monster transported to premises he had leased in The Grove in Southwark before moving to the current Southwark Street building in 1874.

Because the quality of materials such as cast iron initially varied considerably between batches, Kirkaldy's machine tested entire components rather than samples. As a result, it was colossal in size – at 14.5 metres long and weighing almost 120 tonnes, it could test strength in both compression and tension and exert loads of up to 1 million pounds (over 450 tonnes). Solid brick piers and enormous girders were installed in the basement to support its weight; on the first floor a machine room prepared specimens for testing while on the second floor an array of items were tested to destruction in a room known as the Museum of Fractures. Originally the machine was operated by hydraulic power but in 1905 an electric motor was fitted.

Almost as soon as his enterprise was up and running Kirkaldy was commissioned to test materials for the new Blackfriars Bridge in London as well as consignments of steel from Alfred Krupp in Germany. Over the century that followed his firm worked on schemes as far-flung and prestigious as the Eads Bridge in St Louis, US, the longest arch bridge in the world on its completion in 1874; the Sydney Harbour Bridge in Australia, built by a Middlesborough firm in 1932; and the futuristic Skylon tower for the 1951 Festival of Britain.

Initially Kirkaldy supervised every test himself, employing only a foreman, assistant and 'boy' to operate the testing machine, four or five men for the machine room upstairs and three office workers. After his death his son took over the business, followed by his grandson, who finally sold up in 1965. The firm was never a limited company, so with each test not only their integrity but all their personal possessions were on the line.

Since 1984 the premises have been run as a museum by a dedicated team of volunteers, most of them retired engineers or materials testers. Men in overalls feed large chunks of metal into the huge machine, turn a wheel to increase the force until the sample snaps and then make complicated

calculations to measure the load. Visitors have the chance to use smaller pieces of equipment to test the strength of concrete blocks or packaging tape. Most of the building's fittings, including shelving, an old office chair and a rusting range stacked with a kettle and saucepans, are original. In the musty basement is equipment even the knowledgeable volunteers are unsure how to operate, though they can direct you to PhD theses on the subject.

Because these were once working machines, you can see an amount of wear and tear, and moving parts such as cogs and wheels are exposed in ways that would never be tolerated in a modern industrial setting. A can of WD40 sits beside the testing unit and the equipment is carefully maintained rather than relegated to damp warehouses or static museum displays.

Unlike Three Mills or the Brixton or Upminster windmills – relics of a rural past that has been swallowed up by the expanding city – the Kirkaldy testing machine is a rare survival of industrial London that has not been repurposed.

29. Kirkaldy's Testing Works,
    99 Southwark St, SE1 0JF
    www.testingworks.org.uk

2.5 Baths & Bathhouses

The foundations of 2,000-year-old Roman baths were discovered in Lower Thames Street in the City in 1848 (open occasionally through the Museum of London) and more recently at a site across the river in Southwark during the construction of Thameslink. But the facility that for almost 200 years has been known as ㉚ **London's Roman Baths** – sited in the basement of a 19th-century building in the shabby alley of Strand Lane in Westminster – is an oddity in not being Roman at all.

The baths represent something of an archeological puzzle, but the most likely explanations are that they were built in 1612 as a feeder cistern for the grand fountains of nearby Somerset House or were a folly created by Thomas Howard, 2nd Earl of Arundel (1585–1646), who collected antiquities and on whose land they stood. Either way, they took advantage of a natural spring that still flows today.

The facility opened as a public baths in 1776 and two years later proprietor James Smith added a second bath and dressing rooms; a sales notice from 1782 describes an entrance for ladies on Surrey Street and one for gentlemen on Strand Lane. But it is Charles Scott, who took over in 1838, who first tried to boost attendance by

claiming the baths were Roman. The ploy worked: references from the 1840s include a description by New York publisher and politician Thurlow Weed of a visit to a Strand Lane baths 'built by the Romans, over a spring… precisely such as are now seen in all Ancient Roman ruins'. And Dickens' David Copperfield takes 'many a cold plunge' in a bath 'at the bottom of one of the streets out of the Strand'.

The baths closed in 1893 and the dilapidated site was bought in 1922 by the rector of St Clement Danes, who stripped out the Victorian tiles and statues in a vain attempt to restore the feature to its former 'Roman' glory. In 1947 they were taken over by the National Trust, to be run by Westminster Council; today access is mostly restricted to a view of the simple brick-lined pool through a ground-floor window (there is a light you can flick on, but avoid wet days when condensation clouds the glass). Or you can arrange a tour by calling 020 7641 5264. To find the site, walk along Surrey Street from the Strand and turn right down Surrey Steps.

Turkish baths – where visitors progress through a series of increasingly hot rooms warmed by dry air, interspersed with dips in a cold plunge pool, followed by a body wash and massage known to the Victorians as 'shampooing' and a period

31

of often sociable relaxation in a cooling room – became something of a late 19th-century British craze. Surprisingly, their introduction to the UK was largely thanks to a Scottish diplomat and politician, David Urquhart, who advocated their efficacy in his travel memoir *The Pillars of Hercules* (1848). The book was picked up by Irish physician Richard Barter, who in 1856 set up a prototype baths in County Cork, inviting Urquhart to the opening. The fashion soon spread through the UK, beginning in the industrial towns of northern England, bizarrely promoted through the 'working-men's foreign affairs committees', a movement set up by Urquhart around the time of the Crimean War to encourage a more Turkish-friendly foreign policy.

Urquhart's London & Provincial Bath Company opened its first Turkish baths in Jermyn Street in St James's in 1862 and by the turn of the century the capital could boast more than 70 facilities. Most proprietors ran just one establishment, but the Nevill brothers, Henry and James Forder, opened baths on seven different sites, two with separate buildings for 'gentlemen' and 'ladies'. An isolated survivor that gives an idea of the glamour and exoticism of the experience still stands in Bishopsgate Churchyard, just north of Wormwood Street in the City. The site had had baths since 1817 and Turkish baths since the 1860s, but when the Nevills took over the business in 1895 they demolished what was there and started afresh in a bid to attract new clients.

Most of the building, designed by architect G Harold Elphick, was underground, but the tiny above-ground **31** **New Broad Street Baths pavilion** proclaimed its function with blue tiles, Moorish motifs reproduced in terracotta and an onion lantern topped by a finial with crescent moon and star. It would be an extraordinary building under any circumstances, but today it could hardly look more out of place, surrounded by glass-and-steel high-rise offices and with the very English church hall and garden of St Botolph without Bishopsgate just next door. Once inside, bathers went down a spiral staircase with gloriously tiled walls made up of interlocking patterns – which the architect patented – in blues and reds or pinks and creams. The cooling room was decorated in the style of the Alhambra in Granada with Moorish tiled screens while the hot rooms had marble seats, mosaic floors, stained glass and elaborately tiled walls and ceilings. It seems the New Broad Street Baths were presented as a luxurious facility for wealthy businessmen and the entrance fees were higher than at other Nevill establishments.

The baths closed in 1954 and the building was used for storage before opening as a restaurant in the 1970s. It is now owned by Victorian Bathhouse as a venue for special events.

An Act of Parliament encouraging local authorities to provide baths and washhouses was passed in 1846. The act stipulated that two classes of baths and pools must be offered, and while Turkish baths were exempt from the legislation, many conformed to its ethos, despite Urquhart's idealisation of the ritual as a place where people of all classes could mingle.

An extraordinary remnant of a local authority facility is the ghostly skeleton of the **32** **Greenman Street Baths** in Tibby Place in Islington, which was an exact yet very different contemporary of the Nevills' New Broad Street Baths. Where the Turkish baths were inward-looking and cocooned, attracting their clientele with elaborate but retrograde exoticism, Greenman Street used the technologies of the day – cast iron and glass – to create a light-filled building of elegant simplicity.

32

The two-storey complex, which survived until the 1980s, included separate pools for men and women, a substantial laundry and a 'remedial suite' with two beds and a primitive jacuzzi on the upper floor. Pools were housed in double-height halls with glass roofs and a gallery at first-floor level. Decoration was minimal: punched-out gothic roundels marked the junctions between arches and posts and the rivets were exposed to become part of the pattern.

The odd remnant of the baths now stranded in Tibby Place park – a series of graceful arches supported on slender columns

erected on a cruciform plan – is probably part of the upper floor moved here in 1988. Like the Islington Estate on the other side of Greenman Street (see page 141), it is a reminder of an architecture that gave quiet dignity – with a nod to grander precedents – to facilities for improving the health and hygiene of ordinary people.

30. 'Roman' Baths,
    5 Strand Lane, WC2R 1AP
31. New Broad Street Baths pavilion,
    Bishopsgate Churchyard, EC2M 3TJ
32. Greenman Street Baths,
    Tibby Place, N1 8SD

2.6 Finsbury Health Centre

Accessed via a bridge, its half-buried façade a glorious convex curve of glass brick set within a frame of cream tiles, the ❸ **Finsbury Health Centre** on Pine Street in Clerkenwell looks as if it had been beamed in from another planet. Dating from 1938, it is in fact a vision of a never-to-be-realised future imported from the USSR courtesy of the dystopia of totalitarian continental Europe.

London in the 1930s became home to a number of talented émigré Jewish architects from Germany, Eastern Europe and the Soviet Union who brought continental modernism – a sunny vision of streamlined shapes, cutting-edge materials and idealistic social programmes – to a Britain still mired in outmoded traditions of bricks and mortar and rigid class distinctions. Most of the protagonists, who included such prestigious names as Mies van der Rohe, Erich Mendelsohn, Marcel Breuer and Walter Gropius, moved on to the US at the end of WW2, where they trained new generations of architects and helped determine the shape of the 20th-century city. Berthold Lubetkin (1901–1990) and Ernö Goldfinger (1902–1987; see page 151) remained in the UK, where their ideas were first adopted, then rejected, then won limited acceptance as economic circumstances and social ideals changed.

Lubetkin was born in Georgia and studied in post-Revolutionary Moscow and Leningrad before moving to Berlin in 1922 and to Paris in 1925. After emigrating to London at the beginning of the 1930s, he set up the architectural practice Tecton, which won its reputation, bizarrely, though a pioneering design for the Penguin Pool at London Zoo, distinguished by interlocking spiral ramps in gleaming white concrete intended to mimic the birds' natural habitat. This was followed by the Highpoint apartments in Highgate, commissioned by duplicating-machine manufacturer Sigmund Gestetner to provide homes for his staff. Equipped with a communal swimming pool, tennis courts and central heating, as well as a built-in refrigerator in each apartment, the unashamedly modernist blocks were never occupied as intended and instead became sought-after homes for wealthy Londoners with avant-garde tastes.

Four years later, however, Lubetkin was able to marry modernist aesthetics with socialist ideals in the Pine Street health centre, commissioned by the London Borough of Finsbury as the centrepiece of an ambitious plan for the redevelopment of an area that contained some of London's most densely packed slums. A decade before the formation of the NHS, the project was revolutionary in providing healthcare that was free at the point of access, run by an elected local authority with costs met through taxation rather than charitable donations. The project offered a glorious vision of a socialist future in which, as the architect said, 'nothing is too good for ordinary people'.

Still operating today, the health centre consists of a dramatic entrance block – approached via a ceremonial ramp across the void that lets light into the semi-basement – flanked by two wings set at an angle like open arms. The glazed bronze doors are original, as is the roof terrace (an essential component of a modernist building). The basement housed a mortuary, storage, plant and facilities for cleansing and disinfection, the ground floor consultation and treatment rooms (so patients did not need to climb any stairs) and the upper floors offices, with a lecture theatre above the entrance. As an indication of local poverty, the whole

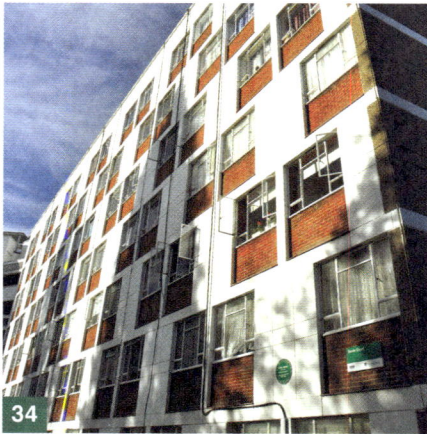

ground floor of one wing was devoted to treating TB and the central block had facilities for 'electrical treatment' (artificial sunshine). Inside, the rooms lived up to Lubetkin's ideals about providing good design for ordinary people, with the glamorous reception area behind the glass bricks dotted with furniture designed by Finnish modernist Alvar Aalto and decorated with murals by Gordon Cullen encouraging patients to 'live out of doors as much as you can' and enjoy 'fresh air night and day'.

It's worth wandering round to the goods entrance on Northampton Road to see the back of the building, where a central projecting block with a cantilevered balcony and dramatically curved roofline rises up from slender pilotis. Ironically, the health centre was built next to the site of a burial ground and bone house; during the mid-19th century, the fumes from illegal bonfires of corpses and coffins dug up to accommodate new interments made local residents ill. An indication of the area's overcrowding, as many as 80,000 people were buried on a site licensed for fewer than 3,000.

As for Lubetkin, he was to continue to accept commissions from Finsbury Council, designing both the Spa Green and Priory Green estates in the late 1940s and early 1950s. His final work for the borough was **34 Bevin Court**, a new housing complex in Cruikshank Street, Pentonville, built on the site of Holford Square, which had been bombed during WW2. Vladimir Lenin had lived in a flat at 30 Holford Square for just over a year from 1902 and the gardens had once contained a bust of the Soviet leader, donated by the Soviet embassy and mounted in an extraordinary angled, Constructivist-inspired casing designed by Lubetkin. Council and architect accordingly agreed that the new complex would be named Lenin Court and that the monument would be placed at its entrance.

As Soviet relations with the west worsened, however, the council reconsidered its promise and at the last moment two letters of the prominent art deco-style entrance sign were recast to incorporate a name change from Lenin to Bevin in honour of trades unionist Ernest Bevin. Angry and disappointed, Lubetkin buried his Constructivist framework beneath the core of the block's dramatic spiral staircase. The bust itself was removed and you can still see it in Islington Museum on St John Street.

You can also still visit the ③⑤ Penguin Pool at London Zoo, though it has now been transformed into a fountain. The penguins voted with their flippers: zoo keepers reported that they seemed much happier when they were moved to alternative accommodation during the pool's renovation in 2004 and so decided against returning them to their modernist dream home.

33. Finsbury Health Centre,
    Clerkenwell, EC1R 0LP
34. Bevin Court,
    Cruikshank St, WC1X 9HB
35. Penguin Pool, ZSL London Zoo,
    Regent's Park, NW1 4RY
    www.zsl.org

35

2.7 Picture Palaces

36

Picture palaces – the grand, purpose-built cinemas of the 1930s – provided audiences with an escapist glamour that matched the fantasies they saw on screen. With their fake-marble lobbies, sweeping staircases and opulent decor, along with attentive service at box office and restaurant, they allowed ordinary cinemagoers to access a kind of environment and experience that had previously been reserved for the wealthy. Some even offered telephone booking and valet parking – aspirational services that were presumably rarely called on, given the low distribution of telephone and car ownership in 1930s Britain.

One of the first London supercinemas was the Regal at Marble Arch, built in 1928 on the site of the present Odeon. Its designers referenced its location on the site where Roman legions allegedly guarded the Tyburn by providing a

Roman amphitheatre and temple with a dome of twinkling stars. In a follow-on from music halls, early picture palaces offered live spectacle as well as movies: the 4,000-seater Davis Theatre in Croydon, the first suburban London supercinema, had a stage that opened up to reveal a lake.

Both the Regal and Davis were demolished in the early 1960s, but other picture palaces have survived. The Brixton Astoria at the south end of Stockwell Road, built in 1929 for an audience of 4,500 and now a concert venue, has an art deco entrance foyer and an auditorium decorated as an Italian Renaissance garden. The auditorium of the former Astoria on the corner of Seven Sisters Road and Isledon Road in Finsbury Park – famous during the 1960s and 1970s as the Rainbow music venue – features a Moorish walled city. It is now a Brazilian Pentecostal church.

Other premises taken over by religious organisations include the ❸❻ **Apollo** (later Ambassador) at 117–19 Stoke Newington Road (1914), now a Turkish mosque with its façades newly clad in blue ceramic tiles and its towers topped by gilded cupolas; the ❸❼ **Carlton Islington** at 161–69 Essex Road (1930), its cream-tiled façade decorated with Egyptian-style columns and friezes; and the ❸❽ **Gaumont State** at 197–99 Kilburn High Road (1937), a truncated art deco skyscraper inspired by the New York Empire State. Access to these buildings is obviously limited, but the ❸❾ **Tooting Granada** at 50 Mitcham Road, now a bingo hall, can still be visited without buying a ticket. Its architects were Cecil Masey and R H Uren and its interior was by Theodore Komisarjevsky, the acknowledged king of picture-palace decoration, whose similarly styled Granada in Woolwich (see below) – now also a church – was dubbed 'the most romantic theatre ever built'.

The son of a Russian opera singer and a Lithuanian princess, Komisarjevsky came to London from Soviet Russia in the early 1920s. He soon established himself as a director of theatre and opera, working at Covent Garden and Stratford-upon-Avon before emigrating to the US in 1939. Unsurprisingly, his eight cinema interiors for Granada drew on his knowledge of set design. His attitudes to those who visited his cinemas acknowledged the illusory

nature of the experience while reeking of condescension: 'the richly decorated theatre… supplies an atmosphere… which the majority have hitherto only imagined. While there, they can within reason consider themselves as good as anyone, and are able to enjoy their cigarettes or their little love affairs in comfortable seats and amidst attractive and appealing surroundings.'

Opened in 1931, the Tooting Granada mixes Moorish with medieval, cathedral with castle. The Italianate moderne façade, its central pediment supported by four tall columns with Corinthian capitals, rises impressively above the local terraces. Like many picture palaces, only the front elevation has any style: wander around the side and you find a windowless, asymmetrical brick block built on a massive scale.

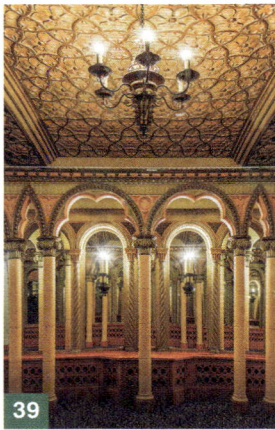

Inside, the foyer is styled as a baronial hall with giant pillars carved with heraldic beasts, gothic stained-glass windows, a 'minstrel's gallery' and a pair of gilded thrones at mezzanine level. A sweeping double staircase at the far end leads to an antechamber with marble columns. The 'hall of mirrors' beyond is a long, low room lined in mirrors fronted by colonnades with Moorish and gothic arches. Lit by rows of 'candles' on sconces, every pink, beige, terracotta or gold surface is decoratively pierced or moulded. The cavernous auditorium combines the fretwork of the (Spanish) Granada Alhambra with the tracery of a gothic cathedral and the tapestry designs of an English castle. Below a grid of intricate Moorish 'windows', two impressive gothic arches on either side of the proscenium are flanked by painted panels depicting medieval knights and minstrels. The impressive accumulation of repeated motifs – with every detail, including the medieval-style door handles, contributing to the story – meant the decoration could be machine made: this is high living for the mass market.

Like many of its contemporaries, Tooting Granada functioned as a theatre as well as a cinema and in the late 1930s screenings were supported by a circus with live elephants. In the 1950s and 1960s it doubled as a music venue: in 1963 the Beatles played here to packed houses. The building closed as a cinema in 1971 and reopened as a bingo hall five years later.

It is a surreal experience to sit in the circle and look down on bingo tables and slot machines. As in the past, the booming soundtrack (yellow 54, green 89, etc) is

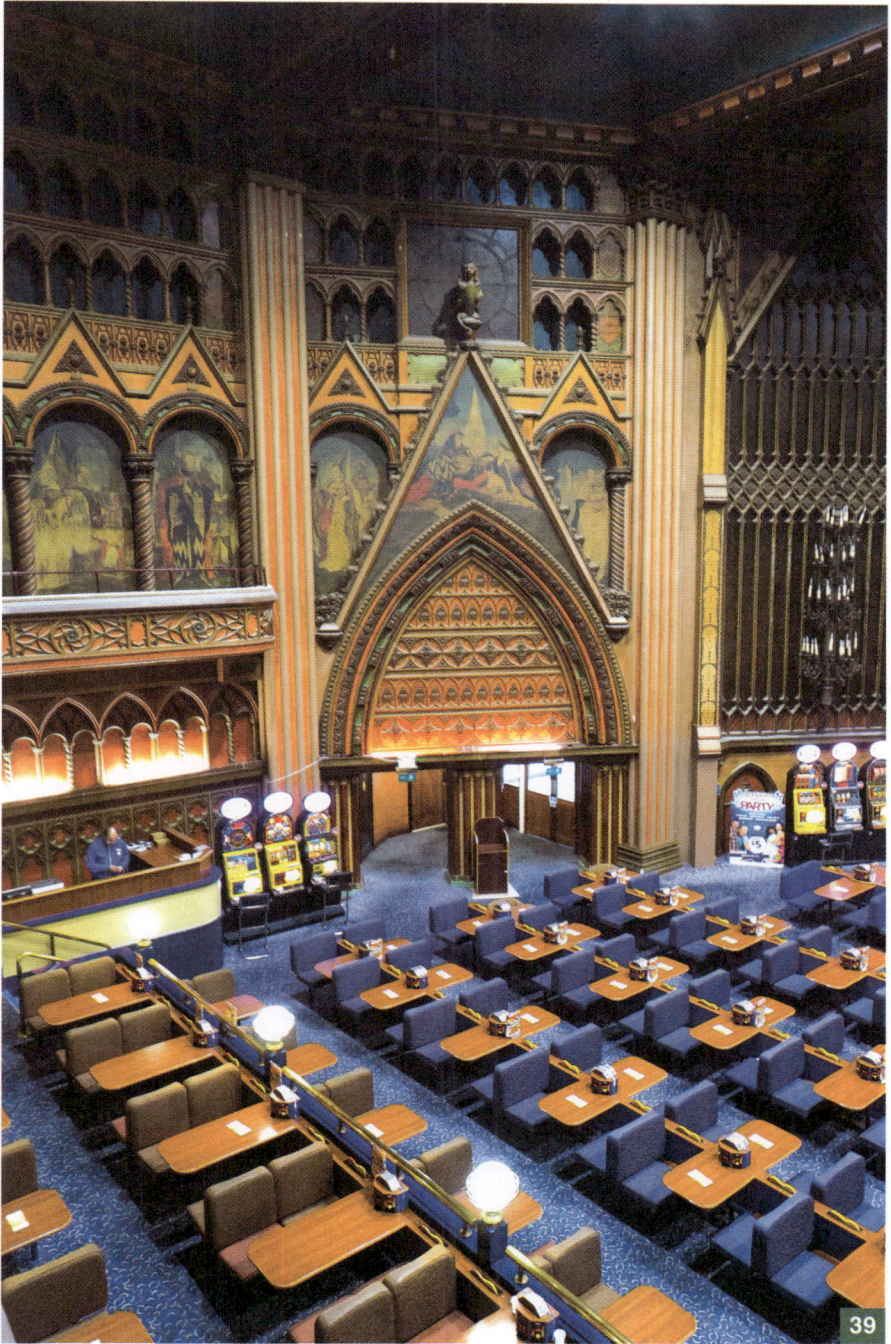

39

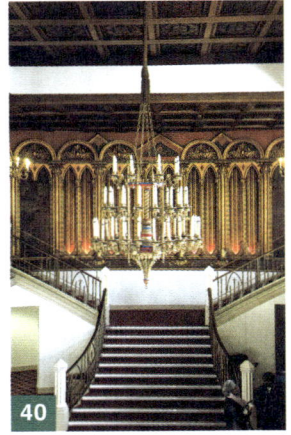

beamed in from another world, as patrons play games against unseen opponents in venues around the UK. Both bingo and Hollywood, of course, offer glimpses of a life beyond our dreams – but for the bingo-players, eyes resolutely down, the environment no longer feeds the fantasy.

Komisarjevsky's **40** **Granada Woolwich,** at the north end of Powis Street, was also owned for some years by Gala Bingo, before becoming a church. Its brick exterior features a sweeping art deco curve and an elegantly spare tower where the letters 'Granada', running vertically, have been replaced by 'cathedral'.

On the other side of the street is an even more flamboyant former cinema – the **41** **Coronet** (later Odeon), designed like the Kilburn Gaumont State by foremost cinema architect George Coles. Painted in two shades of cream, its streamlined moderne profile is topped by a tower, with its sensuous curves outlined in neon tubing. The two rival cinemas filled their huge auditoriums with some 4,000 people, selling glittering visions of a superior life – much like the religious organisations that occupy the buildings today.

36. Former Apollo,
    117-119 Stoke Newington Rd, N16 8BU
37. Former Carlton Islington,
    161-169 Essex Rd, N1 2SN
38. Former Gaumont State,
    197-199 Kilburn High Rd, NW6 6JE
39. Former Tooting Granada,
    50 Mitcham Rd, SW17 9NA
40. Former Granada Woolwich,
    Powis St, SE18 6NL
41. Former Coronet, John Wilson St,
    Woolwich, SE18 6QQ

41

2.8 Black Friar Public House

42

Given the importance of the pub as a British institution, it is hardly surprising that London is dotted with quirky, historically interesting or splendidly decorative places to buy a drink. Some of these are housed in unlikely locations: the Goat on Battersea Rise and the Temperance on Fulham High Street both occupy former Temperance movement billiard halls, set up to keep members away from the demon drink; until July 2017 O'Neills in Muswell Hill Broadway filled a vaulted Presbyterian church; several bars and restaurants have taken over former public toilets. Others retain sumptuous Victorian decoration as with the listed Princess Louise on High Holborn or the Viaduct Tavern in Newgate Street in the

City, a well-preserved former gin palace. Still others have long-lived gimmicky features such as the Windsor Castle on Crawford Place in Marylebone with its bizarre collection of royal and military memorabilia or the Seven Stars on Carey Street near the Inns of Court with its vitrines of stuffed birds and animal skulls topped by wigs.

But perhaps the original theme pub is the ❷ **Black Friar Public House** on Queen Victoria Street, just north of Blackfriars Bridge. Its pseudo-religious styling – a tongue-in-cheek homage to the Blackfriars monastery on whose ruins it stands – is notable for its commitment as well as its craftsmanship, and indeed was created in part by sculptors who were already known for bona fide ecclesiastical works at Westminster Abbey and St Paul's.

Began in 1875, the pub is a triangular wedge of a building, four storeys high; once surrounded by alleyways, it now stands with its distinctive profile fully exposed, its curved prow facing the river. Like a figurehead, a life-size statue of a jolly friar stands at first-floor level above a mosaic frieze interspersed with carved panels depicting monkish corruption and gluttony – grotesque friars feeding pie to a devilish animal, cutting gleefully into a block of cheese to the envy of two nearby starvelings. These were the work of Nathaniel Hitch, a sculptor who also created 28 sedate statues of saints for the exterior of Westminster Abbey.

If the exterior of the pub is odd, the interior is even odder. Masterminded from 1905 by architect Herbert Fuller-Clark at the instigation of then publican Alfred Pettitt, its most striking features are a series of extraordinary copper bas-reliefs related to food, drink and making merry. Above the bar, 'Tomorrow will be Friday' shows monks catching fish; above the entrance to the dining area, 'Saturday afternoon' depicts them busily harvesting vegetables and grapes.

The decoration of the bar was largely the work of Frederick Callcott, but following his death in 1925 the job of completing the Grotto – a small windowless back room excavated from a railway vault – was given to Henry Poole, who had also produced sculptures for the Chapel of St Michael and St George in St Paul's. With an apse at one end and a columned niche at the other, the Grotto gives the impression of a monk's cell – except that it is magnified with mirrors, clad lavishly in marble and boasts a gilded mosaic ceiling, perhaps as a commentary on the wealth and corruption that spurred Henry VIII to dissolve monasteries like Blackfriars in 1538.

Poole's decoration is far superior to his predecessor's in both execution and wit: low reliefs depict monks as pigs; satyrs representing the worldly arts grin down from the cornice; columns have capitals carved with birds and animals to illustrate nursery rhymes and fables. On the end walls a gathering of monks wash dirty linen with the caption 'don't advertise, tell a gossip' while another group pushes a trussed pig in a wheelbarrow with the motto 'a good thing is soon snatched up'.

The pub was condemned in the 1960s but was saved from demolition following a campaign led by poet John Betjeman. Though its uniform theme, expressed in every detail of architecture and decoration, makes it an exemplary Arts & Crafts Gesamtkunstwerk, it injects the sense of fun that the movement's more serious-minded practitioners often lacked.

42. Black Friar Public House,
    174 Queen Victoria St, EC4V 4EG

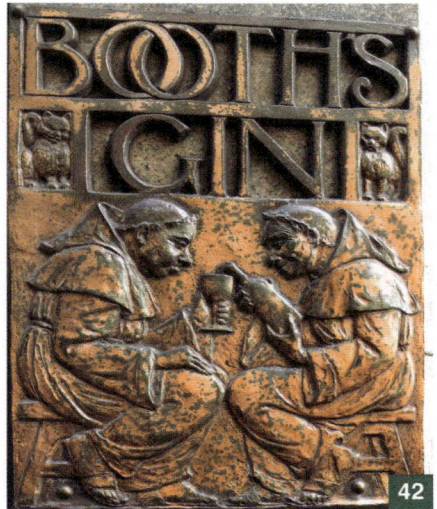

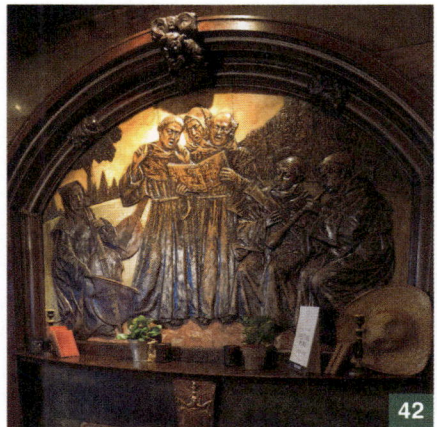

Bollard by Judith Dean, Wakefield Mews, see page 89

Street Furniture

Street Furniture

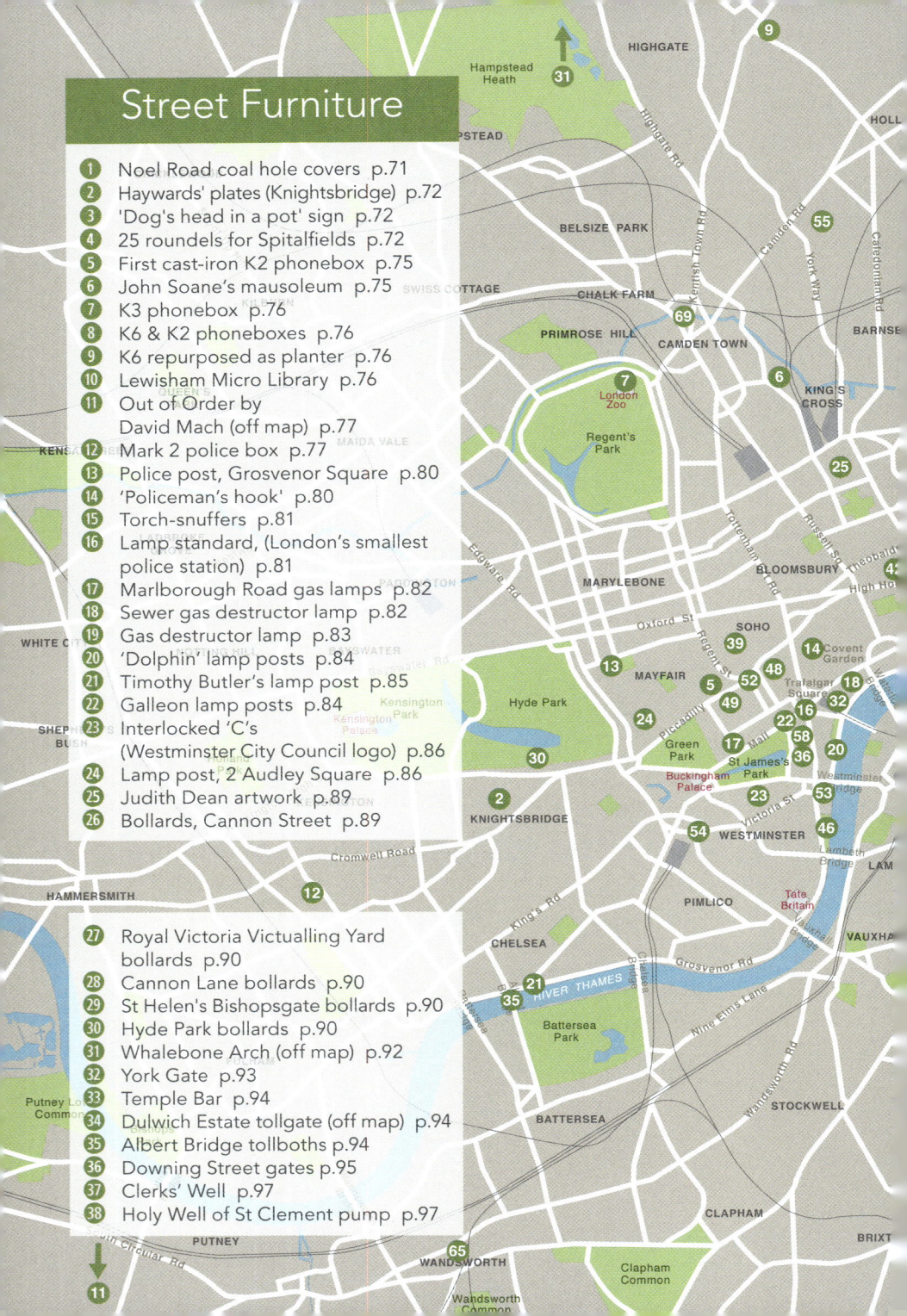

HIGHGATE

HOLL

Hampstead Heath

BELSIZE PARK

55

Camden Rd

York Way

CALEDONIA

PSTEAD

Highgate Rd

Kentish Town Rd

York Rd

CHALK FARM

BARNSE

PRIMROSE HILL

69

CAMDEN TOWN

SWISS COTTAGE

QUEEN'S

London Zoo

7

KING'S CROSS

6

Regent's Park

MAIDA VALE

25

KENSA

Russell Sq

Theobald

BLOOMSBURY

High Hol

PARK

Edgware Rd

Tottenham

MARYLEBONE

WHITE CIT

Oxford St

SOHO

39

Covent Garden

14

WESTBOURNE

Regent St

Hyde Park

MAYFAIR

52

48

Trafalgar Square

18

32

13

5

49

Kensington Gardens

Kensington Palace

24

Piccadilly

16

22

58

20

SHEP

BUSH

Green Park

17

36

St James's Park

Hyde Park

30

Buckingham Palace

23

53

2

54

WESTMINSTER

46

KNIGHTSBRIDGE

Victoria St

Lambeth Bridge

LAM

Cromwell Road

PIMLICO

Tate Britain

HAMMERSMITH

12

King's Rd

CHELSEA

VAUXHALL

Chelsea Bridge

Grosvenor Rd

21

35

RIVER THAMES

Nine Elms Lane

Battersea Park

Wandsworth Rd

STOCKWELL

BATTERSEA

Putney Lo Common

CLAPHAM

PUTNEY

65

WANDSWORTH

Clapham Common

BRIXT

Circular Rd

11

Wandsworth Common

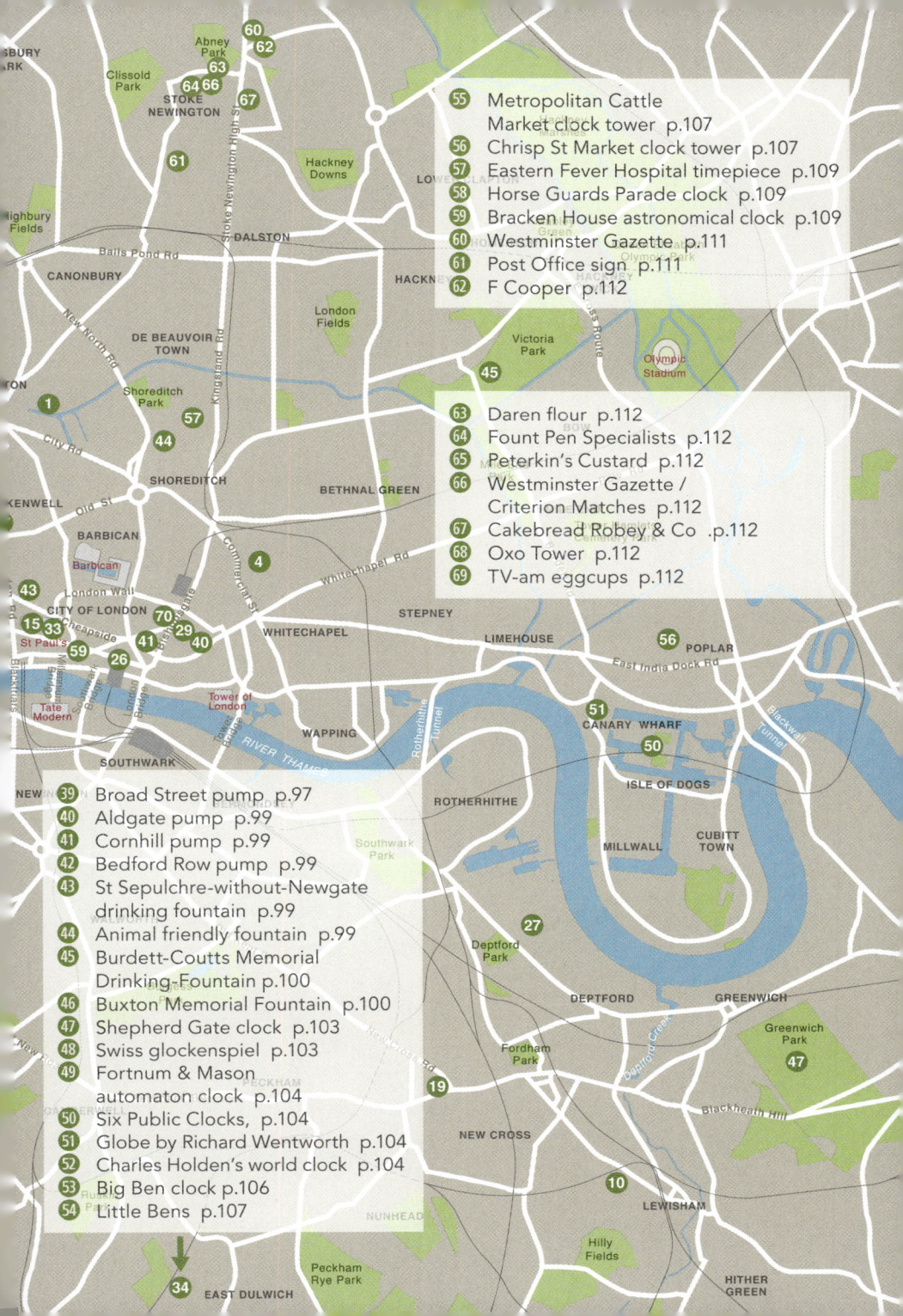

Abney Park
Clissold Park
STOKE NEWINGTON
Hackney Downs
Highbury Fields
DALSTON
CANONBURY
London Fields
DE BEAUVOIR TOWN
HACKNE
Victoria Park
Olympic Stadium
Shoreditch Park
SHOREDITCH
BETHNAL GREEN
KENWELL
Old St
BARBICAN
Barbican
London Wall
CITY OF LONDON
Cheapside
St Paul's
Tate Modern
SOUTHWARK
WHITECHAPEL
Whitechapel Rd
STEPNEY
LIMEHOUSE
East India Dock Rd
POPLAR
Tower of London
WAPPING
RIVER THAMES
CANARY WHARF
ISLE OF DOGS
ROTHERHITHE
MILLWALL
CUBITT TOWN
Southwark Park
Deptford Park
DEPTFORD
GREENWICH
Greenwich Park
Fordham Park
NEW CROSS
LEWISHAM
NUNHEAD
Peckham Rye Park
Hilly Fields
HITHER GREEN
EAST DULWICH

1

1

1

1

1

2

3.1 Coal Hole Covers

Coal hole covers offer an odd, perhaps unique, blurring of public and private. Dotting the pavements of many of London's more affluent streets, they provide a usually unremarked point of entry into adjacent houses and a reminder that beneath us as we walk – as in so much of London – are the caverns and pipes of the city's infrastructure, in this case in the form of private cellars.

Coal holes enabled deliveries of solid fuel to be emptied straight from cart or lorry into a cellar, so dusty sacks were not dragged through the house and owners (or housemaids) could fill scuttles without themselves or the coal getting wet. London coal holes remained in use until 1956, when the Clean Air Act banned the burning of coal within the capital. The act was a response to the Great Smog of 1952, a fog so thick that it stopped trains, traffic and public events and is thought to have led to the deaths of some 4,000 people in its immediate aftermath and double that number over the following months.

With a diameter of 30-35 centimetres, London coal hole covers consist of a cast-iron ring set into the pavement supporting a cast-iron disc that could be easily rolled aside. Hatches lock from the inside to prevent people (or at least starveling urchins) from stealing the coal or gaining access to the houses. Designs vary from manufacturer to manufacturer: most have their maker's name and address as a form of advertising along with a moulded pattern – usually geometric designs or floral motifs – to make them less slippery for pedestrians; some include concrete or glass inserts or small ventilation holes. Often different foundries used the same patterns but added their own names. Once you start to notice the plates, it is easy to become fascinated by similarities and differences (there are plenty of coal hole spotters whose photographs can be found online) and to appreciate their beauty as objects.

Noel Road in Islington – known mainly for the murder of playwright Joe Orton by his lover Kenneth Halliwell in 1967 – has as good a ❶ **collection of coal hole covers** as any. As well as geometric designs with no named manufacturer, including a starburst and a grid of squares, this small stretch of street contains plates that bear the names of about a dozen local ironmongers including P J Boon of Exmouth Street, R Melvill of Essex Road, William Pryor of Dalston Junction, G Aillard of Roman Road, Alfred Syer of Pentonville Road, Alfred Solomons of Caledonian Road and Nicholls & Clarke of Shoreditch. John C Aston of Essex Road, whose plates feature a quatrefoil pattern also used by other firms, was a forerunner of the company that became bathroom retailers Aston Matthews, established in 1823 and still in Essex Road. Moving further afield, there is also a plate by J W Carpenter of Earl's Court Road.

One of the most prestigious coal hole cover manufacturers was Haywards of Borough, and Noel Road boasts one example of a Haywards' self-locking plate. Founded in 1783 by Samuel Hayward, the firm was initially a glaziers based in Cheapside. In 1848 Samuel's descendants William and Edward bought the business of ironmonger R Henly & Co, taking over the Union Street premises whose address features on many of the covers.

Soon afterwards Haywards began to manufacture glazed pavement lights and in 1871 Edward took out a patent for a system that involved using prisms of glass sliced in two to bend the incoming light 90 degrees and so throw it deep into the space

below. You can find ❷ **Haywards' plates** with their characteristic hexagonal lights scattered throughout London, including a well-preserved group in Montpelier Square in Knightsbridge. The same system was used for rectangular gridded pavement lights to allow daylight into the basements of commercial premises and there are still many Haywards-manufactured examples in the West End and City; in comparison with later glass prisms set in concrete, the Haywards system with its cast-iron casing allows a much larger area of the grating to be glazed.

The ❸ **'dog's head in a pot' sign** (the dog signifying fire dogs and the pot a coalscuttle) that hung outside the Haywards' premises appeared on some of their plates in the mid-19th century. According to his friend and biographer John Forster, it was remembered fondly by Charles Dickens; a replica sign and coal hole cover were installed opposite Southwark tube as part of the Dickens bicentenary celebrations in 2012.

Other projects inspired by coal hole covers have included artist Keith Bowler's creation of ❹ **25 roundels for Spitalfields** in the mid-1990s, several of which can still be seen along Brick Lane. Some

ten years later Maria Vlotides designed a series of roundels called the Pavement Poetry Project for Notting Hill Gate using words by local authors Margaret Drabble, Sebastian Faulks, PD James, Michael Holroyd and others. More recently, attention was drawn to the usually ignored ironwork beneath our feet when Labour leader Jeremy Corbyn admitted to a 'zany' interest in the inscriptions on manhole covers as a form of social history.

With living space in London at such a premium, several firms are now advertising ways of enabling homeowners to renovate their coal cellars and occasionally you spot modern glazed covers that presumably allow in more light than envisaged by the Haywards. Perhaps 'working down the old coal hole' – the subject of a characteristically bawdy 1940 song by George Formby – is becoming a reality rather than just a euphemism.

1. Noel Rd, N1 8HH
2. Haywards' plate,
   Montpelier Square, SW7 1JY
3. 'Dog's head in a pot' sign and plate,
   Blackfriars Rd, SE1 8DA
4. Keith Bowler's Spitalfields roundels,
   Brick Lane (& surrounding area), E1 6QL

3.2 Phone Boxes

The UK's original red telephone boxes are in themselves an oddity – strikingly large and conspicuous, with both their shape and decoration unnecessarily overwrought for their purpose compared to the simpler booths you find in other countries. The original Kiosk 2 (K2), produced between 1926 and 1935, stands a full 2.74 metres high, with generous proportions and intricate 'Grecian' fluting on corners and surrounds that make it a thing of beauty in comparison with later models. You can see the original wooden prototype for K2 nestling incongruously within the neoclassical splendour of the portal to the Royal Academy of Arts on Piccadilly, together with one of the **⑤ first cast-iron production models**. Despite the upmarket surroundings, the characteristic acrid phone box smell remains the same.

Yet, looks apart, the strangest thing about the K2 is the source of its inspiration – a mausoleum that stands in St Pancras Old Churchyard in Camden. Created in 1924 by architect Giles Gilbert Scott, the K2 bears a striking resemblance in both overall form and detailing to the tomb designed by architect John Soane to house the remains of his wife Eliza (who died in 1815), and which also contains his own remains and those of one of his sons.

⑥ John Soane's mausoleum consists of a marble cube surmounted by a marble canopy supported on four Ionic columns topped by a shallow dome in Portland stone. The elaborate corners, (relatively) transparent sides, dome and shallow arched entablature – the last two Soanean motifs that you can see in particular in the breakfast room of his own house in Lincoln's Inn Fields (see page 159) – are features of both tomb and phone box, a resemblance that would have been even closer had the kiosks been painted silver as their designer intended, echoing the tomb's once gleaming marble. Soane and his work were presumably at the forefront of Scott's mind as he had recently been appointed a trustee of the Soane Museum and was at the time working on a hall of residence for Clare College, Cambridge, which also drew inspiration from Georgian architecture.

The K2's tripartite division of base, 'column' and entablature, along with its decorative details, may have redeployed the vocabulary of classical architecture, but the materials were modern: cast-iron sections bolted together on a concrete pad, with the door made of teak. Unfortunately, Scott's K2 worked out at almost £36 a kiosk (three times the cost of the GPO's previous K1 model) and was expensive to transport. As a result, only 1,700 were ever installed, almost all of them in London. There are about 200 left nationwide, including ten listed within the City.

In 1929 Scott was asked to simplify his design to make it cheaper. The result was ⓻ **K3**, which retained the iconic shape but was made of concrete, had fewer decorative details and was painted cream. Despite the fact that some 12,000 boxes were manufactured, only two remain – one of which stands outside Penguin Beach at ZSL London Zoo.

K4, known as the 'Vermillion Giant' because of its size, incorporated a post box and machine for buying stamps. It was not a success – the stamps got damp and the noise of the machine disturbed people using the phone. K5 never went into production, but K6 – some 30 centimetres smaller and half the weight of K2, with simplified glazing and fewer decorative details – was rolled out around the country. You can see a ⓼ **K6 and K2** side by side – a case of little and large, with the K6 looking like a cheap toy – outside the Royal Courts of Justice in Carey Street, just north of the Strand.

The ubiquity of mobile phones means phone box use is diminishing rapidly, and in 2008 BT launched the 'Adopt a Kiosk' scheme to encourage local councils and charities to find new uses for boxes. In London some have been converted into coffee stalls, salad bars, mobile phone repair shops, ATMs (you can find one in Borough Market in Southwark) or free mobile phone chargers equipped with a fan of solar panels on the roof (the first green 'solarbox' appeared at the south end of Tottenham Court Road in October 2014).

Other distinctly odd uses for phone boxes include the ⓽ **repurposed K6** on the corner of Giesbach Road and Sandridge Street, just south of Archway tube, which is now home to tiered planters (courtesy of Islington Council). In spring and summer petals poke like the fingers of trapped callers through the open roof and the space where the 'Telephone' sign used to be. Lewisham boasts a ⓾ **micro library** – on the corner of Lewisham Way and Tyrwhitt Road – in a K2 adopted by the Brockley Society in 2013. With a carpet on the floor, seven shelves along the back wall (including a kids' corner at the bottom) and a pleasant smell of wood and books, it feels surprisingly warm and cosy. The ceiling light bears the motto 'It's not what you get, it's what you leave behind' and anyone borrowing a book is asked to contribute another in exchange. The kiosk is open 24/7 – though like many larger libraries, its fragile existence depends on the goodwill of volunteers. Another micro library is now operating close by on Wickham Road,

this time dedicated entirely to children's books.

For his 1987 sculpture **11** *Out of Order,* artist David Mach arranged a series of 12 K6 phone boxes to tumble like dominoes along the pavement at the entrance to Old London Road in Kingston-upon-Thames. At the time it was the artist's comment on a newly privatised public service, but 30 years later it seems phone boxes are refusing to take redundancy lying down.

5. K2, Royal Academy of Arts,
   Piccadilly, W1J 0BD
6. John Soane's mausoleum , St Pancras Old
   Churchyard, Pancras Rd, NW1 1UL
7. K3, Penguin Beach, London Zoo,
   Outer Circle, Regent's Park, NW1 4RY
8. K6 & K2, Carey St, WC2A 2JB
9. Repurposed K6, Sandridge St, N19 3DA
10. Lewisham micro library,
    Tyrwhitt Rd, SE13 7SZ
11. Out of Order, Old London Rd, KT2 6QF

3.3 Police Boxes

Between 1929 and 1937 London's streets were planted with some 700 police boxes that would serve as local mini police stations for bobbies out on the beat. Painted dark blue and topped with a lantern, the kiosks may well have been forgotten had they not served as a model for the TARDIS, the means employed by Time Lord Doctor Who to navigate the universe in the eponymous BBC television series.

None of the original London police boxes has survived, but you can find a lone replica of the **12** **Mark 2** outside Earl's Court Underground. At about 2.8 metres high and 1.35 metres wide, with each side divided into eight panels, the upper two glazed, it was fitted with a CCTV camera beneath the blue light and a direct line to the police switchboard. Installed in 1996, this 'Watchbox' was claimed by the Metropolitan Police to be a prototype for a London-wide safety initiative, though cynics have suggested its sudden appearance was more probably to support the Met's claim to ownership of the Police Public Call Box trademark in a battle with the BBC. At the time *Doctor Who* was being relaunched with a TV film, and presumably the force hoped to benefit from merchandising rights. The courts backed the BBC, however, and the Earl's Court phone was not updated when London phone numbers changed in 2000.

Police boxes were first introduced in Glasgow in 1891, but the model designed by Metropolitan Police architect and surveyor Gilbert Mackenzie Trench did not appear in London until almost 40 years later. As with Giles Gilbert Scott's K2 phone boxes (see page 75), there was an initial wooden prototype, installed in the Beacontree Estate in Barking and Dagenham, followed by a cast-iron version

with a teak door trialled in Richmond and Barnes, which was superseded by a reinforced-concrete version when the initial design proved too expensive. In the days before radios or mobile phones, police boxes allowed patrols to report crime, summon reinforcements or make arrests without wasting time travelling back and forth to the police station. Amazingly, given how small the Earl's Court model appears – as the creators of the TARDIS recognised – each was equipped with a desk and stool, dustpan and brush, fire extinguisher and first-aid kit as well as a small electric heater useful for drying socks.

The boxes were still common in 1963, when the first *Doctor Who* series was made, but were gradually demolished or removed between 1969 and 1981 as radio, walkie-talkies and squad cars rendered them redundant. You can still see an original box at the Peel Centre for police training in Hendon – the best views are from the Northern Line train, looking to your right between Hendon Central and Colindale.

Another piece of street furniture once used for law enforcement is the police post. Equipped with a telephone that could be operated by the public as well as the police, a light, and a locked box containing a first-aid kit, these were introduced from 1907, when the capital's police stations were equipped with telephone exchanges. Most of the surviving examples in London date from the early 1930s, and like Scott's K2 phone box they take inspiration from the classical column, with Soanean details including a shallow arched entablature topped with a lantern mounted on a miniature stepped pedestal. Perhaps because most of the public at the time

Police post outside Postman's Park

were unused to telephones, and simply shouting for help was a more natural (and possibly more effective) response to an emergency, they were little used. Originally painted light blue, around seventy were installed, with eight (non-functioning) examples remaining within the City of London (locations include outside Liverpool Street station, Guildhall, Mansion House and St Martin's-le-Grand near St Paul's, as well as Piccadilly Circus). You can see one in use (ineffectually, of course) outside King's Cross in the 1955 Ealing Comedy *The Ladykillers*.

A poignant comparison of historical British bumbling and present-day US military might was offered until recently through the juxtaposition of the ⑬ **neglected police post** that sits under the watchful gaze of President Eisenhower and the state-of-the-art security guarding the former US Embassy in Grosvenor Square. The embassy moved to a new building in Nine Elms in January 2018.

You can find another memento of 1930s law enforcement in the ⑭ **'policeman's hook'** at 4 Great Newport Street, near Covent Garden. Tucked discreetly into a recessed section of wall, it provided the officer directing traffic at the nearby junction with somewhere to hang his cape or coat.

12. Police box, Earl's Court Underground, SW5 9AA
13. Police post, Grosvenor Square, W1K 6DT
14. 'Policeman's hook', 4 Great Newport St, WC2H 7JB

3.4 Lamp Posts

The function of London's half a million lamp posts stretches far beyond simply lighting our streets. Back in the early 18th century, when an Act of Parliament demanded that householders and businesses burn lights outside their premises from 6pm to 11pm, the justification was a form of social control: to curb undesirable behaviour such as prostitution, theft or violence and make the streets safe for the leisure pursuits of the upper classes. The strategy met with limited success and those who could afford it continued to employ link-boys to walk ahead of them with lighted torches. You can still see houses in wealthy areas with **15** **torch-snuffers** attached to their railings, as in Amen Court, the only surviving residential street in the neighbourhood of St Paul's.

Today lamp posts are coopted for all kinds of other uses, functioning as mounts for bins and hanging baskets, vandal-proof display boards for directions, street names, prohibitions and instructions, and stands for the security cameras that ensure we comply. You could say that lamp posts are the multitaskers of our streetscape.

The strategy of using a lamp post as a form of social control was taken to its extreme in Trafalgar Square. Worried about demonstrations linked to the 1926 General Strike, the Metropolitan Police converted a **16** **lamp standard** in the south-eastern corner into London's smallest police station. The ornamental stone column was hollowed out and fitted with a semi-glazed door, lighting and a direct phone connection to Scotland Yard; decorative openings, spaced at regular intervals like arrow slits in a medieval fortress, provided spyholes. Today the space is used intermittently as a storeroom.

Gas & Gaslights

The first public gas-powered street lighting was installed in Pall Mall in 1807. By the end of the 1820s London had more than 40,000 gaslights lining 215 miles of streets and, amazingly, around 1,500 of these are still in operation. Most of them are looked after by British Gas, which employs a team of five modern-day guardians of the lamp to visit each once a fortnight, climbing a ladder to wind the timing mechanisms, repair broken mantles and clean the glass.

You can identify these lamps by looking for the clocks within their glass cases, the flickering pilot lights that can be glimpsed on dull days or the soft, creamy-yellow glow by night. To appreciate the effect, take an evening stroll down **17** **Marlborough Road,** through St James's Park and along Birdcage Walk, much of which is still lit by gaslight. Many lampstands bear the mark of the reigning monarch: the oldest in London are in Marlborough Road and Birdcage Walk, installed during the reign of George IV (1820-30).

If London still has a surprising number of gaslights, there is only one remaining **18** **working sewer gas destructor lamp.** Patented in the 1890s by Joseph Webb, this was an ingenious invention that gave the gaslight the supplementary function of burning off the potentially poisonous and explosive gases from the city's sewers while at the same time economising on coal gas. (Sewer stink pipes, see page 40, performed the same function of ventilation, but without putting the gases to any useful purpose). The lamps required a conventional gas supply as well: heat from this flame created an updraught

17

to draw up the methane, which would then combust to produce an even brighter light. Each lamp could ventilate three-quarters of a mile of sewer. You can see the only working example in Carting Lane at the back of the Savoy, burning day and night courtesy in part of gas from Joseph Bazalgette's nearby Victoria Embankment sewer. Nicknamed the Iron Lily and now heavily restored after a collision with a lorry, it is inconspicuously elegant, with a fluted shaft ringed by studded collars topped with a single lantern.

On the corner of New Cross Road and Queen's Road in Lewisham is a ⑲ **non-functioning gas destructor lamp** that is the only work outside Glasgow by 19th-century architect Alexander 'Greek' Thomson. Though Thomson died in 1875, the lamp was not installed until 1897, supplying streetlighting with the help of methane from the toilets below. Manufactured by Walter MacFarlane &

Co, also of Glasgow, a prolific foundry whose architectural ironwork was exported throughout the British empire, it is a work of impressive and resplendent magnificence that far outshines the prosaic nature of its function. Newly restored, with its decoration picked out in gold, its fluted column and base have Egyptian papyrus mouldings along with the Greek motifs that gave the architect his nickname – a huge weight of history to support a single, small light. You can see the ventilation holes at the top of the column. There is another, sadly neglected example without a light nearby, at the top of Clifton Rise. The design is based on the standards Thomson created for the Egyptian Halls in Glasgow in 1871, also manufactured by MacFarlane, but exactly how these copies ended up in south London is a mystery.

Pomp & Circumstance

Erected and maintained by borough councils, elaborate Victorian lamp posts were an expression of civic pride. The most iconic central London examples are the **⟨20⟩ 'dolphin' lamp posts** on Victoria Embankment. Created between 1865 and 1870 as part of works to reclaim marshy riverside land for Joseph Bazalgette's sewerage system, the embankment transformed the city's relationship with the river, providing fashionable new carriageways and promenades that required street lighting appropriate to their status. In an unusual exercise in public consultation, several proposed designs were displayed to gauge opinion. Two were chosen: the 'dolphins' by George Vulliamy, architect to the Metropolitan Board of Works, and Bazalgette's simpler lion's paws. Both had reliable classical precedents – Vulliamy's in the Fontana del Nettuno in Rome's Piazza del Popolo. These classical connotations were deliberate: Bazalgette's engineering feat was hailed as comparable with the glories of ancient Rome and the lamp posts were intended to highlight London's prominence as an imperial capital.

In fact, the moulded 'dolphins' are two interlaced sturgeons with their tails rising upwards to wrap around the column. Sturgeons were perhaps chosen as a symbol of continuity (their characteristics have remained unchanged since the earliest fossil records) or of luxury (the source of caviar). Certainly the new sewerage system, which initially discharged directly into the Thames, did little for the river's live fish population. Vulliamy also designed camel and sphinx benches for Victoria Embankment in anticipation of the installation of Cleopatra's Needle near Waterloo Bridge in 1878 (see page 185).

Given the authors of the chosen designs, the lamp post competition sounds something of a shoo-in. Certainly *The*

Illustrated News favoured a design by the artist Timothy Butler in conjunction with the Coalbrookdale Company. This extraordinary fantasia consisted of a base decorated with trident and caduceus surmounted by twin cornucopia overflowing with gifts of plenty representing the rewards of British commerce. The most striking feature, however, is a pair of boys – one naked and one partly draped – climbing the column and exchanging a burning torch. The boys were apparently intended to symbolise the energy of the nation, though they come across more as a pair of cheeky urchin lamplighters. Luckily at least one example of **㉑ Butler's lamp post** was manufactured in 1874 and you can see it today on the Chelsea Embankment, just east of Albert Bridge.

Versions of Vulliamy's 'dolphins' were later placed along the Albert Embankment and The Mall, where the nautical theme of Admiralty Arch is reinforced by standards decorated with scallop shells and **㉒ topped by galleons** installed in the first decade of the 20th century. Mistakenly assumed to be visible to Nelson atop his column in Trafalgar Square, they are said by some to represent each of his battleships and by others to represent the ships he defeated.

Signs & Signals

23

23

24

If London's lamp posts are bursting with symbolism, their decoration is also ripe for misinterpretation. One ubiquitous example in the City of Westminster is the **23** **interlocked 'C's** placed back-to-back on many of the 20th-century columns. The arrangement of the letters and the gold paint have stirred up speculation that this is the Coco Chanel logo, inscribed alongside an ornate 'W' on the instructions of Hugh Grosvenor, 2nd Duke of Westminster, with whom Chanel is said to have had a decade-long relationship from the mid-1920s. (Recently discovered documents unmasking Chanel as a Nazi spy reveal that her codename was Westminster, in reference to the affair.) The reality behind the lettering is more prosaic. According to a council spokesman, 'The fancy W stands for Westminster and the two C's stand for City Council.' Moreover, the lamp posts weren't actually installed until the 1950s.

A lamp post outside **24** **2 Audley Square** in Mayfair has a more recent connection with espionage, having been used by Russian agents in the 1950s and 1960s to signal the deposit and receipt of intelligence documents. The story sounds like the stuff of legend, but seems to have been true. According to Roy Berkeley's *A Spy's London*, an agent who wished to transmit documents to his masters would place a blue chalk

mark below a number on the lamp post. He would then check a bench in nearby St George's Gardens for a similar chalk mark – which was the sign that his signal had been noticed by a KGB officer. After placing his material in a dead letter box (the most popular was behind a column in Brompton Oratory, see page 229), the agent would remove the chalk from the post. His KGB officer would collect the documents and then remove his own mark from the bench.

Today the area is still home to numerous embassies and high commissions and 4x4s with blacked-out windows prowl the streets. Why this particular lamp post, in a relatively open location outside the University Women's Club, was chosen has not been revealed – though Berkeley does suggest that later spies found less obvious ways of leaving marks. By coincidence, 3 Audley Square was during the early 1960s the home of Eon Productions, where Cubby Broccoli and Harry Saltzman cooked up the James Bond films.

In the first decades of the 21st century lamp posts are moving into Bond territory to exercise smarter means of social control through such strategies as bulbs that dim automatically when no one is around and conversely provide bright light where trouble is expected. A huge number of

standards host surveillance cameras and
some cities are introducing 'spy' lamp
posts that can harvest data from mobile
phones. Clearly there is more watching
going on when leaning on a lamp post than
George Formby's innocent 1930s hopes of
glimpsing 'a certain little lady'.

15. Torch-snuffers,
    Amen Court, EC4M 7BU
16. Former police station,
    Trafalgar Square, WC2N 5DR
17. Marlborough Rd SW1A 1BG
18. Sewer gas destructor lamp,
    Carting Lane, WC2R 0EU
19. Former gas destructor lamp,
    New Cross Rd, SE14 5AA
20. 'Dolphin' lamp posts,
    Victoria Embankment, WC2N 6PB
21. Timothy Butler lamp post,
    Chelsea Embankment, SW3 5HH
22. Galleons, The Mall, SW1A 2BJ
23. Westminster lamp posts
24. 2 Audley Square, W1K 1DB

25

3.5 Bollards

Bollards – a word found in dictionaries from the mid-19th century to describe an object previously defined simply as a post – are one of our least-loved items of street furniture. Unnecessarily officious and often useless, their role seems to be to discourage rather than actually prevent access to somewhere we want to go.

Their essence is conveyed brilliantly in an unattributed **25 artwork by Judith Dean** installed in and around Cromer Street, just south of St Pancras, in 2000. Most passers-by probably fail to notice anything unusual – the bollards Dean has added to the streetscape seem to be standard size and colour so it is only when you question their positioning that their oddity, and the artist's joke, become apparent. Taken together, they form a catalogue of redundancy: one is in the middle of a patch of grass in Regent Square Gardens and another (in Wakefield Mews) stands helplessly beside a tree; another (in Loxham Street) is in the centre of a wide pedestrianised zone while opposite it another sits within an already fenced-off courtyard; two others huddle together beside the entrance to Holy Cross Church.

Their sleek, streamlined shape, with polished black granite reflecting street and sky, is perhaps a comment on the overelaboration of the capital's other markers, in particular the massed black, white and red **26 cannon-shaped bollards** installed in the 1990s to control movement through the City of London – you can find a typical throng of them protecting Cannon Street Station from unspecified attack.

The continued use of the cannon – a technology that has been outmoded for well over a century – as a model for London bollards is in itself odd, though it does reflect their function of standing

sentry over monuments and public spaces as well as conferring a false sense of timeless authority. The practice of using actual cannons for bollards dates from the second half of the 18th century and became more common after the end of the Napoleonic Wars in 1815 as a means of redeploying captured guns from French ships that were too large for their British counterparts.

You can see **27** **four massive early cannon bollards** at the dilapidated entrance to the Royal Victoria Victualling Yard in Grove Street (just south of Jodane Street), Deptford. Painted black and white, with cannon balls rammed into their muzzles, their size and solidity – despite damage from collisions – make more modern bollards seem puny by comparison.

A range of **28** **examples from the late 18th and early 19th centuries** guard the entrance to Cannon Hall (the childhood home of writer Daphne du Maurier and one of London's most expensive private residences) in Cannon Place in Hampstead, as well as the parish lock-up (see page 238), built into the wall of the hall in 1730, in Cannon Lane. Here you can see both squat and more slender cannons, with and without cannon balls. An example halfway down Cannon Lane still has the protruding trunnion – used to attach the cannon to its carriage – at its base. At the back of St Helen's Bishopsgate in the City (see page 20) is a **29** **crude and rusting cannon bollard** that is an oddity in being buried muzzle-down rather than muzzle-up.

Just as former military hardware was used to make bollards, so bollards were removed to make guns during WW2. In the late 1980s, a group of Hyde Park horseriders got together to raise funds to replace the bollards that once separated riders from the road. There are now some **30** **600 bollards** marching across the landscape, each inscribed with the name

of a company or individual, and their function – apart from nuisance value – seems to be mainly corporate advertising or self-aggrandisement. They lend the unassuming and unattributed bollards of Cromer Street an extra poignancy.

25. Holy Cross Church, Cromer St, Regent Square Gardens and Wakefield Mews, WC1H 8JU
26. Cannon Street Station, EC4N 6AP
27. Royal Victoria Victualling Yard, SE8 3AY
28. Cannon Lane, NW3 1EL
29. Rear of St Helen's Bishopsgate, EC3A 6AT
30. Hyde Park (Rotten Row), W2 2UH

27

28

29

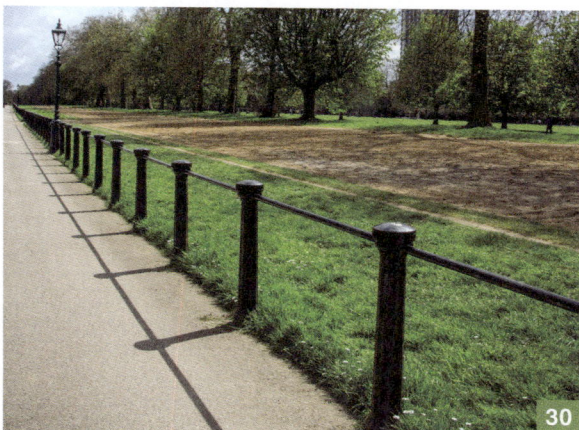

30

30

Whalebone Arch

In Wood Street in Barnet, about 200 metres west of the junction with Wellhouse Lane, stands a **31** gateway imported from the South Pacific. A lofty arch created from the jawbones of a blue whale marks the entrance to Whalebones, a typically English Georgian house recently on the market for £2.5 million. At 7.3 metres high and weighing about a tonne and a half, the bones bring an unexpected touch of South Seas exoticism to a leafy London suburb.

The first set of whalebones on the site were thought to have been installed in the 1830s by polar explorer John Franklin to mark the entrance to his new home. The present bones were imported in 1939 by the house's then owner Gwyn Cowing, whose quest for a replacement for the crumbling original structure was answered by a Norwegian whaling company. According to the firm hired to install the new arch, the cargo that arrived in Barnet stank of rotting fish: the first task was to extract the sinewy nerves responsible for the stench from the bones by tying their ends to a lorry and driving off. Now splintered and worn, with a coating of lichen, the arch looks like a relic of the Jurassic age – a fitting reminder that blue whales have been hunted almost to extinction.

3.6 Gateways

York Gate

Standing at the north end of Victoria Embankment Gardens is another gateway stranded like a fish out of water. For 250 years, **32 York Gate** and stairs provided access to the Thames from the fashionable area around the Strand, enabling the local elite to use the river's taxi service. But in 1862, when the Thames was narrowed as part of the construction of Joseph Bazalgette's sewerage system, the gate and its stairs were left literally high and dry. York Gate now stands almost 150 metres from the river.

Watermen's stairs, which allowed boats to drop off or pick up passengers and goods even at low tide, date from the 14th century; by 1746 John Rocque's map of London shows some 250 access points. York Gate was built in 1626 to serve visitors and residents of York House, the new home of George Villiers, 1st Duke of Buckingham. Sometimes attributed to Inigo Jones, its scale and decoration, especially from the river side, constituted a conspicuous display of wealth and fashionable taste, with motifs in the popular Italianate style exemplified by Jones' Banqueting House in Whitehall. A Portland stone Serliana, with the central arch giving access to the steps and the

side arches providing shelter for waiting passengers, is faced with Doric columns with bands of vermiculation (decoration resembling worm tracks). The central two columns support an ornate pediment bearing the Villiers arms topped by a scallop shell. Above each of the side bays is a seated lion holding a shield with an anchor representing Buckingham's status as Lord Admiral. On the plainer street or garden side, the family motto ('the Cross is the touchstone of faith') is inscribed on the frieze.

Villiers was a favourite (some say lover) of James I and held high office under Charles I before being assassinated by a disgruntled army officer in 1628. Some 50 years later, his son sold the house to be demolished by developers – but the gate remained. Even today, despite its lack of function or purpose, its uncompromising confidence asserts an impressive sense of power.

31. Whalebone Arch, Wood St, EN5 4DB
32. York Gate, Victoria Embankment Gardens, WC2N 6NE

Temple Bar

Dating from the time of York House's demolition, Christopher Wren's glorious **33 Temple Bar** – in its present position on the edge of Paternoster Square near St Paul's only since 2004 – is also an entrance to nowhere. The only surviving gateway to the City of London, it originally stood between Fleet Street and the Strand, replacing a wooden structure that had suffered damage in the 1666 Great Fire, which in turn had replaced a chain and posts installed in the 13th century. Not only traders and passers-by but even monarchs had to stop at the gate to request permission to enter the City.

Temple Bar was dismantled stone by stone in 1877 to allow for the construction of the Royal Courts of Justice. A decade later it was acquired by brewery owner Henry Meux as a grand entrance to his estate in Hertfordshire, apparently at the request of his wife Valerie, a former 'actress' turned flamboyant socialite, racehorse owner and collector of antiquities who drove through London in a carriage pulled by zebras. Temple Bar remained in rural exile, increasingly neglected, until its return to London over a century later.

Tollgates

According to an 1857 article from the *Illustrated London News*, there were once 87 tollgates and bars within a four mile radius of Charing Cross, adding to the cost of goods and travel as well as being a 'vexatious... nuisance so obvious and so palpable that it does not need to be insisted on'. The anti-gate campaign eventually triumphed and London now retains only one functioning **34 tollgate**, positioned near the junction of Grange Lane and College Road to discourage driving through the Dulwich Estate between Crystal Palace and Dulwich Village. The barrier was established in 1789 but the present replica tollbooth was installed only in 1993. If you are wondering where your money ends up, the Dulwich Estate is a charitable trust that funds local public schools.

35 Albert Bridge has London's only surviving bridge tollbooths, though the tolls themselves were abolished only six years after the bridge's opening in 1873. Signs that read 'All troops must break step when marching over this bridge' were addressed to soldiers from nearby Chelsea Barracks, whose marching caused the bridge to vibrate, potentially damaging its structure. The original 'wobbly bridge' – prefiguring the problems that beset the Millennium Bridge over a century later – Albert Bridge was nicknamed the 'trembling lady'.

Tolls charged at Dartford, London's busiest river crossing, were scheduled to be revoked once the costs of building the Queen Elizabeth II bridge in 1991 were covered. Still in place, they have become what a spokesman from the Automobile Association has described as 'a nice little earner which raises around £70 million in a year'.

Downing Street

London's most famous gates today are probably those sealing off the Whitehall entrance to **36 Downing Street** – an oddity in that they perhaps uniquely deny the public's legal right to 'pass and repass... without let or hindrance' part of the capital's public highway. A relatively modest Westminster terrace designed by Wren in the 1680s and advertised in 1720 as homes 'fit for Persons of Honour and Quality', Downing Street has housed Britain's two most senior cabinet ministers (whose honour and quality have been variable) for some 300 years. There have been temporary or partial barriers in place at times since 1920, but the present excessively tall black-painted metal gates and railings were installed only in 1989, under the watch of Margaret Thatcher, as part of the police response to the IRA bombing campaign that also introduced a 'ring of steel' (mainly made up of security cameras) around the City of London. Previous police pressure for tighter security had been resisted: in 1974 requests to create a permanent barrier were turned down by prime minister Harold Wilson, whose private secretary wrote, 'I much regret this further erosion of the Englishman's right to wander at will in Downing Street'.

Even with gates in place, public right of way was not finally denied until 2005, using counter-terrorism legislation. And it seems the policemen at the gates control not only those wishing to go in, but even those wishing to get out, as MP Andrew Mitchell found to his cost when he was challenged for riding through on a bicycle in 2012.

33. Temple Bar, Paternoster Square, EC4M 7DX
34. Dulwich tollgate, College Rd, SE21 7LY
35. Albert Bridge tollbooths, SW11 4PL
36. Downing Street gates, SW1A 2AB

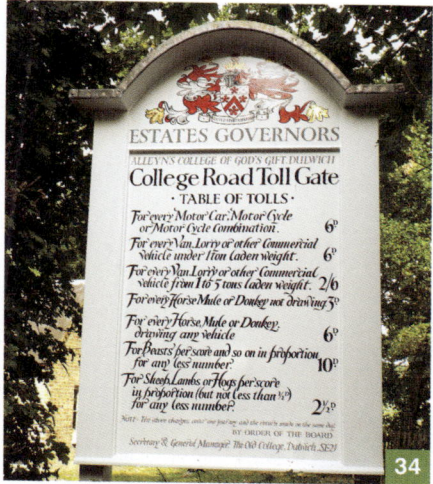

39

3.7 Pumps & Fountains

'There are also about London, on the north side, excellent suburban springs, with sweet, wholesome, and clear water that flows rippling over the bright stones; among which Holy Well, Clerken Well, and Saint Clements are held to be of most note; these are frequented… by scholars and youth of the city when they go out for fresh air on summer evenings.' William Fitzstephen, *Descriptio Nobilissimi Civitatis Londoniae*, 1174

Clean drinking water – essential to our survival but still far from universal – is a surprisingly recent phenomenon for Londoners. Previously the capital relied for water on the increasingly filthy Thames and its tributaries as well as a dozen or so natural springs; two of those noted by William Fitzstephen in 1174, above, are still marked at street level today. The **37** **Clerks' Well**, which gave Clerkenwell its name and was in use until the mid-19th century, was rediscovered during the rebuilding of Farringdon Lane in the 1920s. It can still be glimpsed though the windows of the Well Court office block or visited by appointment. The **38** **holy well or spring of St Clement**, a place of pilgrimage from the early Christian era, was supplied with a pump in 1807 which can still be seen at the eastern end of the grounds of Wren's St Clement Danes in the Strand. The well itself was covered over in 1874 as part of the foundations for the nearby law courts.

London's 'sweet water' did not always prove wholesome, however. The most infamous example of a 'pump of death' was the **39** **Broad Street** (now Broadwick) **pump** in Soho, which was responsible for 616 deaths from cholera in 1854. Soho resident John Snow, a doctor and pioneer of anesthesia who initiated a fashion for chloroform in childbirth after tending Queen Victoria's last two confinements, had been trying for five years to demonstrate that cholera was transmitted through contaminated water: his careful mapping of cases following the Broad Street outbreak (including two women who had moved away from the area but still drank from the pump because they liked the taste) eventually proved his point. Despite denials of negligence by water-company officials, the likely cause was traced to a leaking cesspool into which a woman had emptied water used for washing her infected baby's nappies. The site of the pump at the junction with Lexington Street is marked by a plaque on the front of the John

40

ON
THIS SPOT
A
WELL
WAS
FIRST MADE,
AND
A HOUSE
OF CORRECTION
BUILT THEREON
BY
HENRY WALLIS,
MAYOR OF LONDON,
IN
THE YEAR
1282.

NATHANIEL WRIGHT
ARCHITECT

41

BEDFORD ROW

42

REPLACE THE CUP.

43

Snow pub. There is also a replica of the strikingly simple and functional original pump on the pavement outside.

Another pump notorious for supplying contaminated water is the ㊵ **Aldgate pump** at the junction of Aldgate with Leadenhall and Fenchurch Streets – this time in 1876, when several hundred people died from drinking water polluted with bacteria from human remains from the new North London cemeteries. Previously the water had been praised for its high mineral content – including copious quantities of calcium that was now assumed to have seeped from human bones. The present, sadly neglected, structure – a tapered Portland stone obelisk with rusticated bands – probably dates from the 18th century; the gabled cap is a 19th-century addition that in a typical instance of London monument multitasking at one time supported a gas lamp. After its supply was condemned as unfit for human consumption the pump was converted to mains water so successfully that in the 1920s tea merchants Whittard boasted their kettles were filled from the pump 'so only the purest water was used'.

London also had pumps that brought unmitigated public benefit, some elegantly or idiosyncratically designed as landmarks with forms that far outstrip their modest function. The ㊶ **cast-iron obelisk** outside the Royal Exchange in Cornhill, newly restored, was designed in 1799 by City of London surveyor Nathaniel Wright, who also rebuilt St Botolph Aldersgate in Postman's Park. It was installed over a well discovered in the 13th century and then forgotten for 400 years after the prison it served was demolished in 1380. The pump's construction was funded by the Bank of England, the East India Company and other local bankers and traders as well as neighbouring fire officers; around its top are the emblems of four fire insurance companies. Other

cast-iron pumps that deserve a mention for the elaboration of their appearance include those in ㊷ **Bedford Row** (at the junction with Brownlow Street) and Queen Square in Holborn, dating from 1826 and 1840 respectively. Both multitask as lamp posts and are decorated with the arms of St Andrew and St George at the base and beautifully cast lions' masks towards the top of the column.

The unwholesome condition of London's water, coupled with a desire to stem the consumption of beer and gin, led to the foundation of the Metropolitan Drinking Fountain Association in 1859 to support the provision and maintenance of fountains. The first of these, paid for by the association's founder Samuel Gurney MP and once used by 7,000 people a day, can still be seen against the railings of ㊸ **St Sepulchre-without-Newgate** on the corner of Giltspur Street and Holborn Viaduct in the City. Encased in an elaborate surround, the fountain itself is a simple marble niche – like the setting for a holy relic – within which is a stone scallop shell surmounting a tap above a small basin. Two simple iron cups are attached by chains to the churchyard railings and the legend 'replace the cup' appears along the bottom; drawings show that the original cup was a much more elaborate goblet.

By 1865 (this being England), the association had become equally concerned with the welfare of animals and changed its name to the Metropolitan Drinking Fountain and Cattle Trough Association. Most new fountains were now equipped with low-level drinking bowls for dogs and numerous independent drinking troughs were provided (see page 304). There is an example of a quirky ㊹ **fountain with attached dog bowl** in New North Road in Shoreditch, half in and half out of the mid-19th-century railings of the church of St John the Baptist, which bend to

accommodate it. Perhaps as a nod to its graveyard position, the fountain seems to be topped by a black granite urn – hardly auspicious at a period when drinking water was still widely mistrusted.

Within two years of its founding, the association had installed 85 fountains and wealthy patrons were gushing to commission ever more sumptuous examples. You can find eccentric Victorian fountains all over London, but the **45** **Burdett-Coutts Memorial Drinking-Fountain** near the centre of the eastern side of Victoria Park in Tower Hamlets takes some beating for both size and decoration. Designed in 1862 by Henry Astley Darbishire, the architect to the Peabody Trust, it is said to have cost £6000 – a small fortune, though easily affordable by its patron Angela Burdett-Coutts (1814-1906), who became one of the wealthiest women in England after inheriting £1.8 million from her grandfather in 1837. Among the philanthropic causes she supported were women's education, hospitals and better housing for the people of East London as well as a home for young women who had 'turned to a life of immorality', co-founded with Charles Dickens. She herself spent most of her life in the company of her former governess and 'darling' Hannah

Brown, before marrying her secretary, an American almost 40 years her junior, soon after Brown's death in 1878.

The fountain itself is a miniature temple in the Victorian gothic style, with Moorish touches. A central octagonal chamber is surrounded by a walkway beneath an elaborately vaulted sandstone arcade whose gothic arches are supported on eight pink marble pillars. The structure is topped by a slate cupola with alternating clock faces and windows, finished off with a weather vane. The water is dispensed by four individually sculpted cherubs holding vases, some positioned so the water bizarrely appears to stream between their legs. The inscription reads: 'The earth is the Lord's and all that thereon is.'

Only one-fifth the cost and on a much smaller scale – which makes its juxtapositions of disparate materials and overwrought ecclesiastical decoration look clumsy rather than jewel-like – is the **46** **Buxton Memorial Fountain**, now in Victoria Tower Gardens in Westminster, built to commemorate the abolition of slavery in 1834. Its oddest feature is the gothic spire, clad with brightly coloured enamelled sheet metal; look out for the dog bowl at the base.

While many of London's oldest pumps and fountains are no longer operational, the Metropolitan Association is still in business, installing water fountains in schools and parks in the UK and funding projects to provide clean water in developing countries. It seems that provision of public drinking fountains in London is once more to receive a boost too following concern at the proliferation of single-use plastic water bottles.

London's mains water supply, meanwhile, having been in public ownership for most of the 20th century, is once more in private hands. You wonder if the wheel might turn full circle: one of London's largest water companies, Thames Water, now Australian owned, was fined for pollution more often between 2005 and 2013 than any other UK supplier.

37. Clerks' Well,
    Farringdon Lane, EC1R 3AU
38. St Clement Danes pump,
    Strand, WC2R 1DH
39. Broad Street pump, W1F 7NZ
40. Aldgate pump, EC3A 3DE
41. Cornhill pump, EC3V 3LL
42. Bedford Row pump, WC1R 8BU
43. St Sepulchre-without-Newgate fountain,
    EC1A 2AE
44. St John the Baptist fountain
    with dog bowl, New North Rd, N1 6AU
45. Burdett-Coutts Memorial Drinking
    Fountain, Victoria Park, E9 7DD
46. Buxton Memorial Fountain,
    Victoria Tower Gardens, SW1P 3JU

46

47

3.8 Timepieces

Until recently, London could claim ownership of the standard for all timekeeping. Greenwich Mean Time, which calculates noon by the average (or mean) time when the sun crosses the Greenwich meridian, acted as a national and then worldwide standard from the mid-19th century until the introduction of Coordinated Universal Time in 1972. Mounted on the wall outside Greenwich Observatory is the **47** **Shepherd Gate clock**, the first clock publicly to display Greenwich Mean Time in 1852 and an oddity because it has a 24-hour analogue dial – unexpectedly since the British have proved uniquely resistant to the 24-hour clock embraced by the rest of Europe. Initially, and confusingly, the zero at the top of the circle indicated noon, but this was changed to midnight at some point in the 20th century. Using the clock to tell the time is still a disorienting experience, however, as you find the minute hand in the usual position but the hour hand contradicts expectations.

Made in Switzerland?

Given London's pioneering history, it is perhaps surprising that the capital's oddest clock – the **48** **Swiss glockenspiel** in Swiss Court just off Leicester Square – is a gift from abroad, albeit from a renowned clockmaking nation. The face is the super-legible, number-free Swiss railway clock, an icon designed in 1944 (the prominent red second hand, inspired by a railway guard's signalling disc, was introduced a decade later). The example in Leicester Square stands on a 10-metre-high tower; immediately below it is a glockenspiel of 27 bells, each engraved with the name and shield of a Swiss canton twinned with a Westminster ward, and a drum embellished with cantonal shields. There is no cuckoo, but on top of the drum stand four old-fashioned wooden figures – two peasants and two bourgeois citizens – gazing out from their safe haven at the urban chaos around them. At set times (12.00 daily, then hourly from 17.00 to 20.00 on weekdays and 14.00 to 20.00 at weekends) a procession of herdsmen and nodding cows and goats rises from within the drum, takes a turn to survey the square and then beats a retreat.

Originally attached to the Swiss Centre, a now demolished oddity designed to promote all things Swiss, the glockenspiel was presented to the City of Westminster in 1985 by the Confederation of Switzerland to mark

49

the City Council's 400th anniversary. It was originally programmed to play 200 tunes but since being reconfigured in 2011 by Smith of Derby, the venerable firm that was also responsible for the clock on St Paul's, it plays new music written by the Royal Academy of Music in London and the University for Music and Art in Berne. Swiss railway clocks are controlled electronically from a master clock; the Leicester Square clock is controlled from Derby in the UK.

London's more famous (and arguably more kitsch) **49** **automaton clock** hangs outside Fortnum & Mason in Piccadilly. Despite its rococo appearance, it was installed only in 1964, and the front of the building had to be reinforced to support it. On the hour, to the tune of the 'Eton Boating Song', Mr Fortnum and Mr Mason emerge to bow to each other before retiring inside.

The purity of the Swiss railway clock is subverted in two 1990s art installations in and near Canary Wharf (see page 129). In **50** *Six Public Clocks* in Reuters Plaza, Konstantin Grcic has positioned six scaled-up Swiss clocks with a single numeral added to each. It is disappointing that all the faces tell the same time – perhaps because bankers are easily confused by

numbers. Just outside the Canary Wharf estate's reach, on Westferry Road, Richard Wentworth in his installation **51** *Globe* has mounted seventeen clocks on an anonymous stretch of wall opposite the entrance to the Limehouse Link tunnel. Each is set to tell the time in a different location – Beijing, Tokyo, New York, Alice Springs, Honolulu and Moscow among others – moving clockwise, of course, around the globe. The locations are virtually unreadable – cars speed by too fast and pedestrians are either too close on the pavement beneath or too distant on the opposite side of the carriageway. Back in 1995, the installation was perhaps a way of puncturing the pretensions of London's new international business hub.

A much older **52** **world clock** can be found in Piccadilly Circus tube, designed by London Underground architect Charles Holden (see page 309) when the showcase station was refurbished in the mid-1920s. Perhaps the idea was to appeal to foreign tourists, or to flatter aspiring shoppers that they stood at the centre of the world. Mounted in a handsome 2-metre-high wooden case, the linear clock consists of a map of the world with a central horizontal band marked with the hours in Roman numerals superimposed over it. The strip scrolls across the map at the speed of the rotation of the earth, so the time at any point can be read by drawing a vertical line from a position on the map to the corresponding number on the strip.

47. Shepherd Gate clock, Greenwich Observatory, Blackheath Ave, SE10 8JX
48. Swiss glockenspiel, Swiss Court, off Leicester Square, W1D 6BH
49. Fortnum & Mason automaton clock, 181 Piccadilly, W1A 1ER
50. *Six Public Clocks*, Reuters Plaza, E14 5LQ
51. *Globe*, Westferry Rd, E14 8AU
52. World Clock, Piccadilly Circus Underground, W1J 9HP

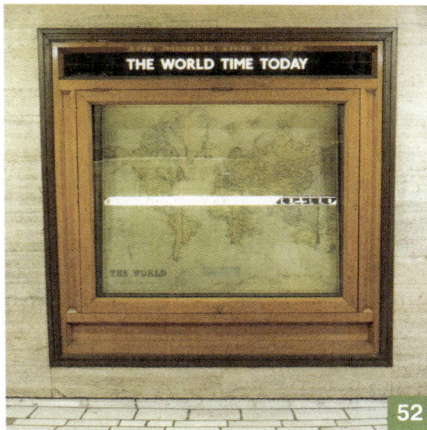

THE WORLD TIME TODAY

THE WORLD

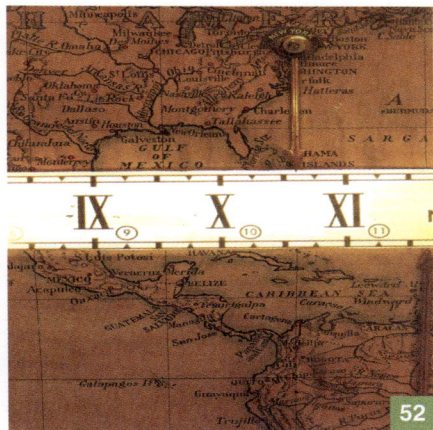

Towering Statements

Like the best of Holden's Underground stations, the Piccadilly Circus clock is understated and elegant, but often clocks and clock towers have functioned as pretexts for building to excessive height and/or indulging in excessive decoration. The flamboyance of the Palace of Westminster, for instance, culminates in the tower built to house London's most famous timepiece, incorrectly known as **53** **Big Ben**, which is in fact the nickname for the bells that have tolled the quarters since 1859 including the Great Bell that still introduces the national news. A symbol of London and one of the world's best-known landmarks, the tower and clock were not included in the competition won by Charles Barry to rebuild the palace following a fire in 1834 but were a rhetorical flourish added later. Subject to stringent regulation, with demands that its performance be telegraphed twice a day to Greenwich to check its accuracy, the clock was the first to have a Double Three-Legged Gravity Escapement mechanism that ensured its pendulum was unaffected by environmental factors such as wind pressure on its hands. Two miniature copies – **54** **Little Bens** – can be found at the junction of Victoria Street and Vauxhall Bridge Road, near Victoria Station, and in Brockwell Park in Herne Hill. The one outside Victoria (installed in 1892 and restored with help from oil company Elf Aquitaine as 'a gesture of Franco-British friendship' in 1981) is permanently stuck on daylight-saving or continental time, so is wrong for five months of the year. Whatever its proclamations of international solidarity, the first line of its dedication, 'My hands you may retard or may advance / My heart beats true for England as for France' is obviously mistaken.

53

54

54

Another eccentric and oversized London clock tower is the **55** **seven-storey centrepiece of the former Metropolitan Cattle Market** just off Caledonian Road in Islington, designed by City of London architect James Bunstone Bunning for the then rural site of Copenhagen Fields. Opened by Prince Albert in 1855, the market was created to relieve the pressure of driving animals through the City to Smithfield; witnesses of the day describe the wonder of watching thousands of cattle stream up York Way from the railway goods yards behind King's Cross.

Photographs show the magnificent tower originally surrounded by a single-storey dodecahedron containing dealers' offices, with the market stalls grouped around it, but today it stands stranded in the otherwise almost bare Caledonian Park. Forty-six metres high (the clock faces at Westminster are positioned at 55 metres), its base is supported by eight elegant arched buttresses. Halfway up are shuttered windows protecting the clock mechanism; above the clock are a balcony and a bizarre Italianate campanile. The clock is still wound by hand every few days, but the 24-hour chimes have been silenced so as not to disturb local residents.

You can find a 20th-century take on the **56** **Victorian clock tower in Chrisp Street Market** in Poplar. Described by its architect Frederick Gibberd as a 'practical folly', it was designed as a focal point for the new Lansbury Estate, built as part of the 1951 Festival of Britain exhibition as a showcase for the new social housing that would revive Britain's bomb-damaged cities. Incredibly, Chrisp Street market was the first pedestrianised shopping area in the UK.

Created as a landmark and talking point, complete with a 360-degree viewing platform near the top, the tower certainly looks extraordinary: two sides are completely open while the brick of the other

55

57

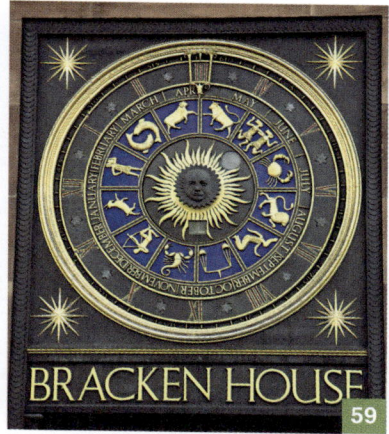

BRACKEN HOUSE

two is punctured by a dramatic diamond lattice. The four clock faces are topped by a pitched roof that gives the effect of a cuckoo clock abandoned on a fairground tower. The structure is spectacularly lit by night but by day its drama is diminished by the development around it.

Another clock oddity has not only outlived its context but has been completely removed from its original setting: the **57** **timepiece that once graced the Eastern Fever Hospital** in Homerton (dating from c. 1870) now sits incongruously in Hoxton Trust Community Garden on Hoxton Street. Instead of providing the visual culmination of a grand building, the baroque clock, topped by a wooden cupola that was probably salvaged from an even earlier structure, is balanced precariously on a metal frame above a greenhouse. It offers a rare opportunity to appreciate at close quarters part of a building that was intended only to be viewed from many metres below.

Funny Faces

Finally, two timepieces are oddities because of anomalies in their faces. The clock on the tower of the **58** **entrance to Horse Guards Parade** has a black mark at numeral II to mark the hour when Charles I was beheaded on 30 January 1649 outside Banqueting House opposite.

The elegant **59** **astronomical clock** on Bracken House in Cannon Street in the City, the former home of the *Financial Times*, was designed by Frank Dobson and Philip Bentham in 1959. It qualifies as an oddity not only because of the strangeness of embellishing a building dedicated to reporting the facts of the economy with a clock that divides time by the signs of the zodiac, but also because the face gazing out from its central sunburst is that of Winston Churchill, a close friend of *Financial Times* chairman Brendan Bracken.

53. Big Ben clock, SW1A 0AA
54. Little Ben, Victoria St, SW1E 5JX
      Little Ben, Brockwell Park, SE24 0PA
55. Caledonian Market tower, N7 9FR
56. Chrisp Street Market tower, E14 6AQ

57. Eastern Fever Hospital timepiece, Hoxton Trust Community Grdn, N1 5LH
58. Horse Guards Parade clock, SW1A 2AX
59. Bracken House astronomical clock, 10 Cannon St, EC4P 4BY

Peterkin's
Custard

Self Raising Flour

Corn Flour

Can be obtained here

3.9 Ghost Signs

Ghost signs – the remnants of hand-painted advertisements on buildings – are a haunting eruption of the past into the present. Most have not been consciously preserved or cared for but linger through benign neglect, changing year on year as sunlight and frost fade and damage their paint, sometimes revealing strata of even earlier messages beneath. To read the layers of a ghost sign is to uncover the history of a building, area or business, to discover changes in ownership, products and services or in presentation and perception.

Most ghost signs date from between the start of the 20th century and the 1950s, when mass-produced posters rendered hand-painted advertisements redundant. You can find them all over London, though the locations with most survivors tend to be on the fringes – areas that once held a wide range of small businesses and have undergone minimal development since. There's a particularly rich selection in Stoke Newington in Hackney – where 'Mr Ghost Signs' Sam Roberts runs guided tours – from which most of the examples below are taken.

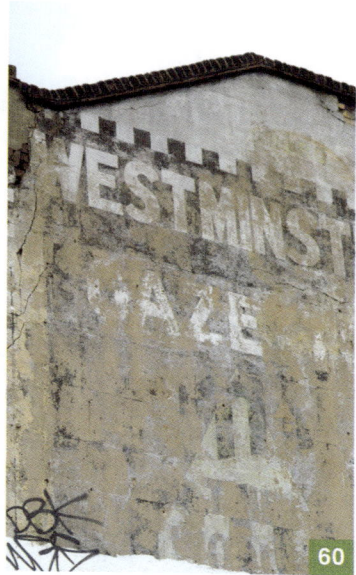

Each ghost sign is an oddity in itself in that each is the product of an individual craftsman either customising a brand's lettering style and logo to fit the proportions of a particular stretch of wall, or producing a one-off advertisement for a local business. You can spot where signwriters have miscalculated the spacing and had to compensate by adjusting the width of individual letters – as in the top line of the **60 Westminster Gazette advert** just north of Stoke Newington station on Stamford Hill – or have added full stops or decorative flourishes to fill out the lines. Sometimes literal mistakes went unremarked or were too costly to overpaint, as with the **61 Post Office sign** on the corner of Allen Road and Milton Grove, which has a capital T in 'SToke Newington'.

Unlike today's mass advertising, the size and complexity of a hand-painted ad was determined largely by the available wallspace. So a small business with a convenient area of brickwork could produce a huge custom-made promotion, like the

sign for ⑥② **F Cooper,** purveyor of Wedding Carriages, Landaus and Broughams, at the west end of Cazenove Road – a glorious example of hand-lettering that uses curved lines of type to evoke wheels – or the more straightforward sign for R Ellis, ironmonger, at the west end of nearby Northwold Road.

Sometimes larger businesses subsidised a sign on the side of premises selling their product, as with the remnant of the sign for ⑥③ **Daren flour** at (Hurst)leigh's bakery in Fleetwood Street. Though most signs are purely graphic – demonstrating the beauty and variety to be gained from using a limited range of lettering in the days before thousands of fonts were available for us to manipulate at the press of a button – others included illustrations as with that for ⑥④ **Fount Pen Specialists** Walker Bros near the junction with Marton Road on Stoke Newington Church Street, one of only two local signs protected by listing.

One of London's best-preserved illustrated signs is for ⑥⑤ **Peterkin's Custard** at the junction of Sangora Road and St John's Hill in Battersea, which mysteriously features a cheeky-looking Dutch boy. Peterkin's was the name of a nearby flour mill owned by Joseph Arthur Rank, who was later to find fame in the film industry. Though Rank's father ran a thriving flour business that was later to merge with Hovis and MacDougall to become RHM, the flour mill venture founded by his son (whom he thought of as 'a dunce') was a failure. As a result, however, the advertisement has been preserved in near-perfect condition, having been covered by a billboard when the business closed.

By contrast, the paint on signs that have been exposed for decades tends to peel or fade away – sometimes revealing previous advertisements beneath, as in the composite of ⑥⑥ **Westminster Gazette and Criterion Matches** on Stoke Newington Church Street or ⑥⑦ **Cakebread Robey & Co** on the corner of Tyssen Road and Stoke Newington High Street, a magnificent

example whose deterioration allows you to map expansions in the product range. Other signs seem odd today simply because they feature slogans that sound incongruous or funny – leather-goods manufacturer A Rubenstein & Son, aka 'Alf the Purse King', also in Stoke Newington Church Street, is a good example.

Ghost signs are advertisements painted on buildings, but buildings can also be advertisements in their own right. One of the first was the ⑥⑧ **Oxo Tower** on the South Bank, an electric power station refurbished in the 1920s by the company that made Oxo stock cubes. Because of a ban on skyline advertising, architect Albert Moore ingeniously incorporated the Oxo letters in the window design, illuminated in red at night. Some sixty years later, architect Terry Farrell pulled off a similar trick in his renovation of a 1920s building in Hawley Crescent, Camden, for the short-lived breakfast channel TV-am by embellishing the canalside roofline with a row of ⑥⑨ **giant eggcups**.

But the most audacious building-as-advertisement is probably the ⑦⓪ **National Westminster Tower** (now Tower 42) in Broad Street in the City. Designed by Richard Seifert and completed in 1980, its plan reproduces the three interlocking chevrons of the NatWest logo – a conceit that can be fully appreciated only from the air.

60. Westminster Gazette, Stamford Hill, N16 6XT
61. Post Office sign, Allen Rd, N16 8RY
62. F Cooper, Cazonove Rd, N16 6PA
63. Daren flour, Fleetwood St, N16 0ND
64. Fount Pen Specialists, Stoke Newington Church St, N16 OUD
65. Peterkins, Sangora Rd, SW11 1RL
66. Westminster Gazette/Criterion Matches, Stoke Newington Church St, N16 OUD
67. Cakebread Robey & Co, Tyssen Rd, N16 8EL
68. Oxo Tower ,South Bank, SE1 9RG
69. TV-am building, NW1 8TT
70. NatWest , 5 Old Broad St, EC2N 1HN

62

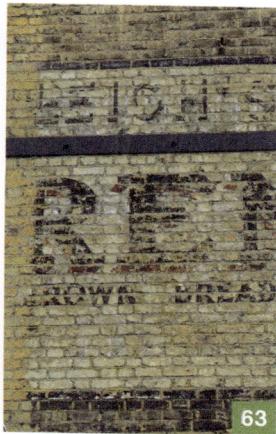

63

64

66

67

68

69

70

More London, see page 131

Private
Public Spaces

4.1 Inner & Middle Temples
4.2 Ely Place
4.3 London Silver Vaults
4.4 Public Space in Private Hands

Private Public Spaces

HAMPSTEAD

SWISS COTTAGE
Adelaide Rd
CHALK FARM

PRIMROSE HILL
CAMDEN TOWN
CAMDEN TOWN

Camden Rd

York Way

KING'S CROSS

BARNSBURY

Holloway Rd

High Fiel

Caledonian Rd

19 18

ISLINGTON

London Zoo

Regent's Park

MAIDA VALE

Euston Rd

CLERKENWELL

Farringdon Rd

Marylebone Rd

Edgware Rd

BLOOMSBURY

Theobalds Rd

8 7

MARYLEBONE

6 9

16 17

PADDINGTON

Oxford St

SOHO

1 2
5 3 PL. 4

Blackfriars Bridge

BAYSWATER

Bayswater Rd

MAYFAIR

Waterloo Bridge

Kensington Park

Hyde Park

Piccadilly

Kensington Palace

Green Park

The Mall

St James's Park

Westminster Bridge

KENSINGTON

Buckingham Palace

Cromwell

WESTMINSTER

Lambeth Bridge

LAMBETH

PIMLICO

Kensington Park Rd

STOCKWELL

Vauxhall Bridge

VAUXHALL

CHELSEA

Nine Elms Lane

Wandsworth Rd

Clapham Rd

Camberwell N

Battersea Park

BATTERSEA

Hackney
Downs

LOWER CLAPTON

Balls Pond Rd

DALSTON

Stoke Newington High

HOMERTON

Mabley
Green

Queen Elizabeth
Olympic Park

BURY

HACKNEY

HACKNEY
WICK

DE BEAUVOIR
TOWN

Kingsland Rd

E Cross Route

rth Rd

Olympic
Stadium

Shoreditch
Park

Victoria
Park

BOW

Hackney Rd

Mile End
Park

Bow Rd

SHOREDITCH

BETHNAL GREEN

MILE END

ARBICAN

Tower Hamlets
Cemetery Park

Commercial St

Whitechapel Rd

Burdett Rd

STEPNEY

OF LONDON

WHITECHAPEL

LIMEHOUSE

POPLAR

East India Dock Rd

The Highway

Bridge

London
Bridge

Tower
of London

Rotherhithe
Tunnel

CANARY WHARF

13

11

10

14

HMS
Belfast

Tower
Bridge

WAPPING

12

15

RIVER THAMES

ISLE OF DOGS

SOUTHWARK

BERMONDSEY

ROTHERHITHE

Jamaica Rd

MILLWALL

CUBITT
TOWN

Southwark
Park

VALWORTH

Tower Bridge Rd

Old Kent Road

Deptford
Park

Burgess
Park

DEPTFORD

GREENW

Deptford Creek

Fordham
Park

PECKHAM

G

Peckham Rd

Blackheath

ELL

4.1 Inner & Middle Temples

Inner Temple and Middle Temple – two of the four London Inns of Court to which all barristers in England and Wales must belong – are oddities within London's system of government as well as being odd in themselves. Covering an area of only about 11 hectares, they form a self-governing island within the City, operating as an independent local authority outside the control of either the Mayor or the City of London Corporation.

This unique arrangement dates to the 12th century, when the Knights Templar – medieval crusaders also known as the Poor Fellow-Soldiers of Christ and of the Temple of Solomon – built the Temple Church and surrounding buildings on the site. From 1169 the Templars were exempted by Papal Bull from local laws, taxes and border controls and deemed to be answerable only to the pope. Following Henry VIII's break with the Catholic church, the Temples reverted to the Crown; in 1608 James I granted them the status of liberties – areas outside royal jurisdiction – on condition that they continue to be used for the accommodation and education of students and practitioners of the law and maintain the Temple Church and its Master.

Like London's 32 other boroughs, the Temple is responsible for its own paving and lighting – mainly gas lamps – as well as refuse collection, water supply, liquor licences and public health and safety. Initially it ran its own police force but from the mid-19th century it allowed the City police to enter its precincts and work in liaison with its own security staff. As with the other two Inns of Court – Lincoln's Inn and Gray's Inn, which form part of the borough of Camden – gates are closed to the public in the evenings and at weekends.

Strolling around inside the Temple, you find yourself cut off not only from the rest of the City, but from the 21st century itself. Though the area was heavily bombed during WW2, damaged buildings were recreated close to their original 17th- and 18th-century forms – for the most part handsome five-storey brick rows with stone dressings – as if modern materials such as steel and concrete had yet to be invented. Walking through the ordered squares and courts feels like being a lowly crew member on the set of a Georgian costume drama, with only the expensive cars parked within the precincts and occasional glimpses of the chaotic contemporary cityscape beyond hinting that all is not what it seems.

The oldest building on the site is the rotunda of ❶ **Temple Church**, built by the Knights Templar in 1162 to recreate the shape and sanctity of the Church of the Holy Sepulchre in Jerusalem, deemed by the crusaders – who captured it at the end of the previous century – to be the most sacred place on earth. A rectangular funerary chapel for Henry III was added to the round church in 1240. James I decreed that the southern half of Temple Church was to be maintained by the Inner Temple and the northern half by the Middle Temple, and even today lawyers attending services are supposed to sit in the appropriate half. The official status of the church is that of 'Royal Peculiar', meaning that it falls directly under the jurisdiction of the British monarch, rather than a diocese; the Reverend and Valiant Master of the Temple, one of two clergymen who run the church, is appointed by the king or queen.

The largest of only four churches built to this form in England and one of the first to use pointed gothic arches, the

Temple Church rotunda has a dramatically central space surrounded by an ambulatory (a characteristic of pilgrimage churches). The ambulatory's delicate fan vaulting springs from slender engaged columns; the soaring central space has six sturdier columns supporting a first-floor gallery surmounted by a clerestory and wooden vaulted ceiling. The columns are the oldest surviving examples to use Dorset Purbeck marble – which in fact is not marble at all but fossiliferous limestone. Temple Church has been made over many times – for instance, the battlements that top the exterior were added by Christopher Wren. Following severe damage during WW2, it was restored to what is believed to be its original form.

Knights Templar were not only crusaders but bankers and power brokers: the Temple provided headquarters for King John during the constitutional crisis of 1214–15 that led to the drawing up of the Magna Carta, which offered his rebellious barons some protection from the whims of the Crown. Three witnesses to the charter's sealing at Runnymede are buried here – William Marshal I, the chief negotiator between the king and the barons, his son of the same name, and Brother Aymeric, then Master of the Temple. Stone effigies of the Marshals and other knights lie on the floor of the church; literally larger than life, and clutching oversized swords and shields, they convey a strong sense of power and privilege, while the broken limbs inflicted by WW2 bombs only intensify awareness of their status as soldiers. Their crossed legs were once thought to denote their role as crusaders but today historians believe they depict movement, emphasising that these were once men of action.

Elsewhere in the Temple, the names of today's power brokers and mediators are listed at the entrances to their chambers. It is relatively easy to distinguish genuinely old buildings from replicas: the constraints of post-war austerity mean that along King's Bench Walk, for instance, rebuilt sections use poor-quality brick, have badly proportioned windows and less detailing or articulation such as stringcourses and stone dressings. Peer into the windows in Pump Court and you can see that rooms on one side have panelling, mouldings and chandeliers while their replicas on the other are plain with strip lighting. Whether mock or genuine, the poky offices with young men and women hunched over computer screens again belie the sense of a world frozen in the 18th century.

Given the density of the City even before the current era of high-rise development, it is extraordinary to find an area within its boundaries with the luxury of so much open space. The 1.2-hectare ❷ **Inner Temple garden** is a sweep of green dotted with mature trees and herbaceous borders that stretches to the Thames Embankment in the distance. It is open to the public for only two and a half hours each weekday, from 12.30pm (except during high winds – lawyers never lose their fear of counter-litigation).

The hall and library of the Inner Temple are post-war reconstructions, but the ❸ **great hall of the Middle Temple** dates from 1562–73, having survived both the Great Fire and the Blitz. A magnificent Elizabethan banqueting hall over 30 metres in length, with a double hammer-beam roof, it was the location of the first known performance of Shakespeare's *Twelfth Night*. Above the polished high table – made of three 8.8-metre planks of a single oak tree donated by Queen Elizabeth I and floated down the Thames from Windsor forest before the building was completed – are oil paintings of various monarchs. The smaller table known as the 'cupboard' is reputedly made from the hatch cover of Francis Drake's *Golden Hind*. Elected Masters of the Bench – or Benchers – still dine at high table and the 'cupboard' supports the book that members sign when called to the Bar. The coats of arms within the panelling that lines the walls are those of successive Readers of the Temple, appointed alongside the Master of the Temple as one of the church's two clergy. Readers with no coat of arms are allowed to create one of their own.

To understand more of the Temple's original magnificence, it is worth looking at the elegant ❹ **Wren doorways** at 4 and 5 King's Bench Walk. ❺ **Fountain Court**, outside the great hall, is perhaps the most charming of the public spaces: an irregular, sloping courtyard with stone paving slabs and cobbles, gaslights, mature trees – including two sprawling mulberries planted in 1887 to commemorate Queen Victoria's jubilee – and a simple fountain dating from 1681 that is reputedly the oldest permanent water feature in London.

From Fountain Court you can exit into the cramped alleys of Devereux Court and Little Essex Street and be reminded once more of the constraints of space that govern the real world. The smallest listed building in London, however, can be found a few hundred metres away in Old Square on the north side of Lincoln's Inn – the former ❻ **ostler's hut,** or porter's lodge, dating from 1852. Built in mock-Tudor style – red brick with stone dressings and

mullioned windows, with four oversized stepped gables behind which sits an elaborately angled roof topped by a central wrought-iron crown – it is a quirky folly, a comic-book building for the working-class characters who waited on the great and good. It probably made a cosy place to rest between stints spent stabling horses, but its diminutive size and cartoonish style could not be a greater contrast with the spacious and stately workspaces that surround it.

1. Temple Church, EC4Y 7BB
2. Inner Temple Garden, EC4Y 7HL
3. Middle Temple great hall, EC4Y 9AT
4. 4 & 5 King's Bench Walk, EC4Y 7D
5. Fountain Court, EC4Y 9AT
6. Ostler's hut,
   Lincoln's Inn, WC2A 3SU

5

4.2 Ely Place

7

with an episcopal chapel (now the church of St Etheldreda), followed by what was to become a magnificent mansion with a cloistered quadrangle, great hall, several apartments and up to 24 hectares of gardens, vineyards, orchards, ploughland and strawberry fields stretching towards the Thames. On becoming Archbishop of Canterbury in 1397, Thomas Arundel leased his apartment to John of Gaunt, who died there two years later. Accordingly, Shakespeare uses the palace as the setting for Gaunt's famous speech in *Richard II* (Act 2, Scene 1) extolling 'this sceptr'd isle… this blessed plot, this earth, this realm, this England'. More prosaically, the episcopal strawberries feature in Act 3, Scene 4 of *Richard III*, where Richard commands the Bishop of Ely to send for 'good strawberries' from his garden in Holborn.

In 1576 much of the palace and its grounds were reluctantly leased to Elizabeth I's Lord Chancellor and court favourite Christopher Hatton – in return for a rent of one red rose picked at midsummer, ten loads of hay and £10 per annum. He was soon to commandeer the land to build Hatton House, designed by Inigo Jones. During his tenancy the crypt of St Etheldreda's was used as a tavern, and drunken brawls and singing would often interrupt the services above. To add to the clergy's discomfort, Hatton's monopoly on the gatehouse meant they had to lead their horses in through the great hall.

In 1772 the bishops moved to Ely House in Dover Street, off Piccadilly. Their Holborn palace – by now in poor condition – was demolished (its only remains are the crypt of St Etheldreda's), to be replaced by the two rows of houses that line Ely Place today. Both the elegant Dover Street residence and the new terraces – handsome Georgian

7 **Ely Place**, off Charterhouse Street in Holborn, is unique in London: a gated street that for centuries was an island of Cambridgeshire marooned within the capital, owned and managed by its own commissioners and administered from East Anglia. The diminutive porter's lodge at the entrance to the cul-de-sac – an 18th-century pillbox built in brick with stone pediments, quoins and a fluted stone chimney – housed a beadle who still closes the gates to cars and cycles at 10pm each night and whose duties until the 1960s included calling out the hour, using the formula '11 o'clock and all's well…'. The Metropolitan Police were not allowed in without invitation, and tales are told of robbers from nearby Hatton Garden, home to London's jewellery trade, diving into the street via Ely Court in the knowledge they could not be followed.

The link to Cambridgeshire goes back to 1290, when John de Kirby left a parcel of land to the See of Ely as a site for a London townhouse for its bishops. Building began

8

townhouses with crisply detailed classical doorcases – were designed by Robert Taylor, who at the time held the prestigious post of architect to the Bank of England.

The most atmospheric time to visit is at weekends, when the street is empty of parked cars and you can imagine yourself strolling back into the 18th century. Only the occupants have changed – now mainly lawyers or diamond dealers spilling over from Hatton Garden. At the far end is a high brick wall with three blind arches and a wooden doorway leading into Bleeding Heart Yard, named in memory of Elizabeth Hatton, widow of Christopher Hatton's heir William, whose murdered body, its heart still pumping blood over the cobblestones, was said to have been discovered in the courtyard.

St Ethelreda's itself is odd on two counts. First, it is one of only two London buildings to have survived from the reign of Edward I; second, it was the first pre-Reformation church to revert to Catholic worship. A sign on the door proclaims that it was 'restored to the old faith' in 1874.

Accessed from Hatton Garden (between Nos 8 and 9) or via an almost imperceptible opening on the west side of Ely Place is the charming, pint-sized alley of Ely Court, home to the **8** **Ye Old Mitre pub**. The stone mitre between the first-floor windows once adorned the gatehouse of the episcopal palace and in the corner of the bar is the stump of a cherry tree around which Elizabeth I is said to have danced with Christopher Hatton. Originally built in 1546 for the palace's servants and rebuilt in the 1770s, the pub was until recently licensed from Cambridge. Letters addressed to the pub at 'Ely Court, Cambridgeshire' are claimed still to be delivered.

7. Ely Place, EC1N 6TD
8. Ye Old Mitre pub, EC1N 6SJ

4.3 London Silver Vaults

whose contents included state papers as well as treasure hoards stashed by thieves, with the entrance protected by guards armed with cutlasses and shotguns. Over time, the rooms were rented by silver dealers to store their stock; merchants then began to invite customers in to view their wares and from there it was an obvious step to open the vaults to the public. However, the sense of wandering into an exclusive club remains: most of the 30 businesses are family owned and many have occupied the same spaces for generations.

It takes a certain amount of nerve to penetrate the **9 London Silver Vaults.** The entrance is seriously underplayed – a discreet doorway in an unassuming building on Chancery Lane in Holborn, with a sign that almost disappears into the Portland stone. Given its proximity to the Inns of Court, you would probably assume Chancery House was home to nothing more glamorous than suites of solicitors' offices.

Walk inside, explain at the security desk that you want to visit the vaults, descend a couple of flights of municipal-looking stairs and you find yourself navigating a series of anonymous cream-painted corridors – the kind of circuitous entry employed as a defensive strategy by builders of fortresses to prevent a full-scale charge. Finally you arrive in a long passageway lined with cells fronted by thick, prison-like metal doors. Peep inside and you'll see each space is crammed with silver ranging in scale from teaspoons to a solid-silver four-poster bed. Taken together, the vaults contain the largest collection of antique silver in the world.

The Silver Vaults were founded in 1876 as the Chancery Lane Safe Deposit, where Londoners could rent strong rooms to store valuables and documents. Press reports from 1890 describe more than 6,000 safes,

With steel-lined walls 1.2 metres thick, the vaults have never been broken into. When the building above suffered bomb damage in WW2, the safe-deposit company took the opportunity to rebuild the vaults as dedicated retail units, with American GIs in search of gifts to take home and diplomats buying silver services to impress foreign colleagues among their first customers. Later, the outlets attracted celebrity collectors such as Rock Hudson and Liberace as well as the props departments on heritage television series such as *Downton Abbey*, who presumably hope the appreciation value will make them a profit.

The experience of shopping here is a little like visiting a souk or bazaar: a street of merchants all specialising in a single commodity who have set up shop side by side. But while the vendors in a marketplace advertise their wares to all-comers, those in the London Silver Vaults – hidden underground and protected by top-level security – expect their customers to know where to find them.

9. London Silver Vaults,
   53-64 Chancery Lane, WC2A 1QS

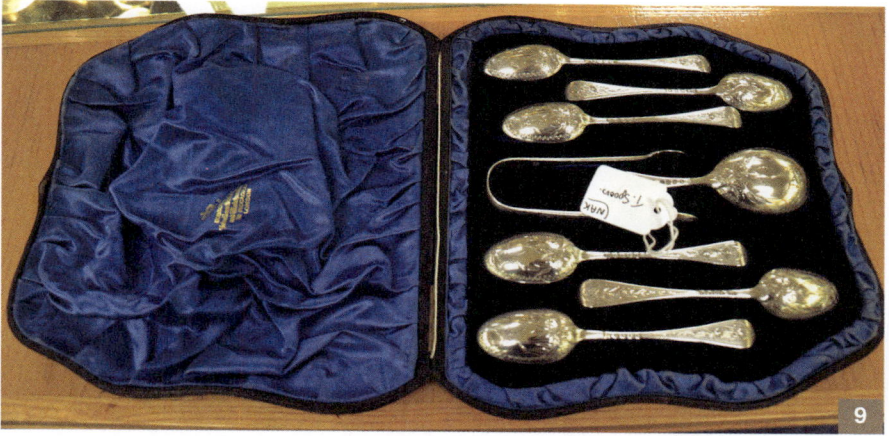

4.4 Public Space in Private Hands

It is becoming increasing difficult for Londoners to know which bits of their city are part of the public domain. Since the 1990s more and more stretches of urban fabric have fallen into private hands, as regeneration projects are devolved to investors and developers who then own and manage (or sell on) the spaces they have created. The trend has accelerated from easily recognisable, largely enclosed shopping malls or office developments and their immediate surroundings – such as Broadgate in the City, opened in 1991 – to outdoor neighbourhoods of streets, squares and parks that seem to be undifferentiated parts of the city. Only when you act in a way that is unacceptable to the corporate owners – such as taking a photograph or participating in a demonstration – does the speedy arrival of private security guards reveal that what is presented as public space is not what it seems.

Canary Wharf

It was Canary Wharf on the Isle of Dogs that set the template for London's privatised public areas. Occupying almost 40 hectares of what was once the world's largest port and still bounded on four sides by water, it is an island state whose control is entirely in the hands of its owners – at the time of writing, an unlikely partnership between the Qatar Investment Authority and Canadian developer Brookfield.

Despite huge protests from soon to be displaced inhabitants, the area's transformation was initiated by the Conservative government in 1981 with the formation of a quango charged with bringing 'these barren areas back into more valuable use'. Canadian developers Olympia & York began building in 1988 but went bankrupt within five years. The site has changed hands several times since, with co-owners

including Saudi business magnate HRH Prince Al-Waleed, New York diamond dealer Simon Glick, the China Investment Corporation and US bank Morgan Stanley. A conglomeration of state-of-the-art premises for banks and businesses employing some of the best-paid individuals in the world, Canary Wharf sits incongruously in the borough of Tower Hamlets, which in 2013 had the highest level of child poverty in the UK and the second highest rate of unemployment in London.

Walking around Canary Wharf is a surreal experience. Because every detail of the 'public' environment has been designed to attract wealthy tenants, streets and open spaces feel like a film set strewn with elements that express a corporate ideal of quality or luxury, art or community. Some 40 mid- and high-rise buildings are arranged in a pattern of streets and squares that replicates Georgian London on a ridiculous scale. The first phase of construction on North and 🔟 **South Colonnade**, largely designed by North American firm Skidmore, Owings and Merrill (who also drew up the masterplan), mimics the

12

13

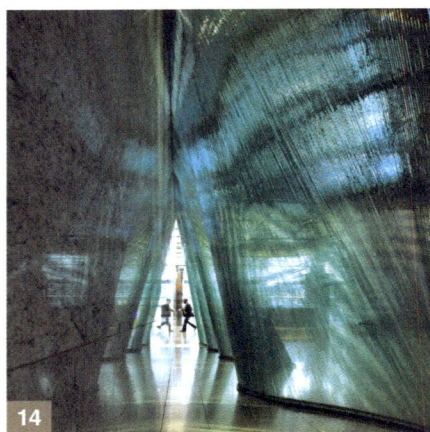

14

neoclassical architecture of the financial districts of Chicago and New York – no doubt to reassure transatlantic tenants that London too means business. Most subsequent buildings follow the lead of **11** **1 Canada Square,** a 50-storey glass-and-steel tower designed by Pelli Clarke Pelli that stretches skyward in seemingly immaculate perfection to a pyramidal cap that is now a feature of the London skyline.

Canary Wharf Group has tried – for business reasons as well as to improve relations with its London neighbours – to make its holding more than a business area. Over 300 shops and restaurants are based in five subterranean malls and the estate also includes concert venues and green spaces such as **12** **Jubilee Park**. No expense has been spared on the largely uninspiring public art: exceptions worth seeking out are **13** *Windwand* by Ron Arad, a 50-metre red needle near Westferry Circus that hints at the potential fragility of the financial megaliths around it by bending alarmingly in the wind, and **14** *Parting the Waves* by Danny Lane, two undulating walls of glass that ripple and crash within the lobby of 20 Canada Square.

Even more so than in London's other privatised public spaces, the level of security is high. In addition to the guards employed by individual businesses and a claimed close working relationship with MI5 and the Metropolitan Police, the estate provides officers, dog teams and some 1,700 cameras. Anyone arousing suspicion is likely to find their steering wheel swabbed for explosives or their right to use their camera challenged. The estate is one of the few parts of London not recorded on Google Street View.

10. South Colonnade, E14 5EP
11. 1 Canada Square, E14 5AB
12. Jubilee Park, E14 5JP
13. *Windwand*, Westferry Circus, E14 4HD
14. *Parting the Waves*, 20 Canada Square, E14 5AB

More London

Other prominent public spaces now in private ownership include Paternoster Square beside St Paul's, completed in 2003, owned by the Mitsubishi Estate Company and home to the London Stock Exchange. But perhaps the oddest example is 🄫 **More London** [sic], which not only surrounds but also includes the former City Hall, seat of the Greater London Authority and London Assembly – once the city's most visible emblem of local democracy. As in other privately owned public spaces, photography is restricted: according to assembly delegates, it took eight years to negotiate the right to record television interviews outside their building.

Covering 5.25 hectares to the west of Tower Bridge, bounded to the north by the Thames and to the south by Tooley Street, the area includes office blocks, shops and cafés clustered around sterile, mostly paved open spaces with the usual fountains, sculptures and sunken amphitheatres – an essential feature of present-day private public space, it seems. The development was completed in 2003 and sold off a decade later to a Kuwaiti property company, which provides cleaning, maintenance – and, of course, security from the threat of camera-wielding bystanders.

15. More London, London Assembly, The Queen's Walk, SE1 2AA

15

Paddington Waterside

It seems the areas of London controlled by private companies are not only multiplying but are getting bigger. At 93 hectares, Paddington Waterside covers a plot the size of Soho: it is bounded by the Westway to the north, Paddington Station to the west and Praed Street to the south, though the site is broken up by the canal, Paddington Basin and Bishop's Bridge Road with limited circulation between the different sections. Developers include British Land (which also owns much of Broadgate) for the Paddington Central area, European Land & Property for Merchant Square, and Tischman Speyer, owners of the Rockefeller Center in New York.

Paddington Central, at the west of the site, rises up around Sheldon Square, a green amphitheatre surrounded by uninspired residential blocks and anonymous corporate-slick offices. It has all the elements of 21st-century public space – water features, sculpture, planters, street food and terraced seating – with none of the sense of place that might attract people who neither live nor work here.

Paddington Basin itself has two distinctly odd moveable bridges. The **16** **Rolling Bridge**, designed by Thomas Heatherwick in 2004, consists of eight jointed sections which curl up like a caterpillar to form an octagon that sits neatly on the wharf. The **17** **Fan Bridge**, designed by Knight Architects a decade later, is hinged at one end, with its deck divided into five steel beams or fingers that open in sequence like a Japanese fan. Both are odd not only for their structural invention but for their redundancy in providing shortcuts across stretches of water that take no more than a couple of minutes to circumnavigate and have little or no boat traffic. It is worth trying to visit them on Wednesday or Friday at 12 noon or Saturday at 2pm to watch them open; the audience is usually outnumbered by security staff in high-visibility jackets.

16. Rolling Bridge, Paddington Basin, W2 1JS
17. Fan Bridge, Paddington Basin, W2 1JS

16

16

16

King's Cross Central

The most successful of the new private public spaces – and an oddity in managing to create a sense of place beyond the corporate – is King's Cross Central, built on 27 hectares of former railway land to the north of the station. Well planned to be full of incident, with unexpected open spaces and signature buildings that are far from bland, it is owned and managed by a bizarre partnership between state-owned property company London & Continental Railways, UK developers Argent, DHL (itself owned by Deutsche Post) and Australian pension fund AustralianSuper. Signs of a corporate presence are largely restricted to notices requesting visitors to 'Please enjoy this private estate considerately' – accompanied by the arrival of security guards to remove those who disobey.

The mix of resources on the site pre-development – handsome Victorian industrial buildings, gasometers, a canal and a nature reserve – provided a rich starting point which the masterplanners built on by refurbishing what was already there rather than tearing it down and starting anew. **18 The Granary,** an imposing warehouse designed in 1852

by Lewis Cubitt, is now a home for the University of the Arts, fronted by an open space the size of Trafalgar Square, its surface animated by a grid of more than 1,000 rising and falling fountains that visitors can programme by mobile phone. One of the skeletal, 25-metre-high gasometers has been transformed into the new **19 Gasholder Park** that doubles as a concert venue; others are bizarrely wrapped around circular blocks of apartments. Constructed in 1853, the gasometers were themselves oddities in using classical detailing – 16 cast-iron columns each, complete with capitals and bases – to support mundane gas storage tanks. The park design leaves the soaring structure that surrounds it free, its strength and mass contrasted with a delicate inner ring of reflective steel columns supporting a pierced canopy.

King's Cross Central has also been given a new London postcode of N1C.

18. Granary Square, N1C 4AA
19. Gasholder Park, N1C 4AB

19

Sir John Soane's Museum, see page 159

Dream Homes

Dream Homes

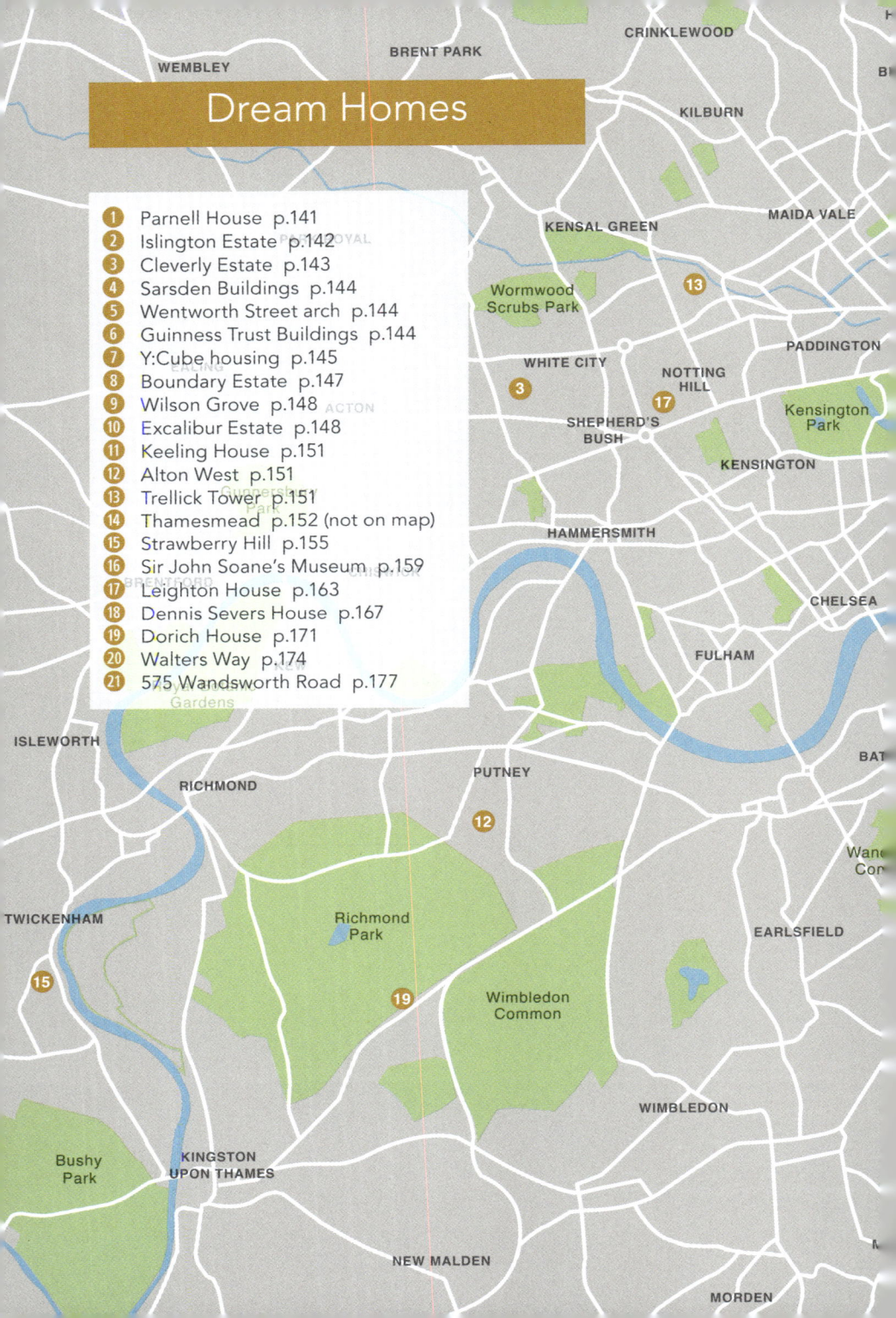

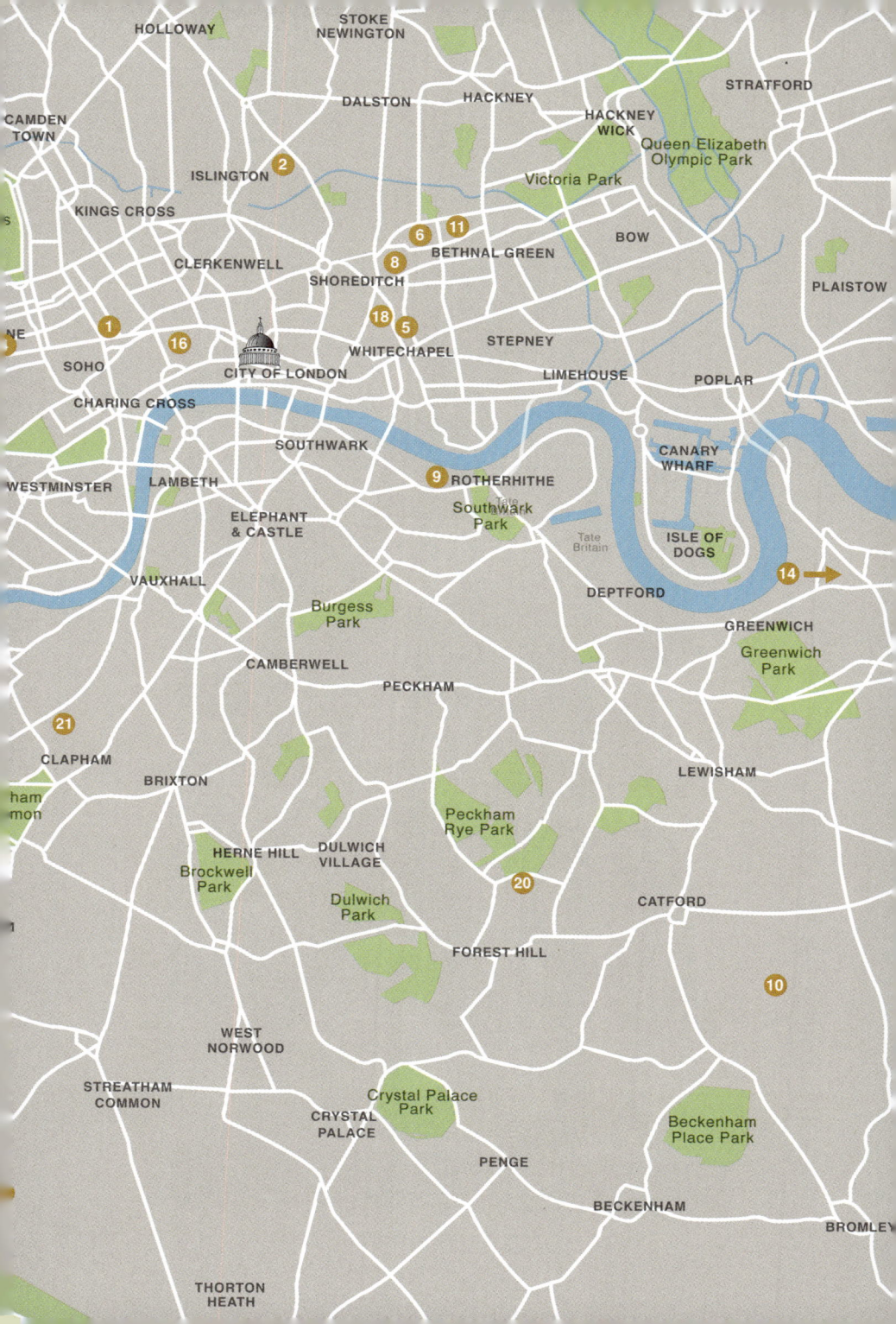

George Peabody (1795–1869)

5.1 Philanthropic Pioneers

You would have to be comatose not to notice that London in the first decades of the 21st century is in the grip of a housing crisis. In just over 150 years, the capital has gone full circle from the first attempts to provide decent, affordable housing for the working classes to a situation where today's workers are forced by sky-rocketing costs to move ever further from the centre. Once impoverished boroughs such as Islington, Hammersmith & Fulham and Chelsea have become unaffordable to all but the wealthiest buyers and renters. Yet even here you can still find surprising remnants of the philanthropic idealism that transformed London's slums in the late 19th and early 20th centuries.

The Model Dwellings movement began in London in the 1840s with the formation of a number of companies that aimed to improve housing conditions while at the same time making a competitive rate of return on their members' investment. This was known as 'five per cent philanthropy'. Among the first was the Society for Improving the Condition of the Labouring Classes which in 1848 superseded the Labourer's Friend Society, credited with founding the allotment movement. One of its earliest developments was ❶ **Parnell House** at the west end of Streatham

Street in Bloomsbury, where you can see the proud declaration 'Model Houses for Families' inscribed on the stucco band at second-floor level. Built in 1849 and still used as flats today, the five-storey scheme is astonishingly modern in plan, with an L-shaped block enclosing an inner courtyard lined with open galleries that give access to the apartments.

Parnell House is now run by Peabody (formerly Peabody Trust), which works exclusively in London and today owns and manages some 27,000 homes across the capital. Ironically, this pioneer of high-quality housing for the 'artisans and labouring poor of London' was set up by one of the caste deemed responsible for London's current crisis – an American banker. George Peabody (1795–1869) moved to London in 1837 and eventually established what was to become the City's largest US merchant bank in partnership with fellow American J S Morgan. Over his lifetime Peabody donated more than £1 million to philanthropic causes, almost half of it to the Peabody Donation Fund, set up in 1862. The fund's first block of 57 homes – on a triangular site fronting Commercial Street and Folgate Street in Spitalfields – is now in private ownership, but the second, the ❷ **Islington Estate** on Greenman

Street, built in 1865, is still owned and run by Peabody.

The Islington Estate replaced houses described in contemporary reports as inhabited by 'a dense population of the worst characters of the Metropolis, who herded together with little or no attention to morality or decency'. Designed by Henry Astley Darbishire, architect of all the trust's housing until the start of the 20th century, the estate was obviously intended to impress residents, visitors and potential investors with its provision of a dignified, civilised and perhaps civilising architecture at affordable prices. Like Parnell House, the scheme ignored the street patterns of the neighbourhood and imposed instead an open square flanked by four five-storey blocks – a plan not unlike the grand Georgian squares found in wealthier areas. Italianate in style, the elevations use London stock brick relieved by bands of a lighter colour, with a dentillated stringcourse and architrave and arched doorways with handsome decorative surrounds. Inside,

each floor had 20 flats of one, two or three rooms arranged on either side of a central corridor, with communal kitchens, baths and lavatories in the stepped-back ranges at each end. The top floor, with its distinctive window arrangement, contained laundries.

Even today, it is easy to imagine the welcome contrast between the overcrowded, dirty and ill-ventilated slums and the calm and considered environment of the estate, with its open spaces, generous windows and state-of-the-art sanitation. However, to live in the Islington Estate – as with all the philanthropic housing schemes – required compliance with a level of social control. The central square, which also served as a playground for children, was closed by iron gates at 11pm to protect tenants from 'evil social intercourse' with their former neighbours. According to Darbishire, the degree of security needed depended on the surrounding area: 'One class of neighbourhood will make high walls necessary; in another, an open railing or wood fence will be sufficient.'

A superintendent, who lived in Peabody House on Greenman Street, controlled access to the site, ensured adherence to regulations and kept records of cases of infectious disease: all tenants had to be vaccinated against smallpox before moving in. Residents were required to sweep the passages and staircases every morning and took it in turns to clean the laundry windows, sinks and lavatories. Typical tenant occupations included labourers, porters, coachmen, printers, messengers and tailors as well as police constables. Peabody Yard, with its entrance on Greenman Street, contained a dozen workshops rented out to tenants.

From the start of the 20th century, new Peabody Trust flats had their own lavatories (the communal lavatories at Greenman Street were replaced in 1911). The ❸ **Cleverly Estate** on Wormholt Road in Hammersmith & Fulham, completed in 1928, was the first to have a bathroom in each apartment, though the economic downturn of the 1930s led the policy to

be reversed, with each dwelling provided only with a covered bath in the scullery that could double as a work surface. From 1910 to 1947 the trust's architect was Victor Wilkins: two more west London estates in areas that have since come up in the world – Chelsea Manor Street (1931) and Dalgarno Gardens in North Kensington (1934–38) – are typical of his work from this period.

Built on a site purchased with money from an anonymous donor and named after the banker William Cleverly Alexander, an art collector and patron of Whistler, the Cleverly Estate is the most elaborate of the pre-war schemes, with both the form of the blocks and their decorative details inspired by Christopher Wren. The stately entrances – double-height Serlianas flanked by engaged columns supporting simple pediments surmounted by four round windows – would serve equally well for an exclusive gated community. Inside, generous courtyards are surrounded by three-storey, red-brick blocks with prominent classical porches topped by

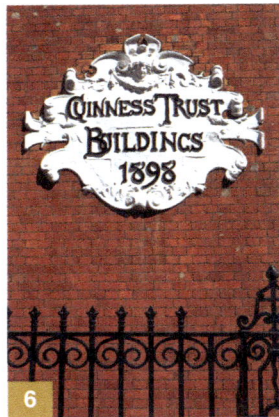

pitched or curved pediments. Dentillated stringcourses, engaged columns, pediments, oculi laced with elaborate swags – the classical language of architecture is used with precision and delicacy. It probably does not matter that what looks like Portland stone is in fact painted concrete, or that behind the grand porches are stark hallways with concrete stairs and walls lined with utilitarian white tiles.

Other odd pockets of social housing within areas now inhabited mainly by the rich – or no longer residential at all – include the ❹ **Sarsden Buildings** in St Christopher's Place off Oxford Street. Within a narrow pedestrianised street of high-end fashion outlets and galleries is a modest doorway leading to five floors of two-bedroom flats linked at the rear by communal walkways and a large terrace; the block has been managed since 1869 by Octavia Housing, set up by social reformer and National Trust founder Octavia Hill in 1862 to 'make lives noble, homes happy and family life good'. Hill's role was to look after the properties financed by others: her first scheme, in Marylebone, was built with money from influential art critic and theorist John Ruskin, who took five per cent of any return on his capital and allowed the remainder to be reinvested in housing. By 1874 Hill had 15 sites with

3,000 tenants whom she and her staff – initially a band of female volunteers – monitored closely through weekly visits to collect rent.

Other benefactors whose companies survive today include Nathanial Rothschild, who founded the Four Per Cent Industrial Dwellings Company (now IDS or Industrial Dwellings Society) in 1885, its members taking a smaller return than other investors and so able to offer lower rents. Near the junction of Gunthorpe Street and Wentworth Street in Whitechapel you can still see the ❺ **monumental brick arch**, with the inscription 'Erected by the Four Per Cent Dwellings Company', that once formed the entrance to the company's first development, the Charlotte de Rothschild Model Dwellings.

Five years later Edward Guinness set up the Guinness Trust: its earliest surviving development, of six six-storey blocks on a triangular site fronting Columbia Road and Baxendale Street in Bethnal Green, still bears the inscription ❻ '**Guinness Trust Buildings** 1898'.

It is extraordinary to think that so many of these 150-year-old housing developments have robustly and successfully survived

The one-bedroom flats, which at 26 square metres are only two-thirds of the recommended minimum for single-person occupancy, were assembled in a Derbyshire factory and arrived on site with services already incorporated. The units have a lifespan of around 60 years and can be moved and re-installed up to five times, meaning that in theory they can be erected temporarily on vacant lots waiting to be developed. Sited on the corner of Woodstock Way and Clay Avenue in Mitcham, the first complex of 36 units, grouped around an inner courtyard, has the trademark RSHP exposed structure – hefty wooden posts and beams, generous walkways and an engineered steel staircase – while the pastels of the street front give way to strong colours (another RSHP trope) around the courtyard, providing a welcome splash of brightness in an otherwise drab neighbourhood. Yet perhaps the greatest oddity is that this economical solution to crowded inner-city living should have landed in the suburbs, opposite a generous playground and small park, where land is relatively cheap and densities low.

social and economic changes when more recent schemes have been demolished as no longer fit for purpose. Yet new responses to the capital's housing problems are in short supply. Peabody is still building in London, using quality architects and sometimes innovative ideas: for its development on the corner of Shepherdess Walk and Murray Grove in Shoreditch, for instance, Cartwright Pickard Architects pioneered a method of construction whereby 30 prefabricated apartments were hung on a steel frame, with a dramatic circular staircase tower at the hinge.

More radical still is the ❼ Y:Cube housing, developed by Rogers Stirk Harbour + Partners (RSHP) in conjunction with charity YMCA London South West as starter accommodation for young people. Though Richard Rogers has put forward ideas for making London a more liveable city and suggested solutions for low-cost modular housing since the 1960s, it is still extraordinary that the practice responsible for Lloyd's of London, 122 Leadenhall Street (the Cheesegrater) and the Neo Bankside tower with its £22 million penthouse should also have designed homes costing as little as £45,000 each – about 70 per cent of the usual local authority new-build per-square-metre price.

Whether this first scheme will survive in situ for longer than Lewisham's post-war Excalibur prefabs (see page 148) is yet to be seen. But whatever its merits and influence, it seems unlikely to provide a philanthropic housing solution for Londoners that will be as enduring as the schemes developed by the YMCA's charitable predecessors a century and a half ago.

1. Parnell House, Streatham St, WC1A 1JB
2. Islington Estate, Greenman St, N1 8SB
3. Cleverly Estate,
   Wormholt Rd, W12 0LA
4. Sarsden Buildings,
   St Christopher's Place, W1U 1DZ
5. Wentworth Street arch, E1 6RG
6. Guinness Trust Buildings,
   Columbia Rd, E2 7RL
7. Y:Cube housing, Woodstock Way, CR4 1BA

5.2 Public Housing

Oddities when built, the public housing schemes described here remain oddities today, though the reasons have changed over time. All were commissioned by local authorities or by the capital's central governing body: from 1889, the London County Council (LCC), superseded by the Greater London Council (GLC) from 1965 until 1986, when it was dissolved by Conservative prime minister Margaret Thatcher because of its socialist policies. The schemes, however, have survived as reminders of progressive ideas or architectural fashions against which we can measure today's new homes.

Boundary Estate

Opened in 1896, ❽ **Boundary Estate**, centred on Arnold Circus on the border of Bethnal Green and Shoreditch, was the UK's first council estate. For its early tenants, a council flat was a step up in the world and the handsome five-storey tenement buildings are far removed from later and lower expectations of council accommodation. Walking through the estate today is like travelling back in time to an idealised version of Victorian Britain.

Boundary Estate can be attributed to Owen Fleming, a 23-year-old housing officer at the newly formed LCC who dreamed up its main features: a central raised public space that ingeniously incorporated rubble from the demolition of the houses it replaced; an orderly plan, with streets radiating from this central circus and blocks interspersed with courtyards and gardens to create a sense of community closed off from the slums beyond; amenities that included shops, a doctor's surgery and schools, but no pubs; architectural details such as decorative polychrome brickwork and doorways inset with tiles to humanise the scale. The contrast with the former maze of insanitary alleys, where as many as 60 people might be crowded into a single house and average life expectancy was only 16 years, could not have been starker – though with rents four times those of slum dwellings, none of the people displaced by the new development could afford to live there.

Instead, the estate attracted artisans and tradesmen, with some 75 per cent of early inhabitants drawn from the largely Jewish local garment trade. From the 1950s flats lay empty as residents moved up and out and the unmodernised apartments proved unattractive to new tenants. Following a successful protest and squatting movement, the estate became home to 60 newly arrived Bangladeshi families in the 1970s; by the turn of this century, the proportion of Bangladeshi tenants had reached 40 per cent.

Today almost half of Boundary Estate is privately owned as Thatcher's 'Right to Buy' scheme has progressively removed some 150,000 London council homes into private ownership (over a third of these are now let back to council tenants by private landlords). In a sign of changing times, one of the former schools houses an art gallery and most of the shops in the once bustling high street are high-end boutiques.

8. Boundary Estate, Arnold Circus, E2 7JT

Wilson Grove

The architecture and ethos of Boundary Estate were not admired by all. In Bermondsey in the 1920s slum housing along what is now **9** **Wilson Grove** was replaced with an estate of two-storey brick cottages that would look more at home in Welwyn Garden City than in Southwark. Official Labour policy was to ease overcrowding by banning tenements and forcing the population out to new towns and suburbs – but in Bermondsey, uniquely, suburban-density development was provided within the inner city. The incoming Labour council of 1922, led by Ada Salter (see page 207), went so far as to promise 'a cottage home for every family... No more Progressive barracks and Coalition skyscrapers!' On becoming the local Labour MP in the same year, her husband Alfred, a doctor with first-hand experience of the disastrous effects of slum dwelling on his patients' health, vowed his party would 'pull down three-quarters of Bermondsey and build a garden city in its place'.

Salter may not have been able to deliver the full scale of his promise, but the council did manage to build an estate of 54 cottages to the designs of Garden City planner Ewart G Culpin. With their Dutch gables, casement windows and Arts and Crafts arched entrances, they were palatial by the standards of the time. However, this relative luxury came at the cost of accommodating only one-third of the population the development displaced, leading to protests from the leaders of neighbouring boroughs who feared an influx of slum-dwellers.

The estate has survived and continues to be well maintained, justifying Salter's praise of the council at the opening ceremony of 1929 for 'not hurriedly throwing up dwellings which in 50 years' time will become slums and therefore a disgrace to civilisation'.

9. Wilson Grove, SE16 4PN

Excalibur Estate

The **10** **Excalibur Estate**, by contrast with Wilson Grove, was intended to last for no more than a decade. Bounded by Persant Road in Catford, the collection of almost 200 prefabricated bungalows, built in 1945–46 by German and Italian prisoners of war, was an interim response to the devastation of the Blitz that unexpectedly endured for well over half a century. Though the Excalibur was slated for demolition at the time of writing, a handful of houses have been listed and hopefully will be preserved.

Visiting the estate today, it is easy to see why it remained popular with residents. Roads lined with detached bungalows, each with its own private garden at both front and back, are linked by pedestrian alleys that foster the sense of a networked community as romantic and remote from the housing models that followed as the Arthurian legends that give the streets their names.

With their flat roofs, corner windows and cantilevered porch details, the bungalows themselves look surprisingly modern – and certainly unlike anything else in London. The two models used on the estate – both manufactured by Uni-Seco, with either a central or corner doorway – had two bedrooms, an indoor toilet, a fitted kitchen with a state-of-the-art refrigerator, built-in cupboards and shelves (saving on furniture coupons), and central heating as well as a coal fire. Some residents have customised the street fronts with decorative mouldings or ornamental fencing; other houses show how readily the timber frames, asbestos panels and metal-framed windows decay if not maintained.

10. Excalibur Estate, SE6 1RW

9

PERSANT ROAD SE6

10

10

10

10

10

10

10

11

13

12

Heroic Visions

Within a decade of WW2, the construction industry had regenerated to the extent that ambitious high-rise schemes ushered in a heroic new era for local authority housing. In London, these are exemplified by a handful of survivals from a time when council housing was at the cutting edge of architectural practice.

Designed by Denys Lasdun, a former partner in Tecton with Berthold Lubetkin (see page 55) and best known for the National Theatre on the South Bank, **11** **Keeling House** in Claredale Street in Bethnal Green stands like an elaborately articulated space rocket among the polite brick terraces that surround it. Completed in 1957 and the first post-war council scheme to be Grade II* listed, it consists of four 16-storey blocks of maisonettes radiating from a central service tower. The effect of walking between the blocks is like moving through a winding medieval alley with the closely set balconies almost meeting above your head. Despite its futuristic form, Lasdun intended the scheme to mimic the conditions of an East End street, with each unit having two storeys and the arrangement of the blocks encouraging easy contact between the outdoor spaces of the balconies.

Described shortly after completion in 1959 as 'probably the finest low-cost housing development in the world', the Alton Estate in Roehampton springs up to startling effect between two golf courses just north of the vast green space of Richmond Park. The architectural accolade did not prevent it from featuring prominently in François Truffaut's 1966 dystopian film *Fahrenheit 451*, based on a Ray Bradbury novel about the dangers of state censorship and the proliferation of mass media. Unusually, the team of LCC architects responsible for the initial phase of the estate's design was headed by a woman, Rosemary Stjernstedt (1912–1988), who had trained in Birmingham and London before moving to Sweden for six years at the start of WW2.

Based on Swedish models, Alton East at the southern end of Roehampton Lane consists of a series of 12-storey concrete blocks juxtaposed with low-rise housing set among trees and walls left over from the gardens of the villas it replaced. But it is the slightly later **12** **Alton West**, off Highcliffe Drive, that looks most extraordinary today. Five 11-storey slabs of maisonettes supported on pilotis stride down a hillside planted with trees. Unique in London, though heavily influenced by Le Corbusier's Unités d'Habitation, the low-density development illustrates how modernist architecture can be integrated into the landscape to spectacular effect, providing suburban council homes that take superb advantage of views of Richmond Park.

Almost a decade later, Balfron and **13** **Trellick towers**, designed by Hungarian émigré Ernö Goldfinger, introduced another continental aesthetic, anglicised as Brutalism. When Balfron Tower, off St Leonards Road in Poplar, was completed in 1967, its architect was excited enough to abandon his Hampstead home for its 26th-floor penthouse, where he and his artist wife held champagne parties to collect feedback from tenants. Goldfinger used their comments to refine his design for Trellick Tower at the north end of Golborne Road in North Kensington, a 31-storey landmark completed five years later.

A gridded slab of raw concrete, Trellick's idiosyncratic profile is created largely by the separate lift and service tower, linked to the main block by bridges, with a cantilevered glazed boiler room near the top that resembles a surreal watch house.

Inside, public areas such as entrance hall and corridors are starkly functional but the split-level flats are surprisingly spacious, with high-quality fittings including cedar panelling.

Keeling House was initially popular, but by the early 1990s a mix of social and structural problems forced its closure. Epitomising the shameful trajectory of London property, it was sold by Tower Hamlets council to a private developer in 1999 and turned into luxury apartments, with the addition of eight penthouses and a glass foyer with an external water feature. Around 40 per cent of the Alton Estate has been sold off to leaseholders with many of the flats now rented to students; in comparison with its surroundings, the area suffers high levels of deprivation and unemployment. Flats in Trellick Tower, by contrast, seem to change hands for mind-boggling amounts, even if the block has retained its gritty edge. Balfron, meanwhile, has been transferred to a housing association and emptied of tenants; to the dismay of many of them, it seems that all the flats may be sold off privately once refurbishment is completed.

Thamesmead

The most ambitious piece of London local authority social engineering is **14** **Thamesmead**, which is unique not just because it is the only new town within the M25. Built in phases from the early 1960s, it straddles the boroughs of Greenwich and Bexley, stretching for about four miles along the south bank of the Thames. Its site was unpromising: built on marshland, it is bounded to the west by a prison and to the east by Crossness sewage works (see page 33). From the abolition of the GLC in 1986 until 1999 the town was run by a private company controlled by residents; since 2014 it has been managed by Peabody (see page 141).

Thamesmead is a true oddity – a place like nowhere else. Concrete towers stand in surreal formation along the shore of a 12-hectare lake, envisaged by optimistic planners as an international yachting marina; high-level concrete walkways and subways provide baffling pedestrian routes above and beneath a network of almost deserted dual-carriageways and roundabouts; small estates of modernist housing are interrupted by man-made hills and ragged fields grazed by tethered horses. Risk of flooding means residential use at ground-floor level is forbidden, so the tall, thin houses have large garages and porches, with living space from the first floor upwards. It is hardly surprising that Thamesmead South – the first and most extraordinary phase of development – formed a haunting location for the dystopian film *A Clockwork Orange* (1971).

A 1970 documentary outlining the City of London's vision for Thamesmead shows it peopled solely by white residents, filmed sunbathing on balconies, walking children to school and asking planners about the likely location of public houses. Today, two of the town's wards house the highest concentrations in the UK of inhabitants identifying as Black African (around 35 per cent in the 2011 census). Residents praise the area's sense of community, open spaces and peacefulness; following consultations, Peabody has embarked on a £200 million project to renovate poor-quality housing, upgrade access to the lake, establish more shops and improve community facilities. So perhaps, at least for now, one of London's heroic housing projects will continue to be occupied and appreciated by social tenants, as intended.

11. Keeling House, Claredale St, E2 6PG
12. Alton Estate West,
    Highcliffe Drive, SW15 4PS
13. Trellick Tower,
    Goldborne Rd, W10 5NY
14. Thamesmead, SE2 9UT

5.3 Strawberry Hill

⑮ Strawberry Hill is one of the oddest houses in London – or perhaps anywhere. Its idiosyncracy is perhaps hardly surprising given the way it was designed, with each component created by its owner Horace Walpole and a small group of friends – known as the 'Committee of Taste' – to replicate at small scale unrelated elements from the architecture of medieval castles and abbeys. On the exterior, battlements and finials, gothic ogee and quatrefoil windows, towers and turrets jostle for attention. The effect is something like a fairytale castle with the expected motifs rearranged at random.

Horace (1717–1797) was the youngest son of England's first prime minister Robert Walpole; at his father's death in 1745 he decided to use part of his inheritance to buy a country house. He was lucky to find one of the last undeveloped plots of land at Twickenham, at the time highly fashionable – he described it to a friend as having 'dowagers as plentiful as flounders'. The house was a relatively modest cottage known as Chopp'd Straw Hall because locals assumed its coachman owner had been able to afford it only by giving his employer's horses chopped straw and illicitly selling off the more valuable hay for his own profit. Over the next half century, Walpole – perhaps in an act of Oedipal rebellion against Houghton Hall, the house commissioned in 1722 by his father from England's leading Palladian architect Colen Campbell – was to use a style previously reserved largely for follies to transform his 'little plaything house' into a sprawling gothic mansion that initiated a new architectural fashion and turned the tide against classicism.

The flamboyance and aestheticism Walpole brought to Strawberry Hill applied to the man himself: he was described by his friend Laetitia Hawkins as 'always enter[ing] a room in that style of affected delicacy, which fashion had then made almost natural… knees bent, and feet on tip-toe, as if afraid of a wet floor.' An avid letter-writer whose first-hand accounts of politics and society are one of our most valuable sources of information on 18th-century English life, he assiduously collected books, pictures, furniture and antiquities – plus such curiosities as Cardinal Wolsey's hat and Charles I's death warrant – with the aim of documenting English history from the Middle Ages to the present. The collection aroused the interest of many visitors, and the auction at which it was sold off by his descendants in 1842 took 32 days. The event was so hyped that spoof catalogues appeared including fake lots such as a mouse that had run over Queen Adelaide's foot. An MP who never visited his constituency, Walpole was also known for his lavish entertainments, at one of which – for French, Spanish and Portuguese dignitaries – he dressed in a wooden cravat carved by Grinling Gibbons and a pair of elbow-length gloves that had belonged to James I.

inheritance: after spending £100,000, she stopped counting.

Frances had the London road diverted to give the house more privacy and was responsible for the tall, highly decorated 'Tudor' chimney pots you see on the present building. After Harcourt died she married Chichester Fortescue, a Whig minister and secretary for Ireland, and Strawberry Hill became the Liberal salon of the day, with guests including Palmerston, Gladstone and the Prince and Princess of Wales. Frances, who was a famous society figure in her own right, was known as the Queen of Dublin.

A flavour of the house can be sensed from the main entrance, outside which is a colonnaded 'oratory' with a basin for 'holy water' and a niche in which Walpole placed a bronze saint. In this cloister was a Chinese bowl in which Walpole's cat drowned trying to catch goldfish, inspiring Thomas Gray's poem 'Ode on the Death of a Favourite Cat' with the lines: 'Not all that tempts your wand'ring eyes/And heedless hearts, is lawful prize;/Nor all, that glistens, gold.' Here both the earnest playfulness of Walpole's vision and the flimsiness of the structure supporting it are apparent, with the stone-effect cloister in fact vaulted with papier-mâché.

The house Walpole bought – an inelegant L-shaped structure at the eastern corner of the present building – could most kindly be described as having potential. You could say he then had the builders in for almost 50 years. His first job was to stamp the unpromising exterior with his personality by adding façades and bays incorporating gothic elements. Inside, new fireplaces were based on designs for medieval tombs and bookcases on rood screens. These 'embellishments' were purely for theatrical effect, with no structural rationale, using insubstantial materials (outside lath and plaster enclosed by brick, inside wood or plasterwork) to mimic stone monumentality.

Following Walpole's death, Strawberry Hill passed eventually to Lady Frances Waldegrave (1821–1879), whose second husband George (a distant relative of Walpole's) took a dislike to the area after being imprisoned by Twickenham magistrates for 'riotous behaviour', an event that led Frances to miscarry her only pregnancy. George decided to sell Walpole's collection and let the house rot (Frances, unbeknown to her husband, bought back Reynolds' paintings of her in-laws). Following George's death from syphilis, Frances made a third marriage, at the age of 27, to the much older George Granvill Harcourt. In 1856 she decided to restore and expand her derelict

Strawberry Hill's entrance hall is also decorated to mimic stone, with the flimsy wooden staircase elaborately carved and painted a greyish cream and the walls covered in trompe l'oeil paper. The idea was to evoke the atmosphere of 'gloomth' that pervades Walpole's pioneering Gothic novel *The Castle of Otranto* (1764). Though the intention was to recreate a medieval great hall, the overall effect is uncomfortably cramped, with a replica in miniature of a staircase from Rouen cathedral stuffed into the too-small space. For Walpole, however, this hall was 'the most particular and chief beauty of the Castle'. The adjacent great

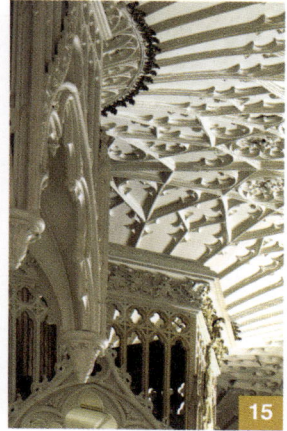

parlour or dining room – the first of Walpole's extensions beyond the confines of Chopp'd Straw Hall – was positioned at the opposite end of the house from the kitchen in the round tower, with no possible indoor route between them.

In 1750 Walpole bought 450 pieces of Flemish stained glass depicting peasants at work, stories from the scriptures, birds, flowers and coats of arms. Scattered throughout the house and sometimes arranged in seemingly random order, the collection is one of the unexpected delights of Strawberry Hill. Walpole, who coined the term serendipity, described 'the adjusting and disposing it [as] a vast amusement'.

Strawberry Hill's wedding-cake elaboration reaches its peak in the long gallery, Walpole's main space for entertaining. Opposite the windows are recesses lined with mirrors edged in fretwork in a Moorish style that reflects the interests of Committee of Taste member Thomas Pitt, who had travelled to Iberia. The ceiling is a series of elaborate gilded papier-mâché swirls up to 2 metres deep that appear to spin out like icing from a cake-decorator's nozzle. (Their origin is less fanciful – papier-

mâché was made by barefoot women and children who risked their lives by treading down rags in lead solution.) Lady Waldegrave spent £20,000 (Walpole's total budget for the house, including the purchase price) on shipping the floor from a Viennese villa she had visited on one of her honeymoons.

In 1923 Strawberry Hill was transformed yet again when what had once been a pleasure palace was bought for St Mary's Catholic Teacher Training College. Since 2002 the house has been leased to the Strawberry Hill Trust, which almost immediately embarked on a lengthy restoration programme aimed at effacing much of Frances Waldegrove's tenancy in favour of recreating its state at the time of Walpole's death.

15. Strawberry Hill,
    268 Waldegrave Rd, TW1 4ST
    www.strawberryhillhouse.org.uk

5.4 Sir John Soane's Museum

Exploring ⓰ **Sir John Soane's Museum** is like wandering through a distorted dreamscape that lays bare its creator's anxieties about education (or lack of it), aspiration, status, family conflicts, the meaning of life and the approach of death. Soane (1753–1837) was one of England's most influential and original architects, his projects including such prestigious commissions as successive stages in the remodelling of the Bank of England (1788–1833), Westminster Law Courts (1820–24) and the Houses of Parliament (1822–23), as well as Dulwich Picture Gallery (1811–17, see page 247) and a string of country houses for the aristocracy of his day. Yet his own house – its fashionable Lincoln's Inn Fields location apart – seems the work of an unemployable maverick, a mix of ostentation, personal whimsy and stubborn defiance of contemporary tastes and values. Soane himself recognised some of the conflicts underlying its creation in a paper of 1812 in which he imagined a future antiquarian speculating on the house's origins and concluding that it was the work of a great architect who suffered for his originality and integrity, was abused by his kin and died of a broken heart.

The son of a provincial bricklayer, Soane came to London at the age of 15, beginning his career as a pupil in the office of George Dance the Younger, whose surveyor had worked with William, John's bricklayer brother. In 1784 Soane married Eliza Smith, the niece and ward of City builder George Wyatt, and dreamed of founding an architectural dynasty along the lines of the Dances. However, the couple's sons John and George both rebelled against the ambitions of their pushy parent, marrying women who brought no wealth or social connections and pursuing largely undistinguished careers – John suffered from chronic ill-health and died in his thirties in 1823 and George, a grimly unsuccessful novelist and later intermittently acclaimed dramatist, was to engage in a lifelong and bitter feud with his father.

Soane began work on Lincoln's Inn Fields in 1792, using a legacy from his wife's uncle to replace the 17th-century house on the site of number 12 with a new home for his family and converting the stables at the back into his office. Lincoln's Inn Fields at the time was a good address, with easy access to shops and markets, galleries and theatres, the Bank of England and the Royal Academy. But Eliza found the unhealthy climate and lack of outdoor space for her young children oppressive and spent most of their holidays with her impoverished in-laws in Chertsey or at Margate, where she socialised with the high society that frequented the then-fashionable Isle of Thanet. Though the marriage had been a love match and Eliza was able to support her husband in setting up his business and courting clients, relations became increasingly strained; in the decade before her death in 1815, Soane was reported to be seen rather too frequently in the company of a certain Norah Brickenden. Described by a pupil as having 'an acute sensitiveness, and a fearful irritability, dangerous to himself if not to others; an embittered heart, prompting a cutting and sarcastic mind; uncompromising pride, neither respecting nor desiring respect; a contemptuous regard for the feelings of his dependants; and yet himself the very victim of irrational impulse; with no pity for the trials of his neighbour and nothing but frantic despair under his own', it seems that Soane was not easy to live or to work with.

Though Soane embarked on his London home with the enthusiasm of a 40-year-old architect who at last has the chance to design a house that expresses his own tastes and showcases his abilities, subsequently he was to bury himself in the project as a distraction from the many unhappy periods in his professional and family life. Extensions and renovations began in earnest once the boys were grown: in 1808 he bought number 13 and rebuilt the stables to form a single-storey extension linked to number 12; in 1812 he rebuilt the front of number 13 and moved into it, renting out number 12; in 1824, nine years after his wife's death, he bought and rebuilt number 14, the back as an extension to the other houses and the front as a separate residence which he also rented out. By this time the building was clearly intended as a showcase for his growing collection of paintings, architectural drawings and antiquities – in 1820 his rival Robert Smirke Jr had won the commission to rebuild the British Museum and Soane, stung by the perceived rejection, perhaps wanted to demonstrate that he could assemble an even more impressive collection in a building of his own design. In 1833, by

Act of Parliament, he disinherited George and bequeathed his house and its contents to the nation as a museum 'for the inspection of amateurs and students in painting, sculpture and architecture'.

13 Lincoln's Inn Fields is immediately recognisable by its façade, distinguished by a three-storey loggia in Portland stone decorated with incised Greek key patterns and topped by statuary. A revolutionary departure for a Georgian terraced house, it may have been a snide response to the grand portico of the recently completed Royal College of Surgeons building on the opposite side of the square – another commission for which Soane was gallingly overlooked, this time in favour of Dance, with whom Soane had fallen out seemingly irrevocably in 1805–06 after he had allegedly schemed to take the professorship of the Royal Academy from his mentor.

Visitors are welcomed by a member of staff and ushered into the ground-floor library/ dining room, painted Pompeian red and home to some 50 urns and vases. Colour scheme and contents are relieved by an ingenious use of mirrors – the one between the front windows makes the wall appear a continuous plane of glass while those above the bookcases reflect the ceiling paintings. A portrait by Thomas Lawrence shows Soane looking benign.

The study and dressing room at the rear are so small in contrast that there is an *Alice in Wonderland* feel about them, as if it is you who has grown, not the scale of the rooms that has shrunk. Roman fragments stretch up to the ceiling and the view of the sculpture courtyard from the east window gives the impression of a ruined temple discovered among London's brick-faced backyards. It is an incongruous mix of worlds that perhaps serves as a metaphor for the way the heady idealism of Soane's two-year scholarship to Italy from 1778 – a time he described as the happiest of his life – was soon overshadowed by the disappointing realities of London architectural practice. Squeeze through a narrow corridor and suddenly the space changes from calm elegance to a chaotic array of artefacts. The picture room at the rear of number 14 juxtaposes serene Raphael cartoon fragments with Hogarth's very English paintings of the debauchery and corruption of *A Rake's Progress* and *An Election*. In an ingenious piece of theatre, the panelling of the north wall swings open to reveal a series of Piranesi drawings of Paestum; the south wall is hinged twice, first for J M Gandy's watercolour perspectives of Soane's fantastic visions and the second time for a view into the yard and monk's parlour below.

The monk's parlour satirises the contemporary passion for all things gothic. Soane invented the character of Padre Giovanni – allegedly buried in the yard in a tomb that in fact holds the remains of Eliza's dog Fanny – and created a melancholic atmosphere for his chamber through restricted space, sombre colours and stained glass. The crypt at the rear of number 13 houses a disturbing collection of prototype tombs, predominantly for women and children, designed by Soane's close friend John Flaxman. In the sepulchral chamber is the sarcophagus of Pharaoh Seti I, which Soane bought in 1824 for £2000 after the British Museum turned down the offer. He celebrated the acquisition over three evenings of parties with some 900 guests including the prime minister, Samuel Taylor Coleridge and his great friend J M W Turner. Above the tomb sit dismembered fragments of classical sculpture – the effect is like an episode of *Casualty* set in stone. Taking pride of place on the upper level of the double-height space, a bust of Soane faces a plaster cast of the Apollo Belvedere, considered the most perfect representation of male beauty.

The breakfast parlour of number 13 contains many of Soane's architectural

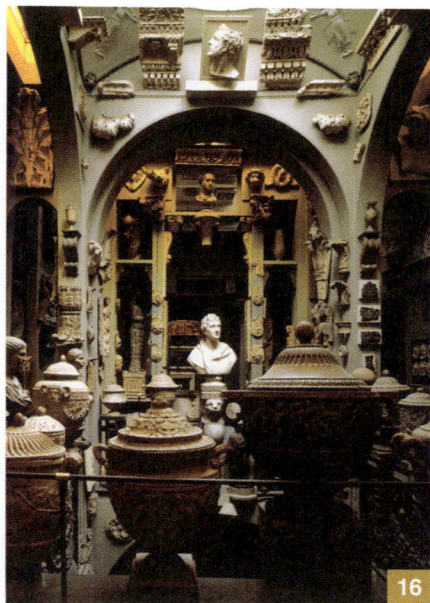

trademarks – a shallow pendentive dome, a central lantern, a mirror reflecting the window with its view of sculptures and fragments – along with books and drawings of Roman architecture. You can find echoes of its form and details in the Dulwich Picture Gallery and mausoleum and in the tomb in St Pancras Old Churchyard (see pages 74 and 246) where Soane, Eliza and their son John are all buried. Despite his continued disappointment and anger with George – whose behaviour he blamed for Eliza's early death – Soane clung on to his dynastic aspirations, arranging an architectural apprenticeship for George's son Fred in 1835. This too led to disaster, with Fred's mentor, ecclesiastical architect John Tarrant, requesting his removal as he was staying out late and keeping bad company.

16. Sir John Soanes Museum,
    13 Lincoln's Inn Fields, WC2A 3BP
    www.soane.org

5.5 Leighton House

17 Leighton House, the home and studio of highly successful Victorian artist Frederic Leighton is indeed an oddity, its relatively conventional brick exterior concealing a fantasy Moorish palace interior in the form of a domed Arab hall lined with tiles, mosaics and marbles. Between its inception in 1864 and its owner's death in 1896, the house consumed substantial amounts of Leighton's time and money. While it was conceived as a retreat in which the artist could work and escape social demands, it also featured so regularly in the press that it came to embody the idea of how a great artist should live.

The son of a doctor whose father had amassed a considerable fortune as physician to the Russian Imperial family, Frederic Leighton moved abroad with his parents when he was just 11 years old because of his mother's ill health. Five years later, in 1846, the family settled in Frankfurt, where Frederic enrolled at the art institute. He then embarked on a European grand tour, involving some three years each in Rome and Paris, before settling in London in 1859.

Handsome, cultivated and cosmopolitan – and with a lifelong private income – Leighton was much sought after by London society, including the Prince and Princess of Wales. However, despite his success, he remains an enigmatic figure, with speculation both that he fathered a child with one of his models and that he was homosexual. As with his house – buttoned-up and closed to the street but with hidden riches inside – he guarded his privacy and perhaps deliberately cultivated an air of mystery. The pinnacle of his career came in 1878, when he was elected president of the Royal Academy, and in 1896 he was created a peer, the only British artist to be so honoured. However, the title was to last only a day – the shortest-lived peerage in British history – as Leighton died the day after receiving the distinction.

Leighton bought the plot for his Holland Park house in 1864 and chose an 'old friend', George Aitchison, as his architect. The young men had met in Rome in the early 1850s: Aitchison's family firm specialised in wharves, warehouses and docks and Leighton House was to be one of only two domestic commissions. Nevertheless, it kept him busy for almost 30 years and led to several requests for extravagant interiors for London's fashionable elite.

The house as originally built was relatively modest: an L-shape containing the present entrance hall, staircase hall, dining room and drawing room with a studio, bedroom and bathroom upstairs – Leighton had no intention of disturbing his working routine by accommodating visitors overnight. The studio space was expanded in 1870 and again in 1890 with the addition of a winter studio, but it was the Arab hall extension of 1877–81 that was to transform a relatively ordinary house into something truly distinctive.

Indeed, nothing in the elegant red-brick façade of Leighton House prepares the visitor for the wonder of the double-height staircase hall, Narcissus hall and domed Arab hall, a continuous open space through which you are irresistibly drawn by the sound of a tinkling fountain. Intended to evoke the world of the Arabian Nights, the Arab hall was created by Aitchison as a setting for the tiles Leighton and his friends had 'acquired' from Rhodes, Damascus, Cairo and Tangier, which he first visited in 1852. All use a similar palette of blues and greens, but their content ranges from inscriptions and abstract patterns to leaves, birds and flowers. Fashionable ceramicist William de Morgan was hired to arrange them and remake some of the broken pieces and the jigsaw effect of fitting the various collections together only adds to the appeal.

Aitchison's design was inspired by the banqueting room at the Moorish palace of La Zisa at Palermo, and Leighton House's black marble basin pays homage to the former's black marble table, which had water running down a central channel in which diners could rinse their hands. Leighton also commissioned contributions from his talented friends: the gilt mosaic frieze of birds and deer was designed by Walter Crane, the capitals of the marble columns at the entrance by Randolph Caldecott and the capitals of the columns flanking the sofas by Edgar Boehm. Aitchison created the copper and wrought-iron chandelier, a modern-day crown of thorns. But the team knew where to stop: the floor is a simple pattern in black-and-white mosaic and the functional fountain is remarkable for its sound rather than its appearance.

It seems a shame to quibble about such a fabulous, magical space. And if the theft involved in this Victorian temple to sensuality and beauty had been purely intellectual, there would be no need. But the 16th- and 17th-century tiles here are cultural and religious artefacts – the large panel above the entrance, 'brought' by traveller and Arabian Nights translator Richard Burton from a hill temple at Sind (then in northern India), contains a passage from the creation myth in the Koran ('He has created man and taught him speech/ [He hath set] the sun and the moon in a certain course…'); the brown 14th-century tiles in the west wall have had the faces erased, and the images of birds on the south wall their throats slit by chipping a line in the glaze, to conform with Islamic edicts against the representation of living things. And while the elaborate Ottoman-style grilles on the windows were an effective way of protecting Leighton's privacy, their connotations of the harem where women were to be heard but not seen introduce sinister overtones into the sensual pleasure of the space.

The library, to the left of the Narcissus hall, was used by Leighton as a study. The fireplace, positioned seemingly nonsensically beneath the window, mirrors that in the drawing room on the opposite side of the hall, its flue rising to the left of the glass. Since Leighton's entertaining was restricted almost exclusively to male company, a withdrawing room was rarely required and the space functioned instead as a gallery for his art collection. The effect of the positioning of the fireplace, its surround of wispy grasses designed by Leighton himself, and the unusual semi-circular bay in the west wall, with a circular sketch by Delacroix (a copy of the original) inset into the ceiling, is thoroughly unpredictable, as if Leighton and Aitchison had taken nothing as given, reworking assumptions from scratch. The doors are made of the ebonised woodwork found throughout the house, with stylised plant forms picked out in gold, and mouldings, in a bizarre joke, derived from picture frames.

The spacious top-lit antechamber above the Narcissus hall leads to a day-bed, also 'brought' from the Middle East, which projects over the Arab hall. With its grille filtering views of the golden dome and tiles and the sound of the fountain, it has fuelled many an erotic fantasy.

Mirroring Leighton's surprisingly modest bedroom is the silk room, built over a former roof terrace in 1894. Windowless but top-lit by a lantern, it was created to display paintings given to Leighton as a mark of respect by his contemporaries: its many portraits include Leighton's cross-looking Desdemona, modelled on Dorothy Dene, an actress whom he befriended and encouraged towards the end of his life (their platonic relationship may have been the source for Shaw's *Pygmalion*), and a sensual, bronzed Pan with the proportions of a Michelangelo nude. More than half of the house's top floor is taken up by Leighton's studio, once overflowing with materials, props and the beautiful objects that served him as inspiration.

While Leighton House was unappreciated for much of the 20th century, it has recently been restored and refurbished, including an ambitious redevelopment that has brought the interiors back to life and created new visitor and learning facilities. Most startling is a new helical staircase within a brick rotunda decorated with a spectacular 11-metre high mural, *Oneness*, by Iranian artist Shahrzad Ghaffari, its colours inspired by the Moorish tiles of the Arab hall.

Leighton's most famous self-portrait, created in 1880, shows a handsome man with a sensitive face and heavy beard dressed in the garb of a Roman senator, reflecting the artist's love for a country and an era he regarded as his spiritual home. His actual home, along with his art and what can be gleaned here of his life, reflect the contradictions of this fantasy of a more glorious age filtered through Victorian constraints. In his home, at least, we should be grateful the fantasy won out.

17. Leighton House,
12 Holland Park Rd, W14 8LZ
www.rbkc.gov.uk/museums

5.6 Dennis Severs House

'The late 20th century may be a fascinating place to visit, but surely… nobody would want to live in it.' Dennis Severs

The **18** **Dennis Severs House**, at 18 Folgate Street in Spitalfields, is full of contradictions. It is a recreation of a historic house that ignores the specifics of history. It is a theatre piece or immersive art installation that was once given life by the changing whims of its creator but is now set in stone. It is a way of evoking the past that was formerly condemned by the establishment but now influences how some of our most prestigious monuments are presented. It is a patch of grimy London reimagined through a prism of Californian sunshine.

The house was bought by Dennis Severs (1948–1999) in 1979. At the time Spitalfields was still a wholesale fruit, vegetable and flower market rather than a mall of galleries and boutiques, and the surrounding area housed Bengali immigrants in overcrowded slums rather than the wealthy city and media personalities who occupy many of the houses today. The son of an impoverished petrol-station owner from Escondido in southern California who had grown up on a diet of BBC costume dramas, Severs scavenged for food along with the area's many tramps, made money from hiring out his horse and carriage, the only privately owned landau in London, and camped with his chamber pot, candle and bedroll in each of his dilapidated house's ten rooms to uncover their particular atmosphere.

Eventually he invented the Jervises, a family of Huguenot silk weavers who fled France soon after Louis XIV banned Protestant worship in 1685, bought the Folgate Street house when it was built in 1724, and whose descendants lived here until 1914. Over the course of 20 years until his death at the age of 51, Severs lived, as he saw it, 'in proxy for the family', creating and furnishing the rooms they inhabited, each frozen at the moment when the residents, startled by the intrusion of modern-day visitors, beat a hasty retreat. As Severs described it: 'This is the only house in Britain that is lived in, maintained, decorated, heated, cleaned – everything – as it was in the 18th and 19th centuries… My job is not to hoard the past but to live in the past.'

Initially Severs offered three-hour tours that began in total darkness in the cellar in an imagined 1197 (the date of fragments of St Mary's Spital found here) and gradually travelled through the upper floors to 1914; artist David Hockney ranked a visit as among the world's great operatic experiences. Today, visitors can roam at will but are cautioned to remain silent for the duration of their stay, and certainly the absence of embarrassed sniggers at stale urine in chamber pots or irrelevant exclamations at the beauty or tackiness of some of the objects on show helps keep the 21st century at bay for those willing and able to suspend their disbelief. Don't be put off by haranguing notices asking you not to touch anything or indeed by Severs' own musings, which dominate the house's website: the key to appreciating the experience lies in allowing your senses to take over rather than trying to deconstruct the psycho-babble with which the project is described.

The house itself – three storeys, with basement and attic, three bays wide and built to a standard L plan – is typical of the area's Georgian terraces, thrown up quickly and shoddily by speculative builders hoping to make money to continue their development. The ground-floor front

room – in which a programme for the coronation of William and Mary in 1689 hints at the occupants' Protestantism as well as the date of their arrival – is set up as a dining room. A notice explains the plot: 'Eighteenth-century silk master Isaac Jervis – his family and descendants – are all still around you somewhere in the house. As you approach – they depart, as you depart – they re-enter, but all so that by not actually seeing them your Imagination might paint a series of pictures: of the various domestic scenes your arrival has forced them to abandon.'

If you are able to keep your scepticism under wraps, then the smells of food that waft around the abandoned table and the soundtrack of domestic exchanges, street noises and cockcrows combined with the chirping of a real caged bird produce an atmosphere that at the least could be described as uncanny. Even knowing that the elaborate ceiling in the hall was created by plastering over plastic fruit bought in

Tesco on Bethnal Green Road in the late 1990s does not quite destroy the illusion.

The most spine-chilling room is the first-floor back, where Severs painstakingly created the scene that might have followed the drunken all-male party depicted in Hogarth's 1733 painting *A Midnight Modern Conversation*, a copy of which hangs above the mantelpiece. Abandoned jackets and newspapers, disordered furniture, overturned glasses and decanters, an overpowering smell of cloves from the empty punchbowl, dying embers and the morning-after-the-night-before gloom are eerie enough, but what is most disturbing is the feeling that the myriad details have been provided with such precision and completeness that the space is in fact fully inhabited, and the visitor an unwelcome intruder.

On the landing a stunning crystal chandelier hints at the more genteel atmosphere of the drawing room. But the most potent indication that we are entering a female domain is the change in smell – from punch dregs to lavender. Presided over by a portrait of Mrs Edward Jervis, the room is set for tea, with a fan draped on what one presumes is the mistress' chair, tea locked in a caddy at her feet, and the startled departure of her guests indicated by an upturned sugar bowl and broken cup. On the table is a book of entertainments dating from 1740, a point at which the halt on imports following the start of the 1740-48 war with France led to a surge in demand for locally produced silk and the prosperity of Spitalfields reached its zenith.

The second floor belongs to a less affluent age. Abandoned wooden toys gather dust at the top of the stairs and the back room is a combined bedchamber/sitting room where the smell of stale urine mingles unpleasantly with the odour of half-eaten food and dregs of tea. The date is 1821, a time when the number of silk weavers dramatically outflanked demand for their product and the influx of veterans from the protracted war with France that ended in the Battle of Waterloo in 1815 had led to social instability and unrest.

The front bedroom, with its flashy display of Delft above the mantelpiece, is dominated by the belongings of another Mrs Jervis, including a chair that seems to hold the impression of her body and might still feel warm to the touch. Disconcertingly, beside the fireplace are a pair of 20th-century men's shoes and socks and tucked behind a screen are a jumper and sweatshirt. It is a discreet reminder that this was also Severs' room and that he chose deliberately, masochistically, to efface his own needs and live in obeisance to a woman created by his imagination.

On the attic landing are lines hung with greying underclothes, and a quotation from Dickens' *Oliver Twist* hints that we are now in the late 1830s. The family has fallen on hard times and padlocks on the doors show that these rooms are let to lodgers, with several people sleeping, cooking, eating and living in each of the spaces.

Severs obviously had fun with his recreation, while at the same time living it with extraordinary seriousness. According to historian and friend Dan Cruikshank, he was eventually overwhelmed by the project, with the house becoming an eternal prison of his own making whose rules he felt compelled to obey. One of his final acts was to replace his original choice of Pompeian red for the first-floor landing with the current pale pink – historically inaccurate, but perhaps an attempt to assert his own taste over the demands of his imaginary housemates.

His creation – bought by the Spitalfields Trust in 1999 – was initially offered to the National Trust, which declined because of historical inaccuracies. Ironically today, evocation of the past through recorded soundtracks, personal stories and artefacts gathered almost at random has become fashionable in historic houses – though unlike Severs, the curators retreat to their own, more comfortable homes once the visitors have departed.

18. Dennis Severs House,
    18 Folgate St, E1 6BX
    www.dennissevershouse.co.uk

5.7 Dorich House

Gordine and Hare designed Dorich House shortly before their marriage in 1936 and lived there for the rest of their lives. They named their new home from a conflation of their two first names, and the building they dreamed up was a highly personal invention, suited to their particular needs and planned with scant regard for architectural norms. Unusually for houses preserved as museums, Dorich House is for the most part the creation of a woman: Hare's family fortune may have provided the means, but it was Gordine who supplied the vision, and it was her personality and the demands of her working life that seem to have shaped its spaces.

Gordine was born in Libau in Latvia and by 1920 had arrived in Paris, where her exotic status as a Russian émigrée enabled her to make connections in the bohemian and art worlds. Following a successful solo exhibition in London in 1928, a commission for pieces for a new government building led her to Singapore, where she married physician Dr G H Garlick. The marriage was short lived. Richard Hare, who had bought one of Gordine's sculptures in London and perhaps proposed, arrived at their door in 1933 after a legacy from his father enabled him to quit his job at the Foreign Office and embark on a tour of south-east Asia. Within a year Gordine and Hare were writing letters in which they planned to build a London home.

19 Dorich House is like no other. Built in brick, with a central tower on the entrance elevation flanked on one side by three long thin windows that from a distance resemble overscaled arrow slits and on the other by matching blind arches, it stands in splendid isolation on the edge of Richmond Park. At first sight it seems like an extraordinary mix of fortress, quarantine hospital and warehouse, or perhaps an ill-conceived Palladian villa stretched to impossible proportions. Its owners – sculptor Dora Gordine (1895–1991) and art collector Richard Hare (1907–1966) – were also an unlikely mix: she a self-taught emigrée Russian artist with a shadowy backstory and a marriage or two behind her; he an aristocrat, academic and one-time government official 12 years her junior. Both were probably attracted to their own sex yet they were devoted enough for him to pursue her over two continents and for their marriage to last happily for 30 years, leaving her bereft at his early death.

Though Gordine was well versed in modernist architecture (while in Paris she had commissioned her neighbour and friend Auguste Perret, the foremost pioneer of reinforced concrete, to build her a studio), Dorich House is not a slave to any style or movement and is modern primarily in its determination to reinvent living conditions to suit the needs of its occupants. Most of the ground floor and the entire double-height first floor contained Gordine's studios and gallery, with the couple's living quarters relegated to a relatively small apartment at the top of the house.

The ground-floor workshop was used for plaster-casting, its shelves a hall of fame of busts of actors, dancers, writers and television personalities alongside Hare's aristocratic and wealthy connections. At the foot of the stairs is a standing bronze of actress Edith Evans, made when she was 50 and embarking on an affair with Michael Redgrave, an actor 20 years her junior. Arms raised behind her head to expose her naked body fully and face turned to one side as if the viewer is of no interest, the statue exudes the sense of a woman who is completely comfortable with both her body and her self. Evans claimed that modelling for Gordine during this unsettled period of her life was better than therapy.

The first-floor modelling studio, with one wall and part of the ceiling made up almost entirely of metal-framed windows that seem to touch the greenery of Richmond Park, feels like a gigantic tree house. Beside the platform where work in progress was displayed is a plaster cast of *Power*, a 1960 commission for the walls of an Esso refinery in Milford Haven that depicts a construction worker lifting a metal girder into place. The relief is intended to celebrate strength and work, but in fact the inspiration was flamenco dancers – and indeed the worker's neat boots, muscular legs, narrow waist and outflung arms are more dancer than builder. On the landing is *Crowning Glory* (1947), a statuette of a nude with elaborate tresses sitting cross-legged as though in meditation. The piece was commissioned as a trademark for Eugène Permanent Wave and reproductions were placed in hundreds of salons that used the company's products; ironically for its

creator, whose straight black hair seems always to have been scraped back into a bun, this was probably her most famous work. The gallery opposite the modelling studio is a temple to Gordine's art – and indeed the double-height space, with its tall triple windows and curved apse, subtly evokes ecclesiastical buildings.

Hare and Gordine's modest apartment on the floor above was supplemented by a roof terrace where the couple and their friends would eat, hold parties and occasionally sleep. The two main rooms are linked by a circular door inspired by the 'moon gates' of Chinese and Japanese gardens. Photographs of the couple show them enjoying domestic life: eating together on the roof terrace, or Gordine in her apron watching Hare proudly pushing an electric polisher across the beautiful wooden floors. Gordine in particular is extraordinarily arresting: a doll-like figure with stylised kiss curls flattened on each cheek, dramatically arched eyebrows and large, heavily lidded eyes. Above the fireplace in the drawing room is a 1929 portrait she made of Hare which seems to draw out his femininity – full lips, exaggeratedly large eyes, finely arched eyebrows and soft skin.

After Hare's death Gordine continued to live at Dorich House for a quarter of a century, but her career more or less ground to a halt. In comparison with contemporaries such as Barbara Hepworth, her style had not developed as she grew older: possibly in marrying the wealthy Hare and moving to suburbia she had prioritised security over creative freedom, respectability over risk-taking? Nevertheless, Dorich House honours her legacy and today operates as an international centre to support and promote the work of female artists.

19. Dorich House,
    67 Kingston Vale, SW15 3RN
    www.dorichhousemuseum.org.uk

19

19

19

19

5.8 Walters Way

20

Walters Way – together with nearby Segal Close – was the brainchild of Walter Segal (1907–1985), who remains the only architect to have two London roads bearing his name. The son of Jewish Romanian parents – his father was an expressionist painter – Segal was brought up in a commune in Switzerland whose members were trying to develop a new way of living in reaction to stuffy late 19th-century norms of diet, clothing and behaviour. As he described it, the colonists of Monte Verità (Mountain of Truth) 'abhorred private property, practised a rigid code of morality, strict vegetarianism and nudism. They rejected convention in marriage and dress, party politics and dogmas: they were tolerantly intolerant.' Segal eventually studied architecture in Berlin and lived with his family in Mallorca before coming to London in 1935 to work first as an Egyptologist at the British Museum and then as a tutor at the Architectural Association.

Walking down the steep slope of **20 Walters Way** from the bricks-and-mortar respectability of Honor Oak Park in Forest Hill is like entering a 1960s hippy commune or artists' colony. An oddity in London, the street's nearest equivalents are perhaps the houseboat communities of south Amsterdam or the wood-framed houses of the Berkeley Hills in California. Though the 13 houses have features in common – timber frames clad in standard-sized panels and flat roofs – their basic forms are customised by the addition of wooden stairways and verandahs, complicated arrangements of balconies, stained-glass windows, glass-brick walls, tiles, large areas of glazing and even a built-in treehouse. What makes this collection of homes even odder is that all of them were built entirely by their original owners.

Segal may have been remembered only as an inspiring teacher, the author of a couple of books and the designer of a block of flats in Knightsbridge and a few North London houses were it not for a serendipitous project developed with the London Borough of Lewisham towards the end of his life. In the early 1960s the widowed Segal met a new partner, Moran Scott, and found himself with a family of six children. When the couple decided to demolish and rebuild their Highgate home to accommodate their changed circumstances, Segal built a temporary house in the garden using simple materials that could be easily reused – even the wallpaper was secured by batons rather than paste so it could be removed when needed. Cooled in summer by a shallow pond on the flat roof, replenished by Segal using a hosepipe, the house was erected by

a carpenter in just two weeks for a cost of £800. Visitors and clients were impressed – and soon demands for 'little houses at the bottom of the garden' poured in. Segal honed his system over the next few years, and when one frustrated client sacked his builders and declared he would complete the project himself, the Segal self-build method was born.

Meanwhile, during the housing boom of the 1970s Lewisham Council had bought up every vacant scrap of land in the borough to build new homes. Unfortunately some sites were unsuitable for conventional construction – too small, sloping, covered in trees or with soil too soft to sustain foundations. Segal was looking for ways to extend the reach of his self-build ethos, and borough architect Colin Ward, who knew and admired his work, persuaded his council colleagues to offer those on the waiting list the chance to build their own homes. Two hundred families drew lots for the initial 14 plots in what is now Segal Close; construction began in 1979, with the 13 homes on Walters Way following in 1984.

Segal's achievement was to simplify the process of building a house so it could be done by amateurs, cheaply and quickly. He worked with the idiosyncrasies of the site, specifying light timber frames that could sit on paving slabs so there was no need to level the ground or lay concrete foundations; other 'wet trades' like bricklaying and plastering were eliminated by using cladding, insulating and lining materials in standard sizes that could be bought at builders' merchants or DIY stores. According to one of the original self-builders, Segal maintained that anyone could build a house: 'All you need to be able to do is draw a straight line and drill a straight hole.' He also recognised that circumstances change and houses need to be adaptable, so his system has no loadbearing walls, allowing both exterior and interior partitions to be moved and new rooms to be added as required.

Most of the future residents took a couple of years to build their homes, working at weekends and in the evenings. For many, it was an empowering experience: as one resident put it, 'He put a turbo charge up you to convince you it could happen.' During the build neighbours helped each other with tasks such as erecting the main frames and all the participants eventually bought the houses they had created. At the end of the project, they had built not only a group of houses, but a community.

20. Walters Way, SE23 3LH

5.9 575 Wandsworth Road

21

Open to the public since 2012, the former Clapham home of Khadambi Asalache is now one of the oddest of National Trust properties – in London and beyond. The exterior of the modest Georgian terrace house is frankly unassuming, with a shabby modern front door looking out on blocks of council flats across the busy Wandsworth Road. Open the door, however, and the fretwork that twists and curls across walls and ceilings like the tendrils of an out-of-control plant transforms ordinary rooms into magical spaces from another world.

The son of the chief of a tribe of herdsmen in western Kenya, Asalache read architecture at the Royal Technical College in Nairobi before making a European grand tour to study art in Rome, Geneva and Vienna. He moved to London in 1960 and turned his hand to literature, publishing poetry and novels that were among the first to describe Kenyan life to a wider world. A polymath by any standards, he gained an MPhil in the Philosophy of Mathematics in the mid-1970s and joined the Civil Service, working in the Treasury and Cabinet Office. Without a recorded birthdate, he was assigned 28 February 1935 by the Civil Service to determine when he could retire.

Asalache bought **21** **575 Wandsworth Road** in 1981 and lived here until his death in 2006. He chose the house because it was located conveniently on a direct bus route to his office in Whitehall, was relatively unmodernised and had a generous ratio of window to wall, with a garden that backed on to a deconsecrated churchyard rather than other terraces. Built in 1819, the simple artisan house – two storeys above a semi-basement – had once belonged to a family of cobblers, though Asalache inherited it from squatters who kept chickens, pigs and a horse in the back garden, walking the horse through the hallway to exercise it on a nearby stretch of wasteland.

Asalache's forays into interior decoration began prosaically with a damp patch in his basement dining room. Like many a DIY bodger, he opted to cover it up in the hope it might go away, or at least cease to reproach him. But having lined the offending wall with old pine floorboards salvaged from a skip, he found the unadorned wood with its strong vertical lines unlovely. So he began to embellish it with handmade fretwork: first an unambitious frieze of arrowheads, then increasingly elaborate shelves and niches decorated with convoluted, irregular patterns as well as images of birds, animals and masks. He started his piercing and sawing in 1986 and finally laid down his tools almost two decades later.

The refurbishment was carried out one room at a time in a series of concentrated bursts. After office hours and at weekends Asalache would saw and drill lengths of scavenged timber or old wine crates into delicate friezes and patterns, working in his garden on a small concrete path above the lightwell to the semi-basement, which he named the crocodile pit. He designed directly on to the wood, marking it up in pencil before shaping it with his only tools – a hand-drill, a pad saw and a fret saw. Irredeemable mistakes were used as kindling but there was no attempt to disguise the process, with blobs of glue and pins left visible and edges unsanded.

While influenced by Ottoman, Moorish and traditional African architecture, Asalache pursued a path that was entirely his own. Symmetry was eschewed in favour of what he termed 'visual balance' and subjects reflect his eclectic interests: friezes depict memories from a holiday in Zanzibar and the journey of the Nile from its source to the sea; a string of dancers commemorates his love of ballet; birds, animals and plants appear throughout, from flamingos to ducks, giraffes to squirrels, palm trees to roses. His interest in mathematics is represented in shelves arranged according to the Fibonnaci sequence of numbers (1,1,2,3,5,8 etc). 'I don't know or believe one needs to bother with concepts from quantum mechanics when doing interior design,' he said, 'but one can try.'

After completing his basement dining room, Asalache moved upstairs to the ground-floor sitting room where he supplemented fretwork with painting. Kilims are enhanced by geometric borders created with lino paint; colour is introduced into holes in the fretwork; a painted duck on the door swims on a pond suggested by the wood grain. As he moved on to the first floor, his designs became more elaborate and incorporated more paint, always applied freehand, though sometimes, bizarrely, mimicking traditional stencil patterns. Across the lower part of the bedroom window is a wooden screen incorporating his own and his partner's initials (Asalache declared himself 'antipathetic to net curtains') and beside the bed is a kennel for her Tibetan Spaniel, lined with red velvet. On the landing is a frieze of gazelles placed at dog's-eye level.

In the downstairs bathroom are portraits of inspiring women, ranging from Sappho, Pocahontas and Cleopatra to Anna Pavlova and Bessie Smith. It is in the hallway, however, that the elaboration reaches its zenith, culminating at the front door, where a peacock sits in a delicate frame and a pair of guardian angels stand to 'accompany home guests'. By now Asalache was a regular customer at timber merchants Travis Perkins: intrigued and impressed by photographs of his work, staff granted him a professional trade discount, of which he was immensely proud.

What began as a short cut to cover a damp patch had become a lifelong project. And it might have pleased Asalache to know that even the National Trust, with its team of experts and superior budget, has failed to solve the problem of his damp basement.

21. 575 Wandsworth Rd, SW8 3JD
www.nationaltrust.org.uk

Mural by Jean Cocteau, Notre Dame de France, see page 195

Commemoration & Neglect

Commemoration & Neglect

HAMPSTEAD HEATH
HIGHGATE
FINSBURY PARK
HOLLOWAY
Highbury Fields
BARNSBURY
KING'S CROSS
ISLINGTON
CLERKENWELL
MAIDA VALE
BLOOMSBURY
BAYSWATER
SOHO
TEMPLE
MAYFAIR
PICCADILLY
Kensington Park
Kensington Palace
Hyde Park
Green Park
St James's Park
Buckingham Palace
Tate Britain
KNIGHTSBRIDGE
WESTMINSTER
Westminster Bridge
NEWINGTON
KENSINGTON
Lambeth Bridge
LAMBETH
CROMWELL ROAD
PIMLICO
VAUXHALL
CHELSEA
Vauxhall Bridge
RIVER THAMES
Battersea Park
Chelsea Bridge
Albert Bridge
Battersea Bridge
NINE ELMS LANE

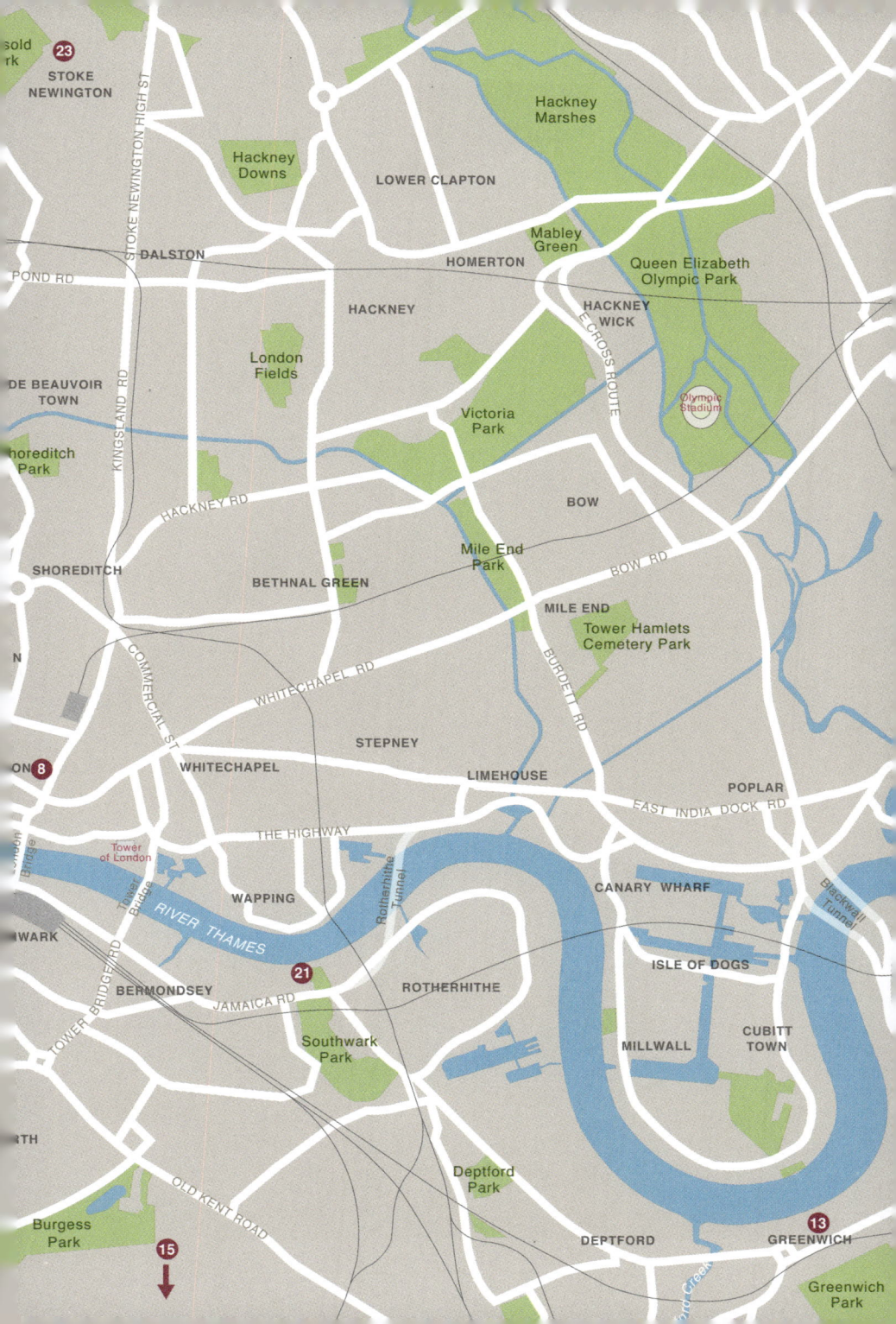

23
STOKE
NEWINGTON

Hackney
Marshes

Hackney
Downs

LOWER CLAPTON

STOKE NEWINGTON HIGH ST

POND RD

DALSTON

Mabley
Green

HOMERTON

Queen Elizabeth
Olympic Park

HACKNEY
WICK

HACKNEY

DE BEAUVOIR
TOWN

London
Fields

KINGSLAND RD

E CROSS ROUTE

Olympic
Stadium

horeditch
Park

Victoria
Park

HACKNEY RD

BOW

SHOREDITCH

Mile End
Park

BETHNAL GREEN

BOW RD

MILE END

Tower Hamlets
Cemetery Park

COMMERCIAL ST

BURDETT RD

WHITECHAPEL RD

STEPNEY

8

WHITECHAPEL

LIMEHOUSE

POPLAR

EAST INDIA DOCK RD

THE HIGHWAY

Tower
of London

Rotherhithe
Tunnel

CANARY WHARF

Blackwall
Tunnel

Tower Bridge

WAPPING

RIVER THAMES

ISLE OF DOGS

London Bridge

TOWER BRIDGE RD

21

BERMONDSEY

JAMAICA RD

ROTHERHITHE

MILLWALL

CUBITT
TOWN

WARK

Southwark
Park

RTH

Deptford
Park

Burgess
Park

OLD KENT ROAD

DEPTFORD

GREENWICH

13

15

Greenwich
Park

d Creek

1

6.1 Out of Time, Out of Place

Sekhmet & Cleopatra's Needle

Above a doorway at 34–35 New Bond Street in Mayfair is a statue that is both out of time and far from home. The black basalt effigy commemorating the ancient Egyptian goddess ❶ **Sekhmet** – half lion, half woman – travelled some 3,000 miles to its current resting place and predates its surroundings by some 3,000 years. The oldest outdoor statue in London, its quiet dignity and simplicity contrast with the attention-seeking façades and banners that line the street.

Sekhmet has presided over the entrance to Sotheby's auction house since 1917, though it has been in the company's possession since the 1880s, when its buyer – who successfully bid £40 – failed to collect it. Perhaps appropriately for an auctioneer, Sekhmet was the Egyptians' warrior goddess, a fierce hunter whose breath was said to have formed the desert.

Egypt was much in vogue in late 19th-century London and a much larger Egyptian treasure – the 21-metre-high ❷ **Cleopatra's Needle** – arrived on the Victoria Embankment in 1878. Surprisingly, it has nothing to do with Cleopatra: it was created in Heliopolis around 1450BCE as an offering from Pharaoh Thutmose III to the sun god and so predates the Egyptian queen by about 1,000 years. The toppled obelisk was offered to Britain by the Viceroy of Egypt in 1819 in thanks for Nelson's triumph at the Battle of the Nile. However, since parliament refused to fund its transport, it remained face down in the desert for 60 years until the money to bring it to Britain was raised by public subscription. Though the hieroglyphs – which include prayers from Thutmose as well as commemorations of victories by Rameses II added 200 years later – were well preserved during three millennia in Egypt, 150 years of London rain and pollution have taken their toll.

Not content with the time capsule the monument represented, the Victorians decided to add objects commemorating the wonders of their own age. Hidden within the pedestal is a box containing a bizarre collection that includes 12 photographs of what were considered the best-looking women of the day, a baby's bottle, toys, a razor and hairpins, a portrait of Queen Victoria, a Bradshaw Railway Guide and copies of the Bible in several languages.

THROUGH THE PATRIOTIC ZEAL OF
ERASMUS WILSON F.R.S.
THIS OBELISK
WAS BROUGHT FROM ALEXANDRIA
ENCASED IN AN IRON CYLINDER
WAS ABANDONED DURING A STORM
IN THE BAY OF BISCAY
RECOVERED AND ERECTED
ON THIS SPOT BY
JOHN DIXON C.E.

George Ryan, Nelson's Column

The Battle of Trafalgar of 1805 is celebrated as a great British victory over the Spanish and French and lamented as the conflict in which Britain's most famous admiral met his death. But the military triumph – like those of WW1 and WW2 – was also thanks to fighting forces from India, Africa and the Caribbean as well as a number of Europeans. Little is known of the crew of Nelson's *HMS Victory* beyond their names, ages and places of birth, which tell us that nine were from the West Indies (perhaps recruited or pressganged when Nelson was pursuing the French in the Caribbean), 21 were Americans (possibly former slaves freed on condition they took up servitude in the Royal Navy), and one was an African: George Ryan, aged 25, who served in the navy until he was invalided out in 1813.

The bronze relief recording the death of Nelson on the Whitehall side of ❸ **Nelson's Column** in Trafalgar Square, created by sculptor John Carew and installed in 1849, places a black seaman near the centre of the action. Standing aboard ship on the right of the image, his gun held in readiness, he seems to be listening to the man behind him, who is pointing towards the recumbent admiral.

The relief, which makes obvious that he is an equal and trusted part of the fighting team, is the only known public image of a black hero created in 19th-century London. Ironically, the man at the top of the column repeatedly spoke out against the abolition of the slave trade.

3

Oceanides

Carved in Carrara marble by sculptor Oscar Spalmach in the Roman studio of Orazio Andreoni towards the end of the 19th century, the ❹ **Oceanides** (or Naked Ladies) make a strange contrast to their setting of clipped lawns and municipal hedges within the riverside gardens of York House, the town hall of the borough of Richmond upon Thames at the west end of Richmond Road in Twickenham. The effect is not improved (except in oddness) by the seven sea nymphs being scattered across a cascade of rough stone, reeds and pondweed rather than forming the closely grouped centrepiece of a marble fountain within an Italian piazza.

The sculptures were brought to England by Whitaker Wright, a corrupt financier who committed suicide at the Royal Courts of Justice following his conviction for fraud in 1904. Five years later they were bought by Indian industrialist and art collector Ratan Tata and transported to Twickenham, still in their packing cases, to be installed in the gardens of York House by J Cheal & Sons. Members of the firm went over to Italy for a summer holiday in order to meet a 'professor' who claimed to know how the statues should be arranged, but struggling with the language barrier and being unprepared to pay their contact to come to England, they were left largely to improvise.

At the summit of the cascade stands Venus accompanied by two winged horses. Below her are seven nymphs, larger than human size, in various awkward poses: one sits in a giant shell, one reaches up to salute the goddess from a kneeling position, one appears to be falling into the water as she studies her reflection, one sits legs akimbo, one lies on her stomach as if half way through a Pilates exercise, one hauls her sister out of the pool. Afraid that the gleaming marble would attract attention, the figures were covered in grey sludge during WW2 and are still under constant threat of being engulfed by English slime and vegetation.

Mahomet Weyonomon

In the grounds of Southwark Cathedral near London Bridge, surrounded by a neat circle of lawn, is an irregularly shaped mound of pink granite that from a distance could be mistaken for a giant anthill or fossilised coils of rope. It seems as out of place in this English churchyard as a Native American might have felt in 18th-century London.

5 **Mahomet Weyonomon**, a chief of the Native American Mohegans, died in London in 1736 but waited 270 years for a memorial to mark his body's resting place. He had come to the UK to plead for justice for his people, who had helped the early New England settlers to survive but had subsequently found their territory reduced to a mere two square miles as the colonisers appropriated tribal land. While waiting with another Mohegan to put their case to George II, Weyonomon contracted smallpox and died.

As a foreigner, he was not entitled to be buried in the City of London so his body was carried across the river to an unmarked grave. The memorial in the Southwark Cathedral churchyard – carved with grooves that represent the paths taken through life – was created in 2006 by sculptor Peter Randall-Page from a stone chosen by tribal leaders in Uncasville, Connecticut, US, in accordance with the custom of naming a boulder after a chief who dies. The Mohegans had to wait until 1994 to be granted land for a tribal reservation, located on Connecticut's own Thames River, just north of the town of New London.

1. Sekhmet, 34–35 New Bond St, W1A 2AA
2. Cleopatra's Needle,
   Victoria Embankment, WC2N 6PB
3. Nelson's Column,
   Trafalgar Square, WC2N 5DU
4. Oceanides, York House,
   Richmond Rd, TW1 3AA
5. Mahomet Weyonomon memorial,
   Southwark Cathedral, SE1 9DA

5

6.2 Messages & Misunderstandings

Albert Memorial

London's grandest – and perhaps oddest – piece of commemorative public art is the ❻ **Albert Memorial** at the south side of Kensington Gardens, a monument to Queen Victoria's husband Prince Albert, who died of typhoid in 1861 at the age of 42. Designed and erected over the course of 15 years at a cost of £120,000 (about £10 million at today's prices), it places the Prince Consort, a man who complained of his 'difficulty in fulfilling my place with the proper dignity [in] that I am only the husband' at the centre of the world, lording it over the continents of Africa, Asia, Europe and the Americas, over the trades and industries of the day and over artists ancient and modern.

Albert had objected to the idea of a statue commemorating his role in the Great Exhibition of 1851, saying that 'if (as is very likely) it became an artistic monstrosity, like most of our monuments, it would upset my equanimity to be permanently ridiculed and laughed at in effigy.' His grieving widow unwisely ignored these sentiments, overseeing every aspect of a memorial that was widely criticised as ill-proportioned and badly composed; in 1928 it was denounced in *The Sunday Times* as 'the ugliest monument in London'.

Part of the problem with the memorial is its jumble of architectural styles: a gothic spire with gilded bronzes representing angels and virtues sits atop a gothic canopy with Moorish arches, which shelters a giant gilded statue of the prince enthroned on a podium decorated with a classical 'Frieze of Parnassus' made up of 187 figures of eminent engineers, composers, painters, architects, sculptors and poets. At the corners of the podium are marble statues in classical dress representing cutting-edge Victorian achievements in the 'useful arts' of agriculture, commerce, manufacture and engineering; below, at the level of the railings, are scantily clad figures surrounding emblematic animals representing the continents.

The overall design was by George Gilbert Scott, grandfather of Giles Gilbert Scott, the architect of the iconic K2 phone box (see page 75), with individual sculptures subcontracted to a number of highly skilled artists. The statue of Albert himself – a seated figure, bare headed, holding the catalogue of the Great Exhibition – proved predictably problematic, with the queen repeatedly dissatisfied and two sculptors (Carlo Marochetti and his successor John Foley) dying on the job. His shoulders slightly stooped, Albert is presented as a thinker and philosopher with no military pretentions (both Scott and the queen repeatedly refused pleas for a grandstanding equestrian statue); his legs akimbo in a very male appropriation of space, he is surrounded by handmaidens representing the intellectual disciplines.

Presumably the decade and a half Victoria spent fretting about the memorial's details was a valuable part of a mourning process that was to last until her death some 40 years later. Without wishing to undermine Albert's contribution to such reforms as the abolition of slavery or his encouragement of the arts and industry, it is as if his widow were demanding that in death the world should recognise his supremacy, granting him a status as head of the empire that in life could be only hers.

6. Albert Memorial,
   Kensington Gardens, SW7 2ET

Shaftesbury Memorial Fountain

London's most famous piece of sculpture is generally referred to as **❼ Eros,** the god of sensual love – a strange choice for a memorial to a Victorian social reformer. Balanced precariously above a fountain on the south side of Piccadilly Circus, the winged figure with his bow and arrow commemorates the philanthropic work of Anthony Ashley Cooper, 7th Earl of Shaftesbury (1801–1885), who campaigned successfully for better conditions for the mentally ill and introduced Acts of Parliament that eradicated the use of children as chimney sweeps, restricted factory hours and prohibited women and children from working down mines. One of the first statues to be made from aluminium, the monument in fact represents Anteros, the brother of Eros and the god of unrequited love.

Sculptor Alfred Gilbert, aged only 32 at the time, had already used Anteros as a subject and argued that the god of selfless love, poised above a source of free, clean water, would better reflect Shaftesbury's altruism than an image of the man himself. Not everyone agreed: the statue was derided following its installation in 1893 and complaints were also made about the fountain, which drenched passers-by and the flower-sellers clustered around its base. Unsurprisingly, objectors to the sensuality of the figure – a young boy poised in motion, arms outstretched to reveal his near-naked body – were not appeased when it was renamed the *Angel of Christian Charity.* Gilbert's model for his Greek god was his 15-year-old Italian studio assistant, Angelo Colarossi.

Cornhill Devils

Conflicts between developers and communities are hardly news in London, but it is rare that the bad guys commemorate the struggle in sculpture. Late in the 19th century, however, a fight to preserve the grounds of St Peter upon Cornhill from defilement by an office development at 54–55 Cornhill resulted in the creation of the **❽ Cornhill Devils,** three fiendish terracotta figures that glare down malevolently at the church entrance as if spitting fury at those who insist on honouring the religion they despise.

One of the oldest church foundations in London, rebuilt by Christopher Wren after the Great Fire, St Peter's is barely visible from the street, reduced to insignificance by an incongruous mock-Tudor building clad entirely in terracotta. The architect of the latter, Ernest Runtz, had tried in his initial plans to encroach on land belonging to the church; when the rector spotted the misdeed he insisted that the scheme be revised.

Legend has it that in revenge Runtz hired W J Neatby, later to become head of architectural sculpture at the Doulton factory in Lambeth, to create three devilish statues, one of them modelled on the offending vicar. The figure on the gable, crouching on griffin-like claws as if preparing to spring, has horns, large pointed ears, dangling breasts and a demonic grin; below it, above the window, is a smaller version; the third statue, its tail whipping round its legs and its mouth open in a silent howl like a Francis Bacon pope, seems to be haranguing anyone entering the church from its perch on the turret. Neatby's other works include the Art Nouveau tiles in Harrods' Meat Hall.

7

7

8

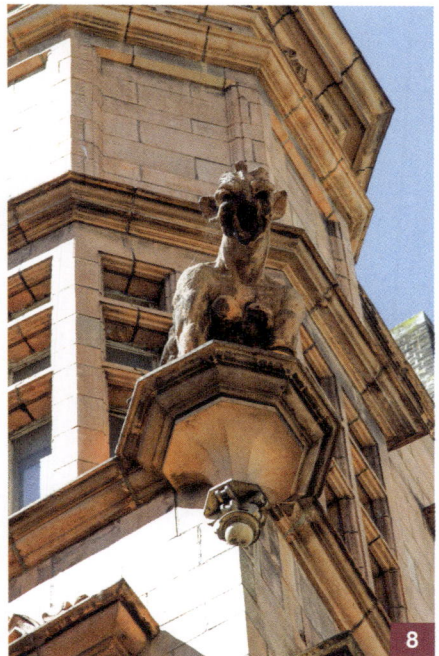

8

Seven Ages of Man

Charles Holden, designer of many of London's finest Underground stations (see page 309), may have regretted his choice of a relatively unknown young sculptor to decorate the British Medical Association building at 429 Strand. Despite the commissioners' request for a frieze of renowned doctors, Jacob Epstein (1880–1959) decided to adorn the building with nude figures representing the ⑨ **seven ages of man** (and woman), arguing that 'surgeons with side whiskers, no matter how eminent, could hardly have served my purpose as models'. Standing 2.5 metres high at third-floor level, the 18 figures appear as if squeezed uncomfortably within tight niches between the windows, their hands and feet, knees and elbows – and sometimes breasts and buttocks – overhanging the plane of the walls. Naked and vulnerable, their genitals exposed to passers-by, they were conceived as a perfect allegory for human frailty within the modern world.

But the statues' nudity and flouting of classical norms – in particular a young pregnant woman and an older woman with withered breasts, both holding children – caused an outcry when they were unveiled in 1908. Despite the *Evening Standard*'s declaration that this was 'a form of statuary which no careful father would wish his daughter, or no discriminating young man, his fiancée, to see', crowds gathered in the streets below and the top decks of buses were filled with standing passengers hoping to get a better view. The National Vigilance Association – whose offices in Agar Street overlooked the offending works – was particularly virulent in stirring up public opinion and unsurprisingly the church weighed in, condemning the work as encouraging 'vulgarity and unwholesome talk, calculated to lead to practices of which there are more than enough in the purlieus of the Strand already'.

Nevertheless, the figures survived until the building was taken over by the South Rhodesian High Commission in the 1930s. Using the pretext that the Portland stone had decayed, they hacked off heads and hands – and, of course, breasts and genitalia. The frieze can still be seen in its mutilated form on what is now Zimbabwe House. Epstein and Holden's tomb for Oscar Wilde in Paris suffered a similar fate (see page 207); in this case the genitalia were salvaged and used as paperweights in the cemetery office.

9. Seven Ages of Man,
   429 Strand, WC2R 0JR

Crucifixion, Notre Dame de France

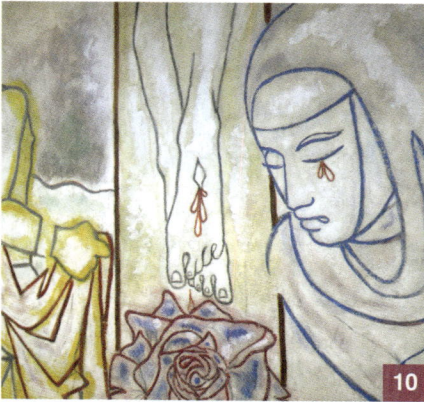

⑩ Notre Dame de France in Leicester Place near Leicester Square, London's French church, is unusual in being circular, taking its cue not as you might expect from the Pantheon in Rome but rather from the original building on the site – the first panorama, created in 1792 by painter Robert Barker, the inventor of both the term and the form. Viewers would stand on a central platform under a skylight to look at two circular pictures, one on the walls and the other on a drum suspended from the roof, with subjects ranging from cityscapes to the battles of the Napoleonic Wars. A century later a cruciform church was inserted into the shell of the building but after this was damaged in WW2 a new place of worship was created using the panorama's circular form.

Notre Dame de France's most extraordinary feature, however, is the Lady Chapel, with murals painted in 1959 by artist, poet, playwright and film-maker Jean Cocteau (1889–1963), a fascist sympathiser and open bisexual who nevertheless decorated several chapels for the Catholic church. The commission was agreed through French cultural attaché René Varin in return for support in securing the artist an honorary doctorate from Oxford University. Cocteau executed his designs over the course of a week, allegedly talking to the Virgin Mary as he worked.

Using bold lines and minimal colour, the frescoes juxtapose cartoon-like muscular soldiers and abstracted heads of grieving women to extraordinary effect. The crucifixion is notable for the near-absence of the main character, with only his feet visible, bleeding into a gigantic rose. The combination of rose and cross, a large letter M on the altar (for Mary Magdalene), a black sun and the numbers on the dice thrown by Roman soldiers have spawned theories linking the mural to the Rosicrucians, a mystical secret society with connections to Freemasonry who developed doctrines based on esoteric truths from the ancient world (Cocteau, along with composers Debussy and Satie, was a member of a subset of the order). Encoded messages or not, Cocteau himself continues to challenge onlookers through an extraordinary larger-than-life self-portrait that dominates the foreground of the scene, one eyebrow quizzically raised as if encouraging us to question all we see.

10. Lady Chapel, Notre Dame de France, Leicester Place, WC2H 7BX

6.3 Coade Stone

Coade stone, the material used to create some of London's most extraordinary late 18th- and early 19th-century statues and memorials, is not stone at all, but ceramic. Unusually for the time, its recipe, manufacture and marketing were developed and driven by a woman: Eleanor Coade (1733–1821), who in 1769 took over a struggling artificial-stone making business on the site of what is now the Royal Festival Hall on the South Bank and managed it successfully until her death. Imitating real stone in

colour, but much easier to shape into complex forms, Coade stone soon attracted advocates including Robert Adam (for the gateway to Syon House), John Nash (for his work on Buckingham Palace) and John Soane, who used it extensively in the Bank of England as well as for the statues on the front of his own house in Lincoln's Inn Fields (see page 159). The material – which Coade preferred to call Lithodipyra, from the Greek for 'stone fired twice' – has proved remarkably durable, with examples surviving without apparent wear and tear for 250 years.

Eleanor Coade succeeded in a business where many of her contemporaries had failed. Not only was Coade stone superior to other similar products in quality and durability – the result of a recipe using ball clay from her native Devon subjected to rigorously controlled firing over a period of up to four days – but Eleanor herself combined artistic taste with shrewd business sense. She employed talented designers including John Sealy, who had trained at the Royal Academy; John Devaere, who had studied in Rome and worked with Josiah Wedgwood; John Bacon, winner of the first Royal Academy gold medal for sculpture; and Benjamin West, a successful history painter and president of the Royal Academy for almost 30 years.

Business acumen seems to have run through the female line of the Coade family: Eleanor's maternal grandmother owned and managed a thriving textiles business and Eleanor set up a drapery company when the family moved to London from Exeter in the early 1760s. Within two years of buying Daniel Pincot's failing artificial stone-making firm she had sacked its former owner for passing himself off as sole proprietor and was running the company herself; Coade's Artificial Stone Manufactory was to trade successfully for the next half century.

The most famous piece of Coade stone statuary is probably the **⑪ 13-tonne lion** that now stands at the south end of Westminster Bridge. With an air of bemused melancholy rather than the pride or ferocity expected of the king of the beasts, it was created in 1837 by sculptor William Woodington to decorate the riverfront parapet of the Lion Brewery, a neighbour of the Coade factory.

Painted red and rising out of the mist across the river, the statue was admired by French novelist Emile Zola as well as by George VI, who demanded its preservation when the brewery was demolished. The beast's air of bewilderment, even dismay, is fitting given its recent history: in 1949, in preparation for the development of the South Bank, it was placed in Waterloo Station (the British Rail logo featured a red lion); when the station was extended in 1966 it was stripped of its coloured coat and moved to its present position, facing what used to be County Hall but is now a set of banal tourist experiences. A recess in its back originally contained a bottle holding two William IV coins and a Coade trade card; these were replaced by the GLC with a coin from 1966 and an article on Coade stone published in the *Times*.

A similar but more **⑫ aggressive-looking lion**, also created for the brewery by Woodington and saved through royal intervention, was presented by the GLC to the Rugby Football Union in its centenary year of 1971. Given a coat of gold leaf in 1991, when England hosted the second World Cup, it now snarls down at a bronze of a player kicking a ball outside the Rose and Poppy Gates to Twickenham rugby ground, just off Whitton Road.

Most Coade stone statuary appears crudely modelled, more suitable to being viewed from a distance or from below than in detail, with the material working best for easily recognisable subjects positioned to dominate their surroundings. Regarded by the company's craftsmen as their finest work, the ⓭ **Nelson pediment** installed in 1812 in the King William Courtyard of the Old Royal Naval College at Greenwich (see page 217) unusually combines drama on a grand scale with fine detail. At the centre is Britannia, her trident representing dominion of the seas, receiving Nelson's body from Neptune. On either side, a putto, lion and seaman hold banners commemorating his victories. To the right are cannonballs and other instruments of war, to the left the ships destroyed by their actions. The composition was adapted by Benjamin West from his painting *The Immortality of Nelson* (who had in fact died in 1805); in a pamphlet explaining his message, West lamented that Coade stone had been unavailable to Phidias for his sculptures for the Parthenon in Athens. There are also four finely cast Coade stone female figures representing Faith, Hope, Charity and Meekness in the vestibule of the Old Royal Naval College chapel: following the conversion of the original hospital for naval pensioners into a training college in 1873, the reference to meekness was erased as inappropriate for would-be officers.

Much of the expense of artificial-stone manufacture lay in creating the moulds, which were therefore stored in the hope they could be reused – for instance by providing old, anonymous bodies with new heads. The ⓮ **caryatids** that guard the entrances to the crypt of St Pancras New Church in Camden, moulded by Charles Rossi in 1822, make a virtue of repetition. Rossi had worked in the Coade Manufactory before setting up his own business at the turn of the century, developing and adapting the Coade recipe. His composition here is a bizarre transposition of the 'Porch of the Maidens' from the Erechtheum (c. 420 BCE) on the Acropolis in Athens to the traffic-clogged

Euston Road: as advisor on the purchase of the Elgin marbles in 1816, its creator was presumably familiar with the original.

Rossi's eight caryatids – four on each porch to the north and south of the church – can take no credit for supporting the pediment above them: instead, they consist of hollow terracotta sections assembled around cast-iron columns that provide structural integrity. Perhaps the overscaled hands and feet that give the statues a sense of mass and power were the artist's attempt to compensate for their actual fragility? Their odd proportions could also be explained by claims that when he arrived to install them – in front of an expectant crowd – Rossi had to cut 30 centimetres from their midriffs (or more probably omit one of the sections, perhaps at mid-thigh or mid-calf) to fit them into the space.

Following the death of Eleanor Coade in 1821 her company survived for less than two decades under the management of distant relative William Croggon and his son John. A devout Baptist who never married, Coade herself left her fortune to charity schools, the Baptist church, her maid and a small number of married female friends with the stipulation that their husbands were to have no access to the legacies. Ironically for the creator of a material popular for commemorative statuary, she is buried in Bunhill Fields (see page 252) in an unmarked grave.

12

14

13

6.4 Dinosaur Court

In and around the lake at the south end of Crystal Palace Park in South London is a bizarre collection of some **⑮ 30 life-size dinosaurs**. Appearance apart, they are odd for several reasons: as an earnest educational display within a place of recreation, as a commemoration of scientific ideas that have since been superseded, and as a progressive and daring public statement that paved the way for Charles Darwin's revolutionary *On the Origin of Species* (1859).

The prehistoric beasts were unveiled in 1854 as an added attraction to complement Joseph Paxton's pioneering glass-and-iron Crystal Palace, which was re-sited from Hyde Park to suburban South London at the end of the 1851 Great Exhibition. Often claimed to be the first theme park, the space was envisaged as an 'illustrated encyclopedia', a place for public education as well as entertainment. Prince Albert and Queen Victoria supported the venture, visiting the installation before and after completion: like the Great Exhibition, which had been Albert's brainchild, the dinosaurs and an accompanying display showing the development of geological strata over millions of years were intended to showcase the pioneering discoveries of the best British minds. The theory of evolution had gained tacit royal support.

The mastermind behind the displays was Richard Owen (1804–1892), who had coined the word 'dinosaur' (meaning 'fearfully great reptile'). A contemporary of Darwin's and initially a friend and fellow-advocate of evolutionary theory, he nevertheless disagreed about the specifics of human development and transmutation and was to become a vehement and vindictive opponent. In 1871, following a dispute over funding, Darwin commented: 'I used to be ashamed of hating him so much, but now I will carefully cherish my hatred and contempt to the last days of my life.'

Owen appointed Benjamin Waterhouse Hawkins, a natural-history artist, sculptor and assistant superintendent of the Great Exhibition, to create the giant creatures under his supervision, extrapolating their likely appearance from studies of fossils and the living creatures descended from them. Having won Owen's approval for his reduced-scale models, Hawkins set up a workshop on site to build the full-size versions, using the largest available bones to calculate their likely sizes. To celebrate the part-installation of the first mould, the iguanodon, he invited some 20 guests – including scientists, writers and journalists – to an eight-course dinner served at a table set within the creature's shell. Made from reconstituted stone on a framework of iron rods supported on brick plinths, the model was the largest ever cast; Hawkins described the complexity of its construction as 'not less than building a house upon four columns'.

To come across the prehistoric creatures – which include marine and flying reptiles and early mammals as well as dinosaurs – lurking in an undistinguished surburban park is still an extraordinary experience. The bright green iguanodon, its toenails newly restored to pristine white, snarls down from its rocky perch; a megatherium (giant sloth) clings to a long-dead tree; crocodile-like ichthyosaurs and snake-headed plesiosaurus dabble in the shallows alongside ducks and geese. It is even more uncanny to think that the everyday birds perched on the statues' huge shoulders are their closest living descendants.

Given that this was the first attempt by anyone to represent such creatures at full

scale as if in motion, it was inevitable that some of the scientific assumptions would prove mistaken. For instance, the megalosaurus should be standing on its two back legs like a T-Rex rather than on all fours; the turtle-like synapsid in fact had no shell; the ichthyosaurus was more like a dolphin than a crocodile; and what was assumed to be an iguanodon's nose horn turned out to be a thumb-claw used for digging out roots. Scientific ideas too are subject to evolution and mutation. Perhaps most surprising, however, is the way the statues are painted: as determining colour was beyond even Owen's imaginative extrapolations, he simply allocated different shades to code the creatures according to the era to which they belonged. The idea of a timeline was further reinforced by distributing the statues over and around three islands representing the Paleozoic, Mesozoic and Cenozoic eras, with the Paleozoic island left empty to demonstrate that at that time all life was still at sea.

Next to the dinosaurs – and easy to overlook as simply a decorative piece of landscaping – is an artificial cliff made up of successive strata of minerals from 400 million years ago to the present day, including sandstone, chalk, limestone, coal, ironstone and gravel. Demonstrating the long history of the world's creation, it was also intended to celebrate the natural resources that had enabled the industrial revolution.

Originally visitors to Crystal Palace Park could walk among the dinosaurs, crossing from one island to another in sequence on bridges. Today, unfortunately, we are kept at a safe distance to protect these enormous yet fragile creatures from extinction.

15. Crystal Palace Park, SE20 8DR

6.5 Postman's Park

16

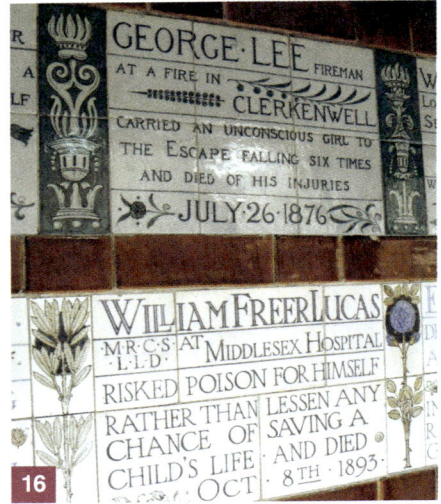

16

16 **Postman's Park** – an amalgam of three City churchyards between St Martin's-le-Grand and King Edward Street – was once a popular lunch spot for workers from the old General Post Office headquarters that bordered it to the south. Its oddity comes not from its name, however, but because it houses the George Frederic Watts Memorial to Heroic Self Sacrifice, built in 1900 at the instigation of the painter and his wife to commemorate the altruistic courage of ordinary men and women.

Watts – whose mawkish allegorical epics were highly popular in late Victorian England – was a socialist who had grown up in poverty and believed in the power of art to encourage social change. Among the causes he supported were an association for teaching art to the working classes, free admission to art galleries, the banning of feathers on hats, and the Anti-Tight-Lacing Society, which encouraged women to loosen their stays. His idea for the Memorial to Heroic Self Sacrifice was inspired by the story of Alice Ayres, who

became a popular heroine in 1885 after returning to a burning house three times to rescue her sister's children at the cost of her own life. Ayres Street, which runs south from Union Street in Borough and was the site of the fire, is named after her. In a letter to the *Times* two years later, Watts proposed that 'a complete record of the stories of heroism in every-day life' would be a fitting way to commemorate Queen Victoria's Golden Jubilee, suggesting that 'intelligent consideration and artistic power might combine to make London richer by a work that is beautiful, and our nation richer by a record that is infinitely honourable.'

After failing to win support for his initial plan for a marble wall in Hyde Park, Watts instead designed a modest memorial for the small open space of Postman's Park. The simple single-storey loggia, with a pitched tiled roof supported on plain wooden posts, shelters a 15-metre-long wall that could accommodate 120 plaques. Though the bodies of those commemorated lie elsewhere, the park itself is built on mounds of corpses from the three churchyards, accounting for its elevation above street level.

Following Watts' death in 1904, his wife Mary – whom he had married in 1876 (when he was 69 and she only 36) after the failure of a short-lived marriage to 16-year-old actress Ellen Terry some 20 years earlier – initially financed the monument and selected the names to be featured from a list drawn up by her husband. Raising funds was a perennial problem and the design of the tablets was gradually downgraded to save money. The first four plaques – including one to popular heroine Mary Rogers, a stewardess who renounced her place on a lifeboat to go down with her ship off the Channel Islands in 1899 – were custom-made by William De Morgan, the Arts & Crafts movement's most brilliant ceramicist and a personal friend of the artist and his wife. Subsequent De Morgan plaques used standard tiles to reduce costs and from 1908 tablets were manufactured by Royal Doulton to an inferior design which Mary – who had trained at the Slade, specialising in pottery and textiles as well as portraiture – disliked.

Though Mary initially declared she would fund the completion of the memorial at her own cost, she was later to go back on her promise. Few tablets were hung after 1910 and by her death in 1938 the memorial had grown to only 53 names. It seems that for Mary, the 'artistic power' of the monument took precedence over its function as an 'honourable record'. Back in 1896 she had created the obsessively odd Watts Memorial Chapel near the couple's home in Compton, Surrey, its spectacular floor-to-ceiling interior decoration the work of women from the village whom she trained in painting and ceramics. After Watts' death she commissioned and maintained a gallery to display his work and designed a much more sophisticated arcaded brick version of the Postman's Park loggia for Compton cemetery.

The tablets that did find their way to Postman's Park tell both heroic and gruesome stories. Following the commissioning committee's requests to professional bodies for nominations, many of those featured are policemen, medical professionals or postal workers, though there are also a surprising number of children. On the whole, it seems that men are more likely to dive heroically into rivers while women return to burning buildings to rescue the young or infirm.

Individual tragedies stack up: Frederick Alfred Croft, who in 1878 'saved a lunatic woman from suicide at Woolwich Arsenal but was himself run over by the train'; Elizabeth Boxall, who died aged 17 in 1888 from 'injuries received trying to save a child from a runaway horse'; Mrs Yarman, who in 1900 'refus[ed] to be deterred from making three attempts to climb a burning staircase to save her aged mother'. The details of some stories have been questioned by historians – for instance, the inquest on Sarah Smith, 'pantomime artiste [who] died of terrible injuries received when attempting in her inflammable dress to extinguish the flames which had enveloped her companion', concluded that her death was a tragic accident as she and another dancer clashed in the wings, with no mention of heroic rescue. Watts used newspaper accounts as his source, and then as now, it seems you cannot believe everything you read...

The only tablet installed since the 1930s commemorates Leigh Pitt, a 30-year-old print technician from Surrey who died in 2007 rescuing a child from a canal in Thamesmead. Nominations for further additions can be made to the Diocese of London.

16. Postman's Park,
    St Martin's-le-Grand, EC1A 7BT

6.6 Benches

17

You can donate and dedicate a bench to a Westminster park or cemetery for around £1000, and London as a whole is dotted with benches with occasionally touching inscriptions to commemorate an individual's particular connection to a specific place. Demand on Hampstead Heath is so high that the City of London Corporation operates a ten-year turnover system, though the waiting list is still long.

There are also many benches commemorating celebrities – from *Oliver!* creator Lionel Bart (Kew Gardens) to singer/songwriter Kirstie MacColl (Soho Square) or comedian Rik Mayall (Hammersmith Bridge Road). Few of these can be classed as oddities, though the ❶ **bench dedicated to musician Ian Dury (**1942–2000), installed in 2002 in Poet's Corner in Pembroke Lodge Gardens, Richmond Park, qualified originally by dint of having solar-powered MP3 players embedded in the armrests that enabled you to listen to a selection of Dury's songs as well as his *Desert Island Discs* choices. Musical chairs, indeed. The bench is inscribed 'Reasons to be cheerful' but few are apparent from this now broken seat in a dispiritingly neglected corner of the park.

18

A handful of London benches not only commemorate the famous but allow you to sit (and be photographed) beside them. The best known is ⑱ *Allies*, a bronze by Lawrence Holofcener of Winston Churchill and Franklin D Roosevelt in conversation, unveiled in 1995 at the junction of New and Old Bond Streets in Mayfair to celebrate a half century since the end of WW2 and temporarily removed in 2017. Roosevelt, with his smartly buttoned suit and all-American smile, is upright and confident, while Churchill leans ingratiatingly towards him. It seems the dynamics of the 'special relationship' have barely changed.

Sitting on the bench designed by John Somerville in 2014 in honour of ⑲ **Spike Milligan** (1918–2002) is an unnerving experience: the comedian fixes you with a friendly – if mad-eyed – stare that is hard to turn away from. Sited near the former stable block in the grounds of Stephens House in Finchley, the suburb where Milligan lived from 1955 to 1974, the bench incorporates motifs from his poems and sketches, most noticeably armrests in the form of elephants. His poem 'Jumbo Jet' namechecks both the animal and the location: 'I saw a little elephant standing in my garden, / I said "You don't belong in here", he said "I beg you pardon?"… / He caught the bus to Finchley and then to Mincing Lane, / And over the Embankment, where he got lost, again.'

Less cheerfully inviting is Maggi Hambling's tribute to ⑳ **Oscar Wilde** (1854–1900), unveiled in 1998 in Adelaide Street near Trafalgar Square. The playwright's ravaged head and shoulders (the hair looks as if it has been growing for some time underground and the eye sockets are empty) rise alarmingly from a coffin-shaped slab of granite where passing tourists often sit to eat lunch. The piece is entitled *A Conversation with Oscar*

20

20

21

21

22

Wilde, and according to Hambling, 'The idea is that he is rising, talking, laughing, smoking from this sarcophagus and the passer-by, should he or she choose to, can sit on the sarcophagus and have a conversation with him.'

The end of the 'bench' is inscribed with a quote from Wilde's play *Lady Windermere's Fan:* 'We are all in the gutter but some of us are looking at the stars.' Following the premiere of the play in 1892 Wilde offended critics by appearing on stage with a cigarette in hand to address the audience by saying: 'Ladies and Gentlemen… your appreciation has been most intelligent. I congratulate you on the great success of your performance, which persuades me that you think almost as highly of the play as I do myself.' Originally Hambling's Wilde was holding a cigarette but this has now been stolen. The playwright's tomb in Père Lachaise in Paris, sculpted by Jacob Epstein (see page 194), suffered an even ruder fate when the allegedly oversized genitals were hacked off by two British women brandishing umbrellas and subsequently used as paperweights in the cemetery offices.

Theft and vandalism are problems for public art: the original ㉑ **memorial to doctor and Labour Party MP Alfred Salter** (1873–1945), which portrayed him sitting on a bench overlooking the Thames at the eastern end of Bermondsey Wall East, was stolen in 2011. A replacement was commissioned from the same artist, Diane Gorvin, along with a new statue of Salter's wife Ada, carrying what may well be the capital's only bronze garden spade. Ada's memorial is one of fewer than twenty commemorative statues in London of women (discounting the royal family), and the group as a whole qualifies as an oddity not least because it includes separate statues of the couple's daughter Joyce and Joyce's cat (the latter two surviving from the original commission). Alfred was a pacifist, republican and temperance supporter as well as a pioneer of free healthcare. Ada was London's first female councillor and the first woman Labour mayor in the UK; she supported women to campaign for better working conditions and formed a 'Beautification Committee' that transformed public spaces into playgrounds and parks (hence the spade). Joyce died of scarlet fever aged eight. You can find examples of the kind of housing the Salters pioneered just down the road in Wilson Grove (see page 148) or join Salter on his concrete bench. Though his attention is ostensibly focused on daydreams of a happier past with his daughter, you can't help but wonder what he might have made of his view of the new monuments to capitalism in the City across the river.

Alfred and Ada devoted their lives to ameliorating conditions within the Bermondsey slums and to campaigning for better housing, food and healthcare. It's a message that bypassed the designers of the ㉒ **Camden bench** – a slab of concrete not unlike the one Salter sits on, but with its top angled to make it impossible for homeless people to sleep on. Introduced by Camden Council in 2012, the benches are part of a range of measures to deter rough sleeping such as installing spikes on ledges or walls. The bench's angles even make it difficult for two people to sit side by side. You can find examples in places where loitering is to be discouraged, such as in front of the Freemason's Hall in Great Queen Street or on the corner of Hatton Garden, home of London's trade in gold and jewellery.

17. Ian Dury bench, Richmond Park, TW10 6JJ
18. *Allies*, New/Old Bond St, W1S 3ST
19. *Conversation with Spike*, Stephens House, 17 East End Rd, N3 3QE
20. *A Conversation with Oscar Wilde*, Adelaide St, WC2N 4HZ
21. *Dr. Salter's Daydream*, Bermondsey Wall East, SE16 4NB
22. Camden bench, outside Freemason's Hall, WC2B 5AZ

6.7 Guerrilla Art

Royal Family Waving from a Balcony

Banksy – Britain's street-art king – has painted scores of London artworks, most of which have been eroded, defaced, or obliterated by officious councils, or removed by companies hoping to make a quick buck. From the bomb-hugging girl or Guantanamo Bay detainee created in protest at the Iraq War and its consequences in the early 2000s to the cocaine-snorting copper, urinating Queen's Guard, or *Slave Labour*, a depiction of a child producing bunting for the queen's Diamond Jubilee of 2012, the artist has provided a sadly ephemeral commentary on the hypocrisies and sins of the establishment and the liberties they take in our name.

One image that looks set to survive against the odds – at least partially – is **❷❸** *Royal Family Waving from a Balcony*, which covers the full height of a side wall of a building in Stoke Newington Church Street, almost opposite Lordship Road. The painting, used in a reworked version as cover artwork for the 2003 Blur single 'Crazy Beat', was created with the consent of the building's owner yet was illegally covered in black paint by council workers in 2009 as part of a clean-up of the borough in readiness for the 2012 Olympics. Luckily the distraught property owner and a gathering crowd persuaded the vandals to stop before they reached the central cartoon of the waving royal family – depicted as clowns – though the original decorative frame topped by an ornate broken pediment has been obliterated.

Councils need permission to remove graffiti from private premises, and Hackney claimed its attempts to contact the owner had failed. 'Hackney Council does not make a judgment call on whether graffiti is art or not,' said an official. 'Our task is to keep Hackney's streets clean.'

23. Stoke Newington Church St, N16 0UH

London Noses

A 2008 Banksy piece near Oxford Street showed a graffiti artist painting the words 'One Nation Under CCTV' in huge capital letters, watched by a police officer with a dog and camera. But Banksy is not the only artist to use street art to protest against the proliferation of CCTV.

Look carefully at buildings and monuments in central London and you may be surprised to find a number of identical plaster-of-Paris **24** **noses** protruding at approximately head height in the oddest of locations. One of the easiest to spot is on the Trafalgar Square side of the inner wall of Admiralty Arch where traffic exits from the Mall. Rumours that it was modelled on Napoleon's nose and set at a height where it could be tweaked by passing cavalry officers proved false: it is in fact part of a Situationist-inspired project by Rick Buckley, a Hackney artist who trained with Nam June Paik in Germany.

Angered by the proliferation of CCTV, Buckley decided to see if he could glue casts of his nose to various London buildings and get away undetected – or at least unpunished. Turning his nose up at authority, indulging in acts of vandalism under the noses of the security forces, castigating official nosiness or simply smelling out trouble – who knows? He succeeded in installing about 35 casts in all: some survived only hours or weeks, but a small number have endured for a couple of decades since their creation in 1997. In addition to the nose job on Admiralty Arch, try looking in Soho, specifically at the Coventry Street end of Great Windmill Street, on the road side of the passageway that runs along the eastern edge of the carriageway; on the Bateman Street end of Quo Vadis at 28–29 Dean Street; and on the Dean Street side of the Milkbar at 3 Bateman Street.

24. Noses:
    Admiralty Arch, SW1A 2WH
    Dean St, W1D 3LL
    Bateman St, W1D 4AG

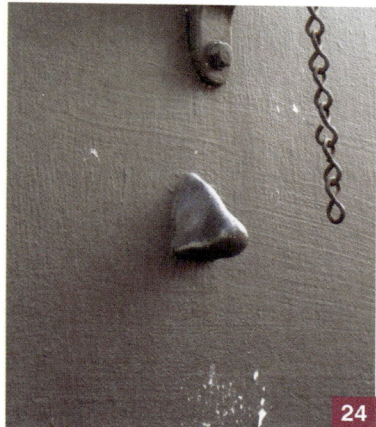

Leake Street Tunnel

A 300-metre tunnel running under the platforms and tracks of Waterloo Station between Station Approach Road and York Road, **25 Leake Street** is covered pavement to roof in graffiti. But what makes it different from other street art is that the site is both legally sanctioned and open to all. Like most graffiti, it is regularly painted over, but the people doing the erasing are fellow artists replacing older images with their own work. Anyone can turn up and add their mark to the walls, making the tunnel an informal training ground for experiments with ideas and techniques.

The area around Waterloo has retained a seedy edge in comparison with the South Bank a few streets away or the privatised developments around King's Cross, Paddington and London Bridge (see page 131). To get to Leake Street, you walk along a dismal road at the side of the station where you will find a set of paint-daubed steps opposite a bizarre rooftop statue of a seated camel that marks the back of the Camel & Artichoke pub. You will soon know you are in the right place: every surface is covered in imagery, whether memorials, slogans, portraits or interlocking patterns, from black on white to day-glo colour. If artists are working, the smell of spray paint hits you before you notice their shadowy figures. The dynamism of some graffiti can make it look like the work of moments, but the intricacy of several designs here, especially on the vaulted roof, demonstrates stamina and painstaking attention to detail. Artists on site seem engaged in a cycle of adding small amounts of paint, moving back to consider the effect, erasing, repainting, then reconsidering once more.

Owned by Network Rail, Leake Street was launched as a site for graffiti during the 'Cans Festival' organised by Banksy in May 2008. The tunnel also holds the entrance to the Vaults – an underground theatre, gallery, bar and restaurant – providing artists with a captive audience of passers-by. The only rules are given on a notice: 'No Sexism. No Racism. No Adverts. Please take empty cans and litter home.' Only the last of these is generally ignored.

25. Leake Street tunnel, SE1 7NN

Admiralty Citadel, see page 223

War & Peace

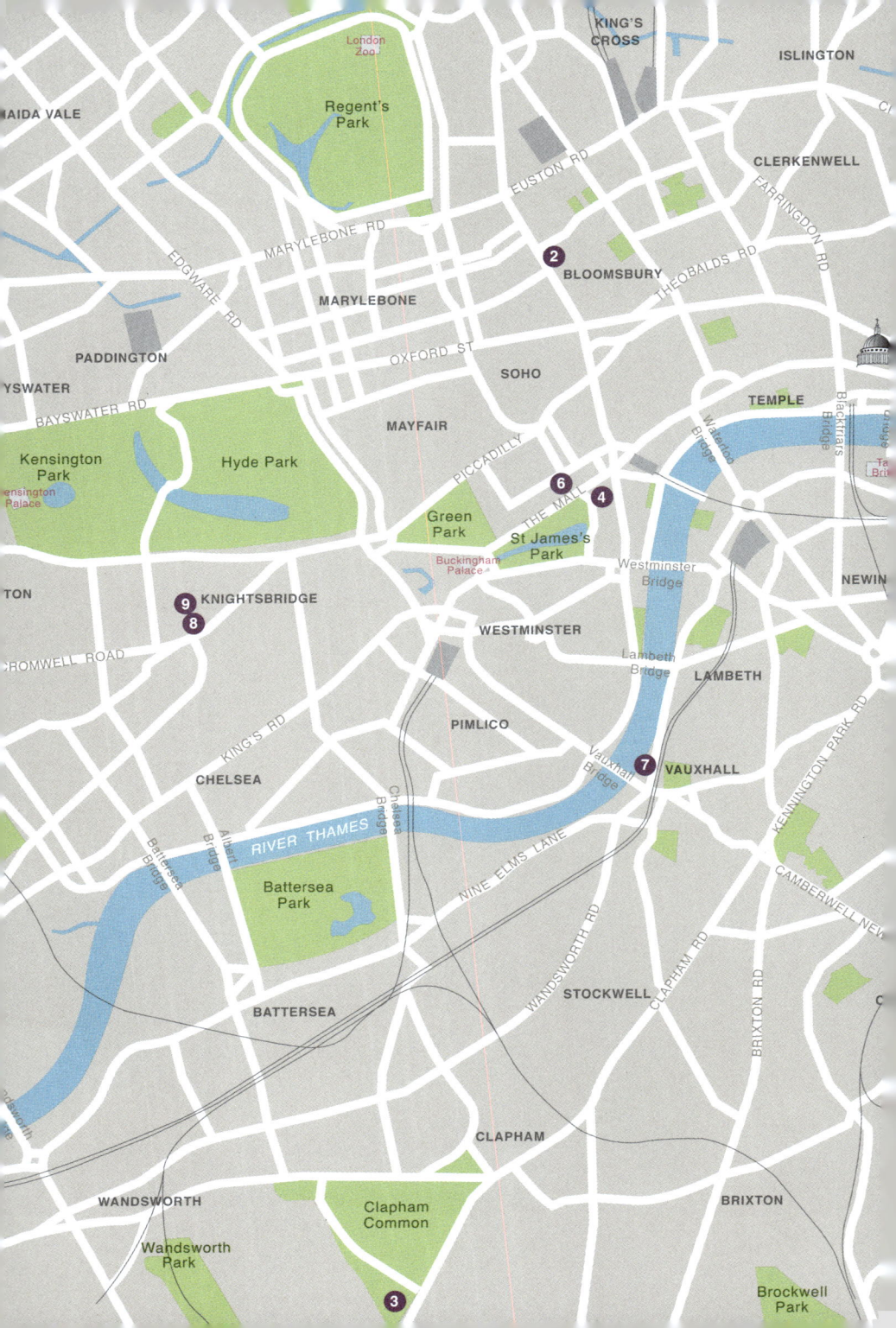

London Zoo

Regent's Park

KING'S CROSS

ISLINGTON

MAIDA VALE

CLERKENWELL

EUSTON RD

MARYLEBONE RD

2 BLOOMSBURY

THEOBALDS RD

FARRINGDON RD

EDGWARE RD

MARYLEBONE

PADDINGTON

OXFORD ST

SOHO

TEMPLE

YSWATER

BAYSWATER RD

MAYFAIR

PICCADILLY

Blackfriars Bridge

Waterloo Bridge

Kensington Park

Hyde Park

Green Park

6 4

THE MALL

St James's Park

Kensington Palace

Buckingham Palace

Westminster Bridge

NEWIN

TON

9 KNIGHTSBRIDGE

8

CROMWELL ROAD

WESTMINSTER

Lambeth Bridge

LAMBETH

KING'S RD

PIMLICO

Vauxhall Bridge

7 VAUXHALL

CHELSEA

Albert Bridge

Chelsea Bridge

RIVER THAMES

Battersea Bridge

Battersea Park

NINE ELMS LANE

KENNINGTON PARK RD

CAMBERWELL NEW

WANDSWORTH RD

CLAPHAM RD

STOCKWELL

BRIXTON RD

BATTERSEA

WANDSWORTH

Wandsworth Park

CLAPHAM

Clapham Common

BRIXTON

Brockwell Park

3

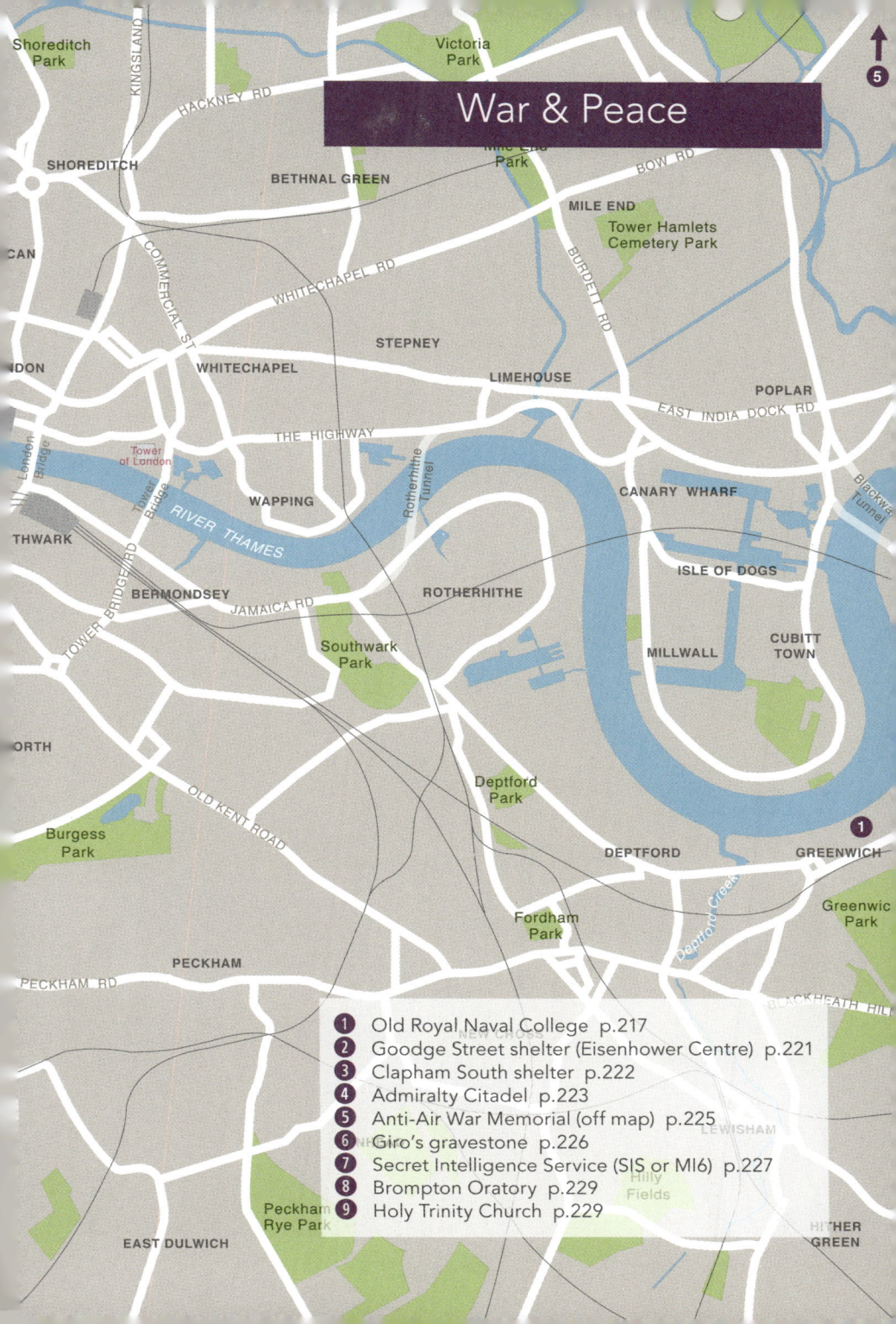

War & Peace

Shoreditch Park

Victoria Park

HACKNEY RD

KINGSLAND

SHOREDITCH

BETHNAL GREEN

Mile End Park

BOW RD

MILE END

Tower Hamlets Cemetery Park

BURDETT RD

CAN

COMMERCIAL ST

WHITECHAPEL RD

STEPNEY

LIMEHOUSE

POPLAR

DON

WHITECHAPEL

EAST INDIA DOCK RD

THE HIGHWAY

Tower of London

Rotherhithe Tunnel

CANARY WHARF

Blackwall Tunnel

London Bridge

Tower Bridge

WAPPING

RIVER THAMES

THWARK

TOWER BRIDGE RD

BERMONDSEY

JAMAICA RD

ROTHERHITHE

ISLE OF DOGS

MILLWALL

CUBITT TOWN

Southwark Park

ORTH

OLD KENT ROAD

Deptford Park

Burgess Park

DEPTFORD

GREENWICH

Deptford Creek

Greenwich Park

Fordham Park

PECKHAM

PECKHAM RD

BLACKHEATH HILL

LEWISHAM

Hilly Fields

Peckham Rye Park

EAST DULWICH

HITHER GREEN

1. Old Royal Naval College p.217
2. Goodge Street shelter (Eisenhower Centre) p.221
3. Clapham South shelter p.222
4. Admiralty Citadel p.223
5. Anti-Air War Memorial (off map) p.225
6. Giro's gravestone p.226
7. Secret Intelligence Service (SIS or MI6) p.227
8. Brompton Oratory p.229
9. Holy Trinity Church p.229

7.1 Old Royal Naval College

The ❶ **Old Royal Naval College** in Greenwich is an oddity in scale and detail, conception and execution. Founded in 1694, the complex was designed as a home and hospital for impoverished, disabled or retired navy veterans. Yet at its core is an unfinished royal palace, surrounded by a collection of equally magnificent baroque buildings with architecture and decoration literally fit for a king.

Sited between the river and College Way, at the bottom of the slope of Greenwich Park, the Old Royal Naval College is built on the ruins of Greenwich Palace, created by the Duke of Gloucester in 1426, rebuilt by Henry VII in c. 1500 and the birthplace of Henry VIII, Mary I and Elizabeth I. The building fell into disrepair during the Civil War of the 1640s and restored monarch Charles II managed to complete only one wing of a planned replacement, the eastern range of what is now King Charles Court. Truly palatial in scale and form, rising to three storeys at each end with imposing central pediments supported on full-height columns, it set a precedent for the architecture that followed when William III, in accordance with the wishes of his late wife Mary II, donated the land as a site for a hospital for seamen. There was one caveat, however: the new building was not to block access or views between the Thames and the Queen's House, designed by Inigo Jones for Anne of Denmark in 1616 and still used as a royal retreat.

Construction began in 1696 but proceeded erratically, stalling when the royal endowment fell into arrears as Queen Anne, George I and George II respectively took the throne and other benefactors defaulted or died. In an early example of a pension scheme, 6d a month was deducted from seamen's wages to finance their retirement. In the end, however, much of the money was raised from the proceeds of crime: loot seized from pirates, fines extracted from smugglers and booty from captured ships as well as rents and profits from the estates of the Earl of Derwentwater, confiscated as punishment for his part in the Jacobite rising of 1715. The first pensioners arrived in 1705 and a century later there were 2,710 former seamen in residence. A decline in numbers led the hospital to close in 1869 after which it was used as a training college for Royal Navy officers until 1998.

Christopher Wren, offering his services free of charge, drew up the overall plan of twinned ranges of buildings and courtyards. The architectural splendour was to convey the nation's power and wealth as well as to show gratitude to those who had served their country at sea. Wren's conception was a masterpiece of baroque design, but since he was still busy with rebuilding St Paul's and the City churches following the Great Fire of 1666, much of the work was entrusted to his assistant Nicholas Hawksmoor (see page 273), who brought a wilful quirkiness to the completed buildings. While Queen Anne Court is a blander, probably cheaper, replica of the pre-existing palace opposite, Hawksmoor gave his imagination free rein in King William Court to the south, which out of necessity mixes stone dressings with bare brick since all the available Portland stone was diverted to St Paul's. Expanding on the grandness of Wren's intentions in ways that contradict classical norms, Hawksmoor played games with proportions and articulation. For instance, the glorious colonnades have become dominant rather than subordinate features while the wall opposite the Nelson pediment (see page 198) has a bizarre frontispiece, with huge engaged columns that support nothing, marking a completely insignificant doorway. The classical language is used eccentrically in detail too, as in the Ionic capitals carved with imaginary sea creatures and shells.

It is the Painted Hall, originally a refectory, that most clearly demonstrates the uncomfortable relationship between the desire of successive royal patrons to advertise their own legitimacy and prestige and the needs of the impoverished invalids the institution was to serve. Created by James Thornhill in two phases between 1708 and 1727, it is the finest piece of decorative painting in England, rivalling the masterpieces of the Italian baroque at least in scale. Entering the domed anteroom is like stepping into a lavishly decorated church, with the interior plan imitating ecclesiastical architecture in its sequence of vestibule, main hall with arched windows and clerestory, and raised platform culminating in a piece of painted theatre. Rather than a mere dining hall, this is a temple to Protestantism, with the overall theme glorifying the accession to the throne of William and Mary and their Hanoverian successors as well as extolling the importance of Britain's naval forces and maritime trade.

The central panel in the ceiling of the lower hall depicts the victory of peace and liberty, as personified by William and Mary, over tyranny and arbitrary power in the person of the Catholic Louis XIV. Panels at each end celebrate naval victories and landmarks in navigation. By the time Thornhill came to decorate the upper hall, George I was king and the theatrical painting at the end celebrates his succession: the royal family, dressed in powdered wigs and armour or silk dresses, sit primly below sensual semi-clad figures representing values such as justice and providence. Thornhill himself stares from the frame at the bottom right; in the background is St Paul's, a reference not only to Wren but to Thornhill's own paintings within the dome.

The scene is surrounded by trompe l'oeil columns supporting a pediment, from which putti swing on garlands of flowers. Cannons and other modern weaponry feature prominently at the base. Trompe l'oeil is used liberally throughout the

1

building, presumably as an economical way of achieving architectural grandeur without having to hire stonemastons or sculptors: giant columns at the entrance are painted with vertical stripes to mimic fluting; the magnificent fireplace surrounds in the upper hall turn out to be illusions created in grisaille. The Nelson Room, where the admiral was laid in state after his body was returned to London, pickled in brandy within a water cask, is surprisingly modest.

Once Thornhill's decorative scheme was complete, the dining hall became a lucrative paying attraction and the pensioners were relegated to the undercroft below, itself an imposing vaulted space, as you can see from its twin in Queen Mary Court, now a café. The Painted Hall's status as an everyday refectory was not restored until 1939, when it served as an officers' mess until the closure of the training college. Other survivals from the site's time as a hospital include a skittle alley, created in 1864 to provide the pensioners with entertainment, and the chapel, its interior reworked by James 'Athenian' Stuart in 1789 after the original

was destroyed in a fire. In contrast with the muscularity of the courts and colonnades and the Painted Hall itself, its decoration is surprisingly delicate and feminine. The only remnant of the original Greenwich Palace, a vaulted undercroft below the present Queen Anne Court, is not open to the public, though video footage from the 1970s shows it in use as a bar and disco for naval officers. The University of Greenwich and Trinity Laban Conservatoire of Music and Dance are now accommodated on site.

Dr Johnson was no fan of the Royal Hospital For Seamen, complaining to his companion James Boswell in 1763 that it was 'too magnificent for a place of charity, and… its parts… too much detached to make one grand whole.' He was probably right – and indeed his criticisms pinpoint exactly those aspects of the complex that make it an oddity.

1. Old Royal Naval College, SE10 9NN
   www.ornc.org

7.2 Somewhere to Hide

Pairs of odd, pillbox-shaped structures with no apparent purpose pop up next to stations along London Underground's Northern Line. These are not disused ticket offices or ventilation shafts but entrances to the deep shelters built following the onset of the Blitz. Despite official discouragement, Londoners had been crowding into Underground stations during air-raids since the bombing intensified, eventually forcing the authorities to sanction the use of some 80 stations as shelters, equipped with toilet facilities and sometimes canteens. Disused stations and tunnels also provided storage for documents and precious objects: Aldwych station on the Strand, for instance, was used to safeguard treasures from the British Museum (see page 314).

Underground stations did not always make safe havens, however: bombs could penetrate 15 metres below ground and at the end of 1940 there were fatal incidents at Marble Arch, which suffered a direct hit, and Balham, which flooded after damage to a water main. As a result, the government ordered the construction of ten deep shelters, with the idea that London Transport could use the facilities to extend its network after the war. Designed to accommodate 8,000 people, each shelter consisted of two parallel tunnels about a quarter of a mile long, equipped with bunks, medical facilities, canteens, sanitation and piped music.

Deep shelters were built at Clapham South, Clapham Common, Clapham North, Stockwell, Goodge Street, Camden Town, Belsize Park and Chancery Lane; one at Oval was cancelled because of flooding and one at St Paul's because of fears that excavations were undermining the cathedral. The scheme turned out to be something of a white elephant: bombing had slackened off by the time the shelters were completed, maintenance proved expensive and post-war austerity put paid to London Transport's plans to use the sites as stations for north–south and east–west express lines.

Even during the war, several shelters were requisitioned for new, sometimes secret purposes. Soon after its completion towards the end of 1942, part of the Goodge Street site became General Eisenhower's London headquarters while five other shelters billeted US and British troops. As the bombing intensified again there were calls to open the underground tunnels to the public, but it took the arrival of flying bombs in the summer of 1944 to persuade the government to issue locals with admission tickets to Clapham South, Clapham North, Stockwell, Camden Town and Belsize Park. Despite the ferocity of the German attack, demand for places averaged less than one-third of capacity.

The ❷ **Goodge Street shelter** – now named the Eisenhower Centre – remained strictly off limits. Reports describe its facilities as a great deal more luxurious than those for the public, with a wood-panelled boardroom equipped with maps and a projector where the US general would hold meetings with the British War Cabinet around an oval mahogany table. There were also adjacent private bedrooms for Eisenhower and his driver and secretary Kate Summersby. You can still see one of the entrances on Chenies Street: two single-storey concrete structures – one octagonal and a squatter, near-circular one with a rectangular ventilation shaft on its roof – linked by a brick rectangle. Scored with horizontal lines as decoration and arranged as if created from a child's building blocks, the streamlined windowless pavilions look puzzlingly out of place, even if the specifics of their site are eerily appropriate. The shelter entrance stands directly in front of Minerva House, built as a car showroom in 1912, with a prominent statue of the goddess of battle holding a spear and shield; in front of the central rectangular section is a WW1 memorial.

After WW2 most of the shelters were used for storage of various kinds. Chancery Lane, which had been a centre for intelligence and signalling, served from 1954 until the 1990s as a bomb-proof telephone exchange that included the London terminal of the first Transatlantic cable and part of the 'hot line' connecting the US and Soviet presidents. With as many as 200 staff at its peak, it had its own water supply from an artesian well, emergency power for up to six weeks and fake windows looking out on to painted landscapes. Clapham Common has been converted into a hydroponic farm where the Zero Carbon Company has been growing salad greens since 2015.

3 **Clapham South**, which still contains some of its original bunks and signage

(Transport for London runs occasional tours), was used to accommodate some 200 Jamaicans who arrived on the *Windrush* in 1948. As the nearest labour exchange was at Coldharbour Lane in Brixton, the area gradually became home to a strong community of West Indian settlers. The shelter was also used as lodgings for school parties, as a budget hotel during the Festival of Britain and as accommodation for Commonwealth troops in London for the coronation of Queen Elizabeth II in 1953. You can still see one of the former shelter's entrances on Balham Hill, opposite Gaskarth Road – now smartly tiled and wedged under a new apartment building. There are plans to convert the other entrance – at present a much tattier affair at the south-east corner of Clapham Common – into a café and exhibition centre. Most of the other deep-shelter superstructures – usually following the formula of a circular concrete pillbox containing a spiral staircase topped by a ventilation intake shaft with a

3

separate square brick building that served as an out-take shaft and hoist for supplies and equipment – also look distinctly dilapidated.

As well as in the Eisenhower Centre, the War Cabinet gathered in the Cabinet War Rooms under the Treasury building in Whitehall – and before that was ready in the disused Down Street Underground station off Piccadilly (see page 314). There was also another, little-used war room and bunker in Brook Road in Neasden, beneath what is now a housing estate. The location of wartime government operations was kept largely secret, but one bunker was highly visible – the ❹ **Admiralty Citadel** on Horse Guards Parade. Built in 1940–41 as a bomb-proof operations centre containing some 156 rooms with a telephone exchange staffed around the clock by 700 people, it was linked by tunnels to Whitehall. In the event of a German invasion it could serve as a fortress, with loophole firing positions to fend off attack.

The massive structure, its foundations 9 metres deep and concrete roof 6 metres thick, sits incongruously beside its refined brick and dressed-stone neighbours. During wartime its roof was covered in grass to blend with nearby St James's Park and in summer it is now camouflaged by walls of Russian vine – though such a big structure really has nowhere to hide. In the 1990s it became HMS *St Vincent* – a bizarrely named 'stone frigate' or land-based naval centre. Aptly described by Churchill as a 'vast monstrosity which weighs upon the Horse Guards Parade', it is still used by the Ministry of Defence.

2. Eisenhower Centre,
    13 Chenies St, WC1E 7EY
3. Clapham South,
    Balham Hill, SW12 9EE
4. Admiralty Citadel,
    Horse Guards Parade, SW1A 2AX

7.3 Pleas for Peace

'There are thousands of memorials in every town and village to the dead but not one as a reminder of the danger of future wars. The purpose of the monument was to create a lasting reproach to those whose morality was untouched, whose consciences were unmoved and whose emotions were unaffected.' Sylvia Pankhurst

Under some trees beside Woodford Green High Road, just north of Mornington Road, stands an inconspicuous ❺ **stone monument** protected by iron railings. Closer inspection reveals it to be a sculpture of a bomb, its nose embedded in a pyramid mounted on a substantial if ugly plinth. Engraved on the base is a dedication: 'To those who in 1932 upheld the right to use bombing aeroplanes'. The monument was commissioned by Sylvia Pankhurst – suffragette, communist, lifelong champion of the poor and mobiliser against the continued colonisation of Africa. An anti-war memorial is, as she identified, an oddity in itself, but even odder is a public monument whose inscription uses sarcasm to make its point.

Sylvia Pankhurst (1882–1960) had campaigned for female suffrage alongside her mother Emmeline and sister Christabel from 1906. But soon their political differences became irreconcilable: while Emmeline and Christabel wanted to extend the right to vote to women on an equal basis with men, where a qualification based on property ownership disenfranchised the poorest 40 per cent, Sylvia aligned her struggle with the Labour movement and called for votes for all. She opposed WW1, arguing that the working classes of Europe had a common interest in uniting against the powerful rather than becoming puppets in a conflict that served the financial interests of their masters. In 1918 she was invited to Moscow by Lenin

and in 1920 she attended the Second Congress of the Third International.

Sylvia and her partner, Italian anarchist Silvio Corio, moved to Vine Cottage on Woodford Green High Road – which they soon renamed Red Cottage – in 1924. Three years later their refusal to marry following the birth of their son Richard led to a lifelong estrangement from Sylvia's mother. Though the family moved to a larger house nearby, on what is now Pankhurst Green, in 1933, they continued to own Red Cottage for the next 30 years. While Sylvia focused on writing and campaigning, Silvio ran the premises as a café offering lunches, teas and suppers to travellers 'on the way to Epping Forest'. The anti-war memorial, incongruously, stood outside the tearoom's front door.

The anti-war memorial was commissioned following the 1932 World Disarmament Conference at the League of Nations in Geneva, at which a motion to ban aerial bombardment was defeated with support from the British delegation, who thought bombs might be necessary to maintain

6

control in north-west India. Designed by Dorset mason and sculptor Eric Benfield, the monument avoids both sensationalism and sentimentality, with no reference to human casualties or ruined homes, perhaps reflecting the way air strikes remove the aggressors from direct contact with their victims. The bomb itself is a small-scale, seemingly benign object, with any evocation of its deadly power left to the viewer's imagination.

Installation in October 1935 coincided with Mussolini's invasion of Ethiopia, Africa's last independent state. That country's liberation – along with freedom from colonisation across Africa – was to become the subject of Sylvia's final campaign. Working with Silvio, who had trained as a typographer and printer in Italy, she published *New Times and Ethiopia News* – described as Britain's anti-fascist weekly and smuggled into occupied Ethiopia – to support the cause. Her politics won her few friends in the UK: in 1948 MI5 considered strategies for 'muzzling the tiresome Miss Sylvia Pankhurst' and in a perhaps unconscious reference to the force-feeding she endured as a suffragette, the Foreign Office wrote to the British minister in Addis Ababa in 1947 in support of 'your evident wish that this horrid old harridan should be choked to death with her own pamphlets'. At the age of 74, following Silvio's death, Sylvia moved with her son to Addis Ababa

at the invitation of Haile Selassie, working to improve healthcare and publishing a political newspaper much as she had done in London for the previous half century.

The Woodford stone bomb met with sadly predictable condemnation: it was covered in creosote by protestors on the night of its installation and was later stolen. A near-replica, also made by Benfield, was unveiled in July 1936 at a ceremony attended by representatives from Germany, France, Hungary, British Guyana and Ethiopia. During the 1980s the monument won new recognition as a focus for nuclear-disarmament campaigns.

Another memorial from the mid-1930s that commemorates efforts to prevent a second world war can be found next to the former German embassy at 9 Carlton House Terrace in Mayfair. Often referred to sensationally – and mistakenly – as the only London memorial to a Nazi, it is in fact the **6 gravestone of Giro**, the pet terrier of German ambassador Leopold von Hoesch. Giro and von Hoesch – the latter described in his obituary as charming, well-dressed and the host of glamorous parties – arrived in London in 1932 as representatives of the Weimar Republic. Following the Nazi accession to power in 1934, von Hoesch continued to work to improve Anglo-German relations and wrote to Hitler to denounce such actions as the 1936 invasion of the Rhineland. After his death later that year von Hoesch was honoured by the British with a funeral cortege to accompany his body to Dover; back in Germany, no Nazi party representative attended his burial. Giro, meanwhile, remains in London, his death in 1934 recorded on a stone that reads 'Giro Ein treuer Begleiter!' ('Giro A Faithful Companion!').

5. Anti-Air War Memorial,
    Woodford Green High Rd, IG8 0RD
6. Giro's gravestone,
    9 Carlton House Terrace, SW1Y 5AH

7.4 Secret Services

On the south bank of the Thames, just beside Vauxhall station, is an overblown late 20th-century building that stands out through its extraordinary bulk, its extravagantly stepped form and its post-modern rhetoric. A more conspicuous setting for the UK's ❼ **Secret Intelligence Service** (SIS or MI6) could hardly be imagined.

MI6 – whose remit is to work secretly overseas 'to help make the UK a safer and more prosperous place' – was set up as the Secret Service Bureau in 1909 following public concern about Germany's imperial ambitions. The first head, Mansfield Smith-Cumming, had neither intelligence experience nor linguistic skills but was apparently recommended for the role thanks to 'special qualifications'. If meetings were not going his way he would stab his leg dramatically with a paper knife – stopping opponents in their tracks until they remembered he had been fitted with a wooden limb following a car accident. It was Smith-Cumming who established the practice of writing in green ink that is still followed today; his nickname 'C' has been given to all subsequent SIS chiefs.

Smith-Cumming set up the SIS's first offices on Vauxhall Bridge Road using a bogus firm of shippers and exporters as cover; potential employees were interviewed at another secret location in Kingsway. Following WW1 he moved the premises to Holland Park, though would-be visitors had to be directed there orally after first reporting to an office off the Strand. In 1926, new 'C' Hugh Sinclair relocated the SIS to 54 Broadway, near St James's Park, where it remained until 1964, followed by a move to Century House on Lambeth Bridge Road near Waterloo.

There is nothing remotely undercover about the SIS's present home of Vauxhall Cross, which the organisation has occupied since 1994. In fact, it is well enough known to have featured prominently in two James Bond films. Architect Terry Farrell, who won the commission to develop the site following a competition, took inspiration from Mayan and Aztec temples as well as 1930s architecture such as Battersea and Bankside power stations. Though then prime minister Margaret Thatcher insisted that the government buy the finished building outright from the developers to keep the identity of its intended occupants secret, the relocation in fact coincided with the first public acknowledgement of MI6's existence through the 1994 Intelligence Services Act, which defines its role and the legal parameters under which it operates.

Looking at Vauxhall Cross today, it seems emblematic of an institution wanting to show off its might and muscle rather than operate under a veil of discretion. The street elevation on Albert Embankment, opposite a motorcycle showroom and gay sauna under the railway arches, consists of a relentless grid of prison-like windows with triple glazing and obscured glass. It is the river front, however, that is most astonishing, with Farrell's eclecticism given full rein. The overall form is an

7

7

8

9

Aztec ziggurat, complete with a 'sacrificial' platform at the summit, behind which sit the huge, 21st-century antennae that presumably capture worldwide communications. Below are art deco curves, Egyptian pylons and a central, deep red pharaonic column (the only splash of colour) with a pair of tempietti on the riverside walkway. For no apparent reason, the building has 60 different stepped terraces and roof areas, like a lavish Hollywood set waiting to be peopled by a crowd of extras, or as if its inhabitants might suddenly burst forth to sing out their secrets to passing tourist boats. Anyone who did not know the building's function might imagine it to be a massive hotel or conference centre – perhaps a cunning disguise, after all, or a form of hiding in plain sight.

MI6 agents historically congregated in the Old Star pub in Broadway and the 'In & Out' (the Naval and Military Club) in Piccadilly, using the Blue Bridge in St James's Park for clandestine meetings. Soviet agents, by contrast, seem to have gravitated to Kensington and Chelsea, home of Kim Philby and the location of regular meeting places such as the Markham Arms pub on the King's Road and Daquise's Polish restaurant near South Kensington Underground.

Intelligence from Oleg Gordievsky, a Soviet double agent who worked for MI6 from the late 1960s, revealed that spies would whizz around Harrods in Brompton Road to make sure they were not being tailed before continuing on foot to one of two west London dead-letter boxes where they could leave packages to be picked up later by their handlers.

One is inside ❽ **Brompton Oratory**: enter by the right-hand door and you see a marble pietà and WW1 memorial; material would be left in the small space behind the two marble pillars on the left of the statue.

An even more unlikely drop was in the garden of the nearby church of ❾ **Holy Trinity**. Walking from Brompton Road, turn left before you reach the church and you will find a small statue of St Francis of Assisi; agents would leave sensitive information below the tree next to the wall. Allegedly, they would then walk across Hyde Park to Audley Place in Mayfair to make or erase a chalk line on a lamp post (see page 87) to indicate that there was information to exchange.

Post-modernism – as exemplified at Vauxhall Cross – is a style that borrows from a more illustrious, imagined past. Whatever their seeming amateurism, tales of Soviet agents sneaking around department stores and churchyards and communicating via chalk marks at least have more romance than the petrified arrogance embodied in the current SIS headquarters.

7. MI6, 85 Albert Embankment, SE1 7TP
8. Brompton Oratory,
    Brompton Rd, SW7 2RP
9. Statue of St Francis, Holy Trinity Garden,
    Brompton Rd, SW7 1JA

Old Operating Theatre, see page 247

Bodies & Bones

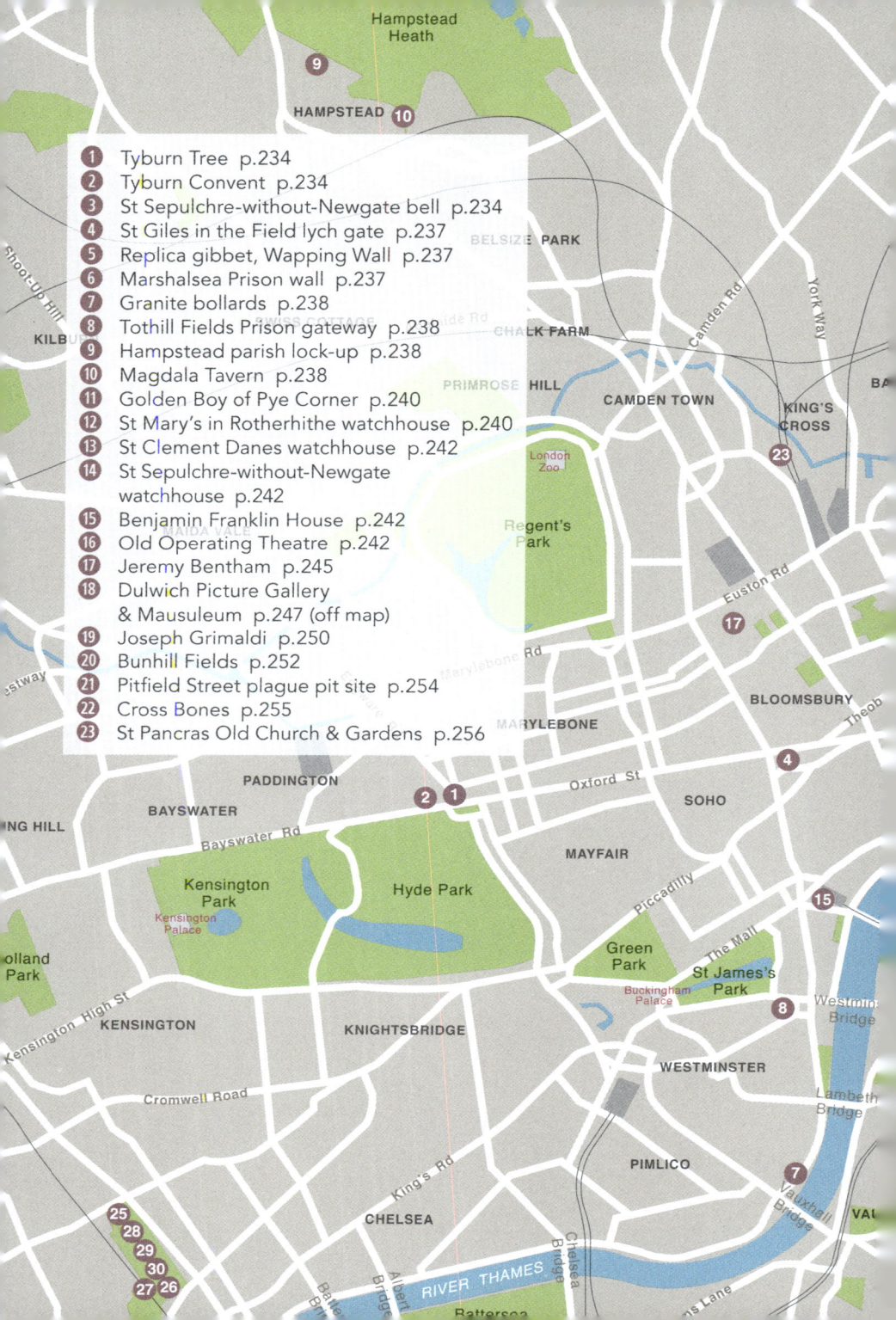

Bodies & Bones

Clissold Park

STOKE NEWINGTON

Hackney Downs

LOWER CLAPTON

Mabley Green

Highbury Fields

DALSTON

HOMERTON

CANONBURY

HACKNEY

HACKN WICK

London Fields

Balls Pond Rd

DE BEAUVOIR TOWN

Victoria Park

SLINGTON

Shoreditch Park

BOW

City Rd

Mile End Park

KENWELL

SHOREDITCH

BETHNAL GREEN

MILE END

Old St

Tower Cemete

BARBICAN

Commercial St

Whitechapel Rd

STEPNEY

CITY OF LONDON

WHITECHAPEL

LIMEHOUSE

East In

Blackfriars Bridge

Millennium Bridge

Southwark Bridge

London Bridge

Tate Britain

The Highway

Tower of London

WAPPING

Rotherhithe Tunnel

RIVER THAMES

CANA

SOUTHWARK

Tower Bridge

Bermondsey

ROTHERHITHE

NEWINGTON

Tower Bridge Rd

MI

WALWORTH

Old Kent Road

Deptford Park

Burgess Park

DEPTFO

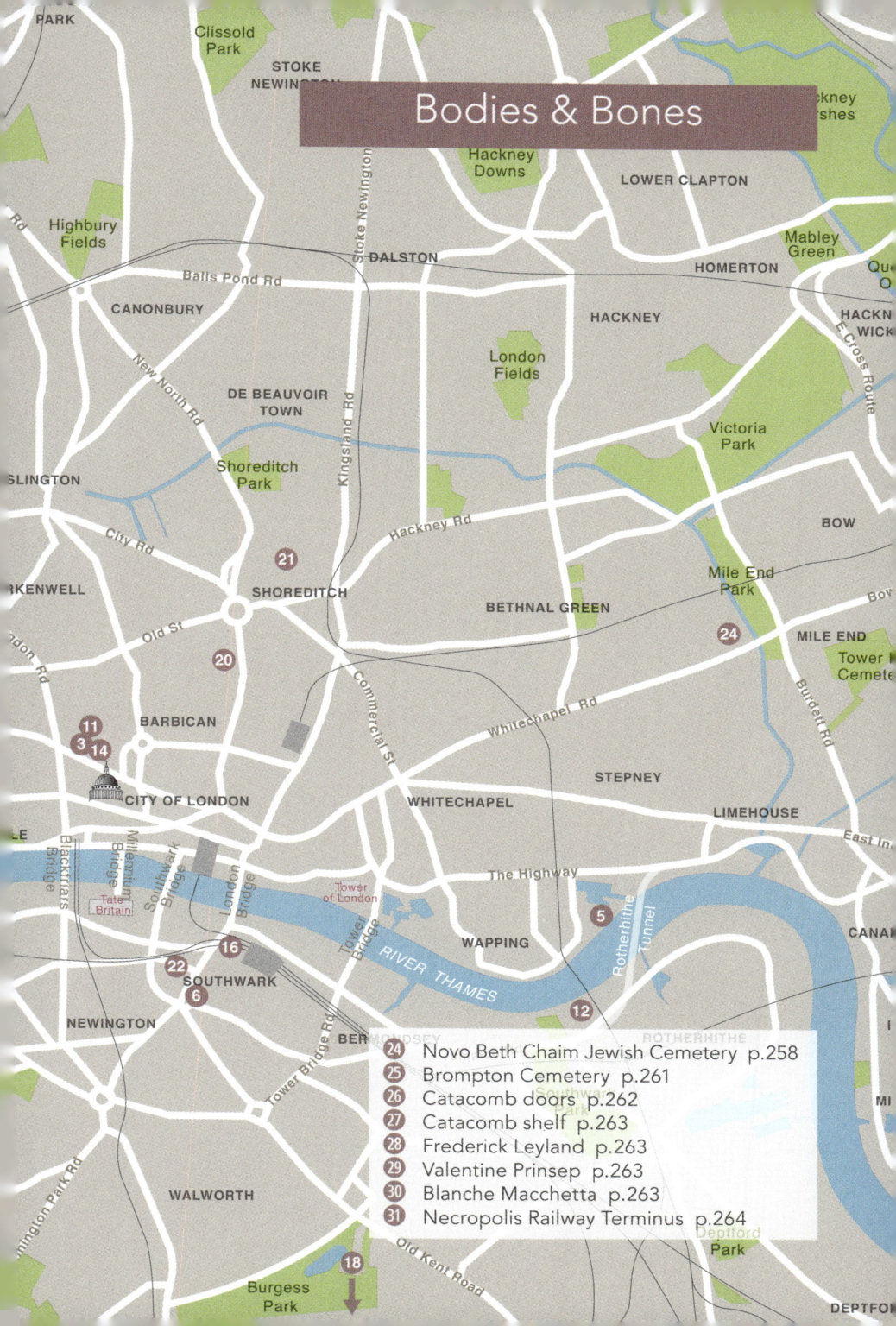

8.1 Crime & Punishment

Though capital punishment in most of the UK was abolished in 1965, its legacy can still be traced in London, sometimes to disturbing effect. The most obvious reminder is the marker commemorating the ❶ **Tyburn gallows** on a traffic island at the Marble Arch end of Edgware Road. Though the plaque itself is no more than a simple circular stone set into the paving, the site has oddity value as a place of special significance for both the Catholic church and upholders of free speech.

Tyburn was used for public executions from 1196 to 1783, but the famous Tyburn Tree – a forbidding triangular structure made up of three 3-metre-long cross-beams supported on 5.5-metre-high posts – was not put up until 1571. Huge crowds – highwayman Jack Sheppard's execution in 1724 attracted some 200,000 onlookers – would gather to see as many as 24 victims hanging at a time. The plaque marking the gallows' location was installed in 1964 and restored in 2104, with three puny oak saplings unsuccessfully evoking the massive triangular form. Within the bustle of Oxford Street, however, it is easy to imagine the holiday atmosphere surrounding the spectacle – and to wonder how many of those vaping, texting and shopping today might have once turned up to cheer.

Among an estimated 50,000 people executed at Tyburn were 105 Catholics who refused to renounce their faith: their fate is commemorated at the nearby ❷ **Tyburn Convent** in Hyde Park Place on Bayswater Road. High up on the façade is a relief with an image of the gallows in the top left-hand corner and in the basement chapel that houses the Shrine of the Martyrs are two fragments said to be wood from the Tyburn Tree as well as the hair, fingernails and blood-soaked linen of martyred individuals. Catholics and others convicted of high treason would be sadistically hanged, drawn and quartered: tied to a hurdle and drawn to the gallows by horse, hanged and then disembowelled while still alive before being beheaded.

The convicted were allowed to address the crowds as a final act: Catholics often used the occasion to make a declaration of faith while others would openly criticise the government or the monarch. Possibly as a result, the corner of Hyde Park opposite the gallows was designated by an 1872 Act of Parliament as a Speakers' Corner – a place where citizens have the right to meet and speak freely. The act was a response to three days of riots after participants of a Reform League march in support of universal male suffrage were locked out of the park. As well as attracting soapbox orators promoting alternative religions, radical politics or wacky theories, the site has been the start or end point of mass demonstrations from the suffragettes in the early 1900s to mobilisation against the Iraq war a century later. When German chancellor Angela Merkel came to London in 2014, she made a point of visiting Speakers' Corner, which she described as 'for us as East Germans... legendary, the very symbol of free speech'.

Tyburn hangings were always on a Monday, and many of the condemned were held in Newgate Prison, on the corner of Newgate Street and Old Bailey in the City. At midnight the previous day, the bellman of St Sepulchre-without-Newgate, the church opposite the gaol, would walk via an underground passage to the cells on death row. Outside each cell he would give 12 tolls on a handbell and recite a verse advising the inmates to repent before their approaching encounter with the Almighty. You can still see the ❸ **St Sepulchre-without-Newgate bell** in a glass case attached to a pillar inside the church.

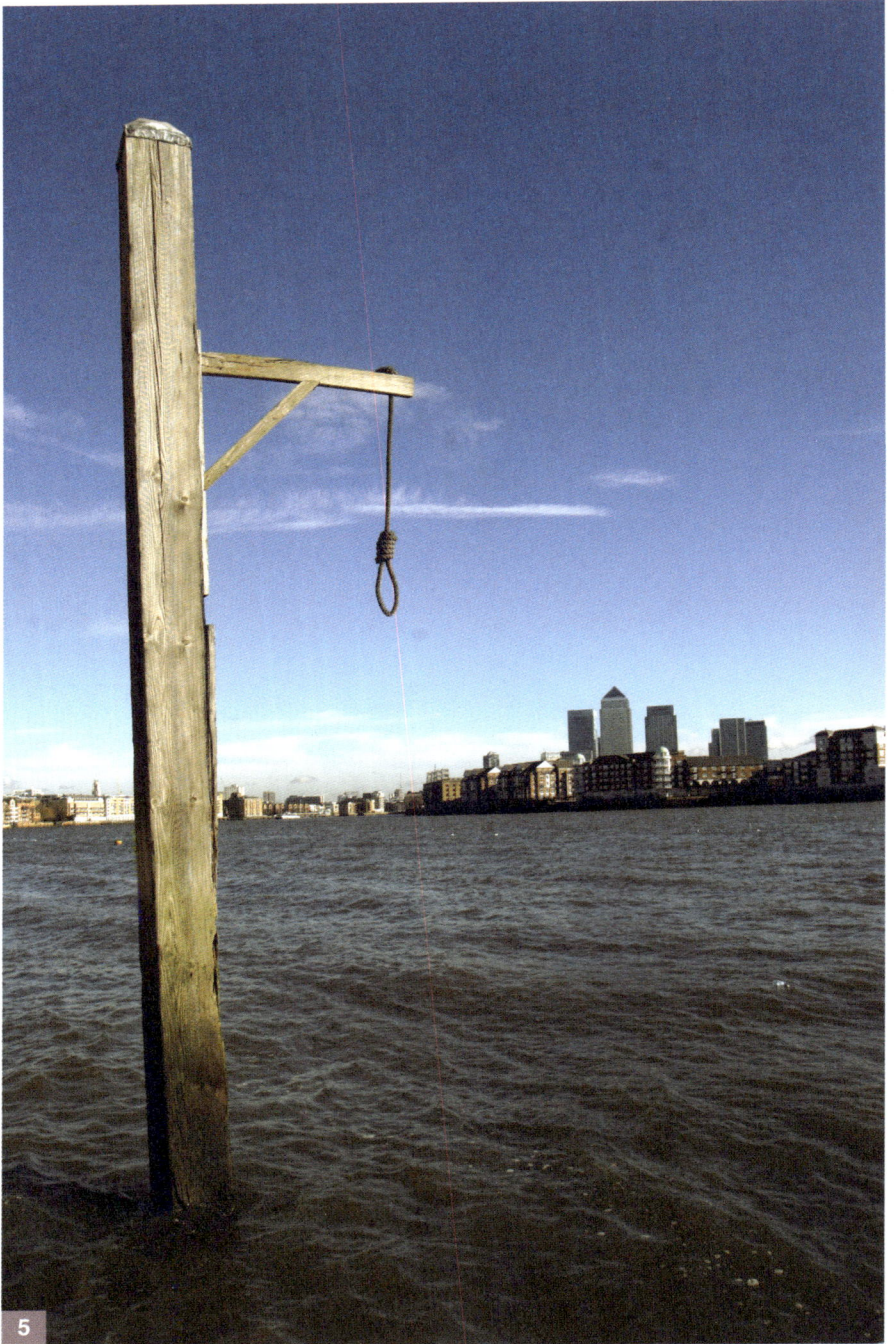

5

Next morning the prisoners would be loaded into open carts and driven through Holborn to St Giles in the Field, near the southern end of Tottenham Court Road. No doubt their attention would be drawn to the ④ **lych gate** with its dramatic low relief of the Last Judgement, contrasting the resurrection of Christ with the fate of sinners condemned to hell. The original gateway on St Giles High Street was a simple brick arch with the image on the tympanum carved in wood; it was replaced in 1800 by a much grander Palladian structure (now at the Flitcroft Street entrance) with the relief reproduced in stone. You can find the original wooden version in the church vestibule. The condemned are also said to have been offered a last drink at a pub called the Bowl (probably now the Angel, next to the church) before proceeding down Oxford Street to Tyburn. The phrase 'on the wagon' is sometimes claimed to derive from the fact that the prisoners were allowed only one drink before being loaded back on the carts.

Other execution sites included the Tower of London, Smithfield and Execution Dock in Wapping, where pirates were hung and their bodies displayed until three tides had washed over them. You can see a ⑤ **replica gibbet**, its noose dangling over the water at high tide, outside the Prospect of Whitby pub on Wapping Wall. Pirates on death row were held at Marshalsea Prison in Southwark, as were debtors such as Charles Dickens' father (the author used the gaol as the setting for *Little Dorrit*). He may have been pleased that part of the site is now a library – though you can still see a tall section of overrestored ⑥ **Marshalsea Prison wall** in St George's Churchyard Gardens off Tabard Street, with metal gates leading through to the former prison grounds on Angel Place.

Prisoners merely sentenced to transportation were held at Millbank Penitentiary before being escorted to underground cells, some of

which are said to form part of the basement of the Morpeth Arms near Vauxhall Bridge on Millbank. One of the derivations of 'POM', the Australian nickname for the English, is 'Prisoner of Millbank', with which convicts were branded. The practice of transportation is commemorated on brass plaques on the massive **7 granite bollards** that once lined the steps to the river where prisoners would board their ships. One now stands in Riverside Walk Gardens, opposite the pub.

Prefiguring today's vicious campaigns against 'shirkers' and 'skivers', paupers categorised as indolent – without the excuse of physical disability or illness for their penury – would find themselves in Tothill Fields Prison, a 'house of correction' founded in 1618 and enlarged in 1655. By the turn of the century it also catered to criminals; in 1834 it was superseded by a larger prison on the site of what is now Westminster Cathedral (see page 293). The roughly hewn **8 stone gateway** from 1655 now stands in Little Sanctuary in Westminster, surmounted by a plaque that reads: 'Here are several sorts of work for the poor of this parish St Margarets Westminster... for such as will beg and live idle in this city.' Though the gate is mounted within the railings that surround what is now the Supreme Court, it is a doorway that leads nowhere.

Another odd survival of former punishment regimes is the **9 doorway to the Hampstead parish lock-up**, built in about 1730 behind the imposing red-brick wall that surrounds Cannon Hall in Cannon Lane. For many years the hall's stable block served as a magistrates' court, and convicted prisoners would be kept in the dark single cell while awaiting their court appearance. You can still see the small barred arched windows, but as you might guess from the number above the door, this is now the entrance to a private house.

London has had its share of notorious murder cases, usually, like the 'Jack the Ripper' killings of prostitutes, by men of women. An exception is the murder of racing driver David Blakely by Ruth Ellis (1926–1955), the last woman to be hanged in the UK. Ellis' story is a bleak one. Following a short-lived violent marriage, she worked as a model, prostitute, hostess and nightclub manager before becoming involved in relationships with two of her clients: former RAF pilot Desmond Cussen (who supplied her with a gun and gave her lessons in how to use it) and Blakely, whose physical abuse a few months earlier had caused a miscarriage. On Easter Sunday 1955, outside the **10 Magdala Tavern**, opposite Hampstead Heath Overground in South Hill Park, Ellis shot Blakely five times – the last three at close range when he was already dying on the pavement. In answer to the only question posed by the prosecution at her trial, she said: 'It's obvious when I shot him I intended to kill him.'

Over 60 years later, you can still see bullet holes from the first two shots under the window nearest the door of the pub. But the legacy of Ellis' crime is much larger: public debate and revulsion at her sentence helped strengthen support for the abolition of the death penalty a decade later.

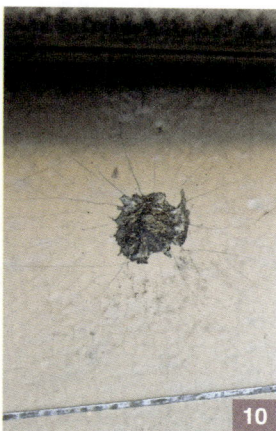

1. Tyburn Tree,
   Marble Arch, W2 2EN
2. Tyburn Convent,
   8-9 Hyde Park Place, W2 2LJ
3. St Sepulchre-without-Newgate bell,
   Holborn Viaduct, EC1A 2DQ
4. St Giles in the Field lych gate,
   60 St Giles High St, WC2H 8LG
5. Replica gibbet, Prospect of Whitby,
   57 Wapping Wall, E1W 3SH

6. Marshalsea Prison wall,
   St George's Churchyard, SE1 1JA
7. Bollards, Riverside Walk Gardens,
   SW1P 4RL
8. Tothill Fields Prison gateway,
   Little Sanctuary, SW1P 3BD
9. Hampstead parish lock-up,
   Cannon Lane, NW3 1EL
10. Magdala Tavern,
    South Hill Park, NW3 2SB

8.2 Kill or Cure

The relationship between the medical profession and the criminal underworld in the 18th and 19th centuries was a grisly one, involving crime and punishment, exhumation and extortion, bodies and bones. Among its physical relics are watchhouses: small buildings at the edge of churchyards where sentries would keep a nightly vigil to deter or catch criminals intent on stealing bodies from freshly dug graves. Body snatchers, also known as resurrectionists, colluded in a lucrative trade with medical schools and hospitals, whose surgeons needed cadavers for research and training. You can find surviving watchhouses in St Marychurch Street in Rotherhithe (opposite the church of St Mary's and close to Guy's and St Thomas' hospitals), in Strand Lane, Westminster (formerly guarding the graveyard of St Clement Danes), and in Giltspur Street in the City (attached to St Sepulchre-without-Newgate, conveniently located opposite St Bartholomew's hospital).

There was strong public revulsion at the idea of dissection, with many fearing that the practice would render their bodies unrecognisable in the afterlife. Dissection was illegal from the 16th century, and until the mid-18th century the Royal College of Physicians and College of Barber-Surgeons were granted an annual quota of just ten corpses between them. The 1751 Murder Act allowed anatomists to carve up the bodies of hanged criminals: this was regarded as an additional punishment that might act as a deterrent, but those who arrived to claim the bodies were often attacked by onlookers. Surgeons were deemed to have little respect for the cadavers they worked on and it was rumoured that human remains ended up as offal, a procedure alluded to in the last plate of Hogarth's 1751 *The Four Stages of*

Cruelty. Many also feared that dissection would render their bodies unrecognisable in the afterlife.

During the 18th century, capital punishment was meted out for relatively trivial crimes but by the early 19th century the number of people receiving the death penalty had fallen to about 50 a year. As a result, legally obtained corpses were in short supply and body snatching was rife: by the 1820s reports to parliament claimed there were some 200 resurrectionists working in London alone. Relatives or friends of the dead would often guard their bodies before and after burial while those who could afford it invested in heavy iron or lead coffins or protected graves with iron bars or stone slabs.

An inscription below the ⑪ **Golden Boy of Pye Corner** (see page 18), at the corner of Giltspur Street and Cock Lane, describes a gruesome scene, alleging that the statue was originally built into the front of a pub called the Fortune of War, which was 'the chief house of call north of the river for resurrectionists in body snatching days years ago. The landlord used to show the room where on benches round the walls the bodies were placed labelled with the snatchers' names waiting till the surgeons at Saint Bartholomew's could run round and appraise them.'

The ⑫ **watchhouse for the graveyard** of St Mary's in Rotherhithe dates from 1821, when grave robbing was at its peak. A single-storey brick lean-to with a sturdy parapet on the street side, it was built as an integral part of a new burial ground – oddly enough, with a matching engine house a few metres down the street. The watchhouse was staffed by a beadle or parish constable and 14 watchmen, working in shifts, whose duties included

calling out the time, seeing residents safely home (for a small fee) and fire prevention – in addition to guarding the churchyard and apprehending criminals, who would be locked in the basement cell before being handed over to magistrates next morning.

A much more elegant affair, the ⓑ **St Clement Danes watchhouse** bridges Strand Lane. Records dating back to the early 18th century indicate that it was run by two beadles and 28 watchmen whose duties included guarding the churchyard. Remodelled in the early 19th century, it is now part of King's College. The ⓮ **St Sepulchre-without-Newgate watchhouse** was built in 1791 along with new vestries attached to the church; it was destroyed in WW2 and rebuilt in 1962. Often derided as elderly, incompetent and drunk on duty,

the watchmen – and their watchhouses – were shut down from 1829 following the formation of the Metropolitan Police.

In 1998 the renovation of ⑮ **Benjamin Franklin House** in Craven Street near Charing Cross where US statesman Benjamin Franklin (1706–1790) lived during his ambassadorship to London was halted because of the discovery of the remains of some 15 corpses in a small pit in the basement. The bones, which amounted to more than a thousand separate fragments, some of which showed dissection marks or evidence of trepanning, were discarded remnants from the anatomical school run by medical pioneer William Hewson (1739–1774), the husband of Franklin's landlady's daughter. You can see some of them on display today alongside Franklin's weathered wallet and a letter to his sister. Hewson trained under anatomist William Hunter, whose younger brother John – a surgeon and teacher at St George's Hospital – amassed some 15,000 plant, animal and human specimens that form the basis of the collections of the Hunterian Museum, now housed in Lincoln's Inn Fields in Holborn.

The ⑯ **Old Operating Theatre** in St Thomas Street near London Bridge provides an uncomfortable insight into medical practices of the early 19th century. Not only is it the oldest surviving operating theatre in Europe, but it also has oddity value by being housed in the roof of a church. Following the relocation of the adjoining St Thomas' Hospital in 1862, the space was closed up and forgotten for almost a century until an intrepid researcher climbed a ladder into the garret and took a look around.

Visitors today climb the narrow spiral staircase in the tower of St Thomas' church (built in 1703) to the attic space known as the Herb Garret, where plants used in medical compounds were once cured and stored – a practical arrangement as the exposed roof timbers absorbed moisture, preventing the plants from rotting. A narrow passage leads to the operating theatre, created in 1822 to treat the hospital's female patients. Built entirely of wood – not the easiest material to scrub clean – it consists of an amphitheatre with a much used operating table at the centre surrounded by tiered stands where up to 120 students and apprentices would jostle for position. A glazed roof ensured the surgeon had plenty of light.

Anyone who could afford it would choose to be treated at home, so a charitable hospital like St Thomas' took in only those

with no other option, including many of the area's prostitutes. A sign at the front of the theatre reads 'Miseratione non mercede' (Compassion not gain). Patients would arrive on Thursdays to petition to be included in the following day's operating schedule: those suffering from infectious diseases would be sent to neighbouring Guy's; those accepted would be subject to procedures such as the setting of fractures, amputation, removal of bladder stones, trepanning, blood letting and the lancing of boils. Hygiene was virtually non-existent – the surgeons' aprons would be stiff with blood and pus and often they would come straight from dissections without washing their hands (simple hygiene was not part of medical practice until the transmission of germs was discovered in the mid-19th century). There was no anesthetic until 1846, when ether and chloroform were introduced.

As a teaching hospital, St Thomas' required a ready supply of cadavers. One of its chief sources was the London Borough Gang, headed by Ben Crouch, a former hospital porter and prizefighter known for his love of gold jewellery and dandy's clothing. 'Contracts' and territories were protected through cartels: in 1816, when the Borough Gang's threat to increase their rates was met with resistance by the hospital, the resurrectionists burst into the dissecting rooms to attack surgeons and students until the hospital capitulated.

The 1832 Anatomy Act increased the legal supply of corpses by giving hospitals access to unclaimed bodies, usually from workhouses or prisons. It spelled the end of the careers of operators such as Crouch, who retired to Margate, where his earnings allowed him to open a pub and guesthouse. Eventually his past caught up with him, however, and when the publicity put an end to his new venture he returned to London. No one seems to know where he was buried – or if his body is still in its grave.

11. Golden Boy of Pye Corner,
    Giltspur St, EC1A 9DD
12. Rotherhithe watchhouse,
    72 St Marychurch St, SE16 4HZ
13. Strand Lane watchhouse, WC2R 1AP
14. St-Sepulchre-without-Newgate
    watchhouse, Holborn Viaduct, EC1A 2DQ
15. Benjamin Franklin House,
    36 Craven St, WC2N 5NF
    www.benjaminfranklinhouse.org
16. Old Operating Theatre,
    9a St Thomas St, SE1 9RY
    www.oldoperatingtheatre.com

8.3 Jeremy Bentham (1748–1832)

Jeremy Bentham (signature)

In a glass-fronted case near the entrance to the new University College London Student Centre in Gordon Square, Bloomsbury, sits the skeleton of ⑰ **Jeremy Bentham** – though you would never recognise it as a skeleton, since his bare bones have been padded out with straw and clothed in a frilly shirt, shiny waistcoat, tailed black jacket, fawn knickerbockers and gloves, and a magnificent straw hat. Reliable sources state that he is also wearing underpants and two pairs of socks. In place of his head is a wax model: his real head, mummified and conserved in a bell jar, now sits in a wooden safe within the UCL Institute of Archaeology.

A philosopher, jurist and social reformer whose theory of utilitarianism maintained that 'it is the greatest happiness for the greatest number that is the measure of right and wrong', Bentham advocated the abolition of slavery and capital punishment, equal rights for women, universal suffrage,

the separation of church and state, free-market economics, the decriminalisation of homosexuality and the right to divorce. He believed that anything that did no harm to others should be legal. His link to UCL goes back to its formation in 1826, which he helped with the purchase of a £100 share in support of its stance as the first university to accept students regardless of race, creed or political belief. His rationalist insistence on following his ideas to their logical conclusion could lead him to inhumane solutions (including, arguably, his desire to be dissected after his death by one of his friends) – most notably the panopticon, a prison where inmates' behavior was regulated by constant threat of surveillance.

Living at a time when cremation was illegal and burial the only option, Bentham condemned the sometimes ruinous cost of funerals and the health hazards associated with piling up bodies in churchyards. He believed that, 'generally, in the present state of things, our dead relations are a source of evil… they generate infectious disease; they send forth the monster, Typhus, to destroy… Why do we not prevent it?'

His solution was the auto-icon – a self-image of the deceased whose appearance (for himself, at least) he specified in some detail, including the clothes, chair, pose and case or box in which he was to be contained. Among other advantages, his invention would do away with the need for expensive marble statues. Hardly a modest man, he imagined that, 'If it should so happen that my personal friends and other disciples should be disposed to meet together… for the purpose of commemorating the founder of the greatest happiness system of morals and legislation, my executor will from time to time cause to be conveyed to the room in which they meet the said box or case. Apparently his executor, doctor and sanitary reformer Thomas Southwood Smith, retained Bentham's auto-icon at his dinner table for 18 years until his future wife objected; thereafter he donated it to UCL, where it has remained ever since.

Before the creation of the auto-icon came the dissection. This was performed, as requested, by Southwood Smith in front of an audience that included Bentham's friends and followers James Mill, an economist and political theorist, his son John Stuart Mill, who was to develop Bentham's philosophy of utilitarianism, and the Lord Chancellor Henry Brougham, one of the founders of UCL.

Bentham had declared that he wanted his corpse to be dissected as early as 1769, as soon as he came of age, at a point when only the bodies of executed criminals were made available to the medical profession. He died a month before the introduction of the 1832 Anatomy Act (see page 243), which allowed anatomists access to unclaimed cadavers and those of consenting individuals, making him probably the first person to donate his body to medical research. His did so out of 'the desire that mankind may reap some small benefit in and by my decease' and hoped that 'I shall have made to the fund of human happiness a contribution, more or less considerable'.

Bentham is occasionally wheeled out of his case at UCL to attend meetings and events as well as being regularly removed for inspection and cleaning. Perhaps the oddest part of his story, however, is the fate of his head, which he planned to have preserved through a Maori process of mummification, with the eyes replaced by glass orbs that he chose himself and delighted in showing to friends. Though initially his head was literally screwed to his body, the mummification process

soon proved inadequate and a wax replica – including straggling strands of Bentham's own hair – was commissioned by Southwood Smith from French sculptor Jacques Talrich. After the move to UCL, the real head was at first displayed at the auto-icon's feet before being removed to a box located until recently above the entrance to the cloisters. In 1975 it was kidnapped by rival students from King's College in return for a ransom payable to charity; King's students also stole the wax head in 1990.

It seems that initially Southwood Smith had intended Bentham's head to remain with his skeleton as it was discovered in 1898 inside the chest cavity – a position that in life might have been occupied by his heart.

UCL Student Centre, 27-28 Gordon Square, WC1H 0AW
www.ucl.ac.uk/culture/auto-icon

8.4 Dulwich Picture Gallery & Mausoleum

Designed in 1811 by architect John Soane, **18 Dulwich Picture Gallery** was the first public art gallery in England. Its revolutionary use of top-lighting created a template still followed by art museums today, but its status as an oddity comes from the inclusion in the plans of a mausoleum to house the remains of the gallery's three founders, Francis Bourgeois (1753–1811), Noel Desenfans (1745–1807) and his wife Margaret (1731–1813). Far from being tucked away in a discreet corner, the mausoleum forms the centrepiece of the west front and is the first thing visitors see when they enter the museum.

Bourgeois, a court painter to George III, and Desanfans, an art dealer and collector, bought the paintings on display – which include masterpieces by Rubens and Van Dyck as well as important Italian and British works – on commission for Stanislaus Augustus, King of Poland, to form the basis of a new national collection. When Stanislaus abdicated in 1795, the dealers were left without a buyer. Desenfans bequeathed the collection to Bourgeois on condition it should be donated to an institution for public exhibition, and Bourgeois in turn left it in his will to Dulwich College.

The idea of including a burial chamber alongside a display of paintings seems to have been Soane's. Bourgeois had left £2000 in his will to create a gallery in one of the existing buildings of the college, in whose grounds he hoped to be buried, but the architect persuaded his widow to triple the sum and commission an entirely new gallery with a mausoleum attached. Apparently Soane had already been asked to design a tomb for the back yard of the Desenfans' Charlotte Street house but the idea was dropped when the family failed to obtain the necessary permissions. Perhaps the combination of art and death is less surprising in the context of Soane's other works – certainly the objects in his house in Lincoln's Inn Fields (see page 159), which include the sarcophagus of Egyptian king Seti I along with the tomb of his wife's dog Fanny, demonstrate his fascination with death and the dramatic possibilities inherent in highlighting its presence among us.

From the outside, the mausoleum lends the gallery's main façade a distinctly bizarre appearance. There is no mistaking its purpose: a cruciform block projecting from the centre of the west elevation, it has a full-size sarcophagus sitting at cornice level on each of its three arms, while the square lantern has an urn at each corner and another forming a central finial. The design of the lantern is very similar to that of Soane's own tomb in St Pancras Old Churchyard (see pages 74 and 256), built in 1815 following the death of his wife, which in turn inspired Giles Gilbert Scott's iconic K2 phone box (see page 75). The three low external doors – which lead nowhere – may be 'spirit doors' inspired by Egyptian funerary architecture.

Inside, the burial space forms an appropriately gloomy contrast to the light-filled galleries. A circular anteroom with a shallow dome supported by six exaggeratedly massive Doric columns leads to the cruciform chamber. Its three projecting niches house plain sarcophaghi painted a rich red to mimic Egyptian porphyry. Glazed in square panes of yellow, orange and red, the lantern casts a glowing amber light. Decoration is minimal – a Greek key pattern, snakes signifying eternity and stylised angels symbolising victory over death.

Soane complained when once he found the door connecting gallery and tomb closed and imagined the theatrical effect his memento mori might have on an occasion such as the banquet of Royal Academicians held annually within the gallery: 'To increase the enjoyment of this splendid scene we have only to fancy the Gallery brilliantly lighted for the exhibition of this unrivalled assemblage of pictorial art – whilst a dull religious light shows the Mausoleum in the full pride of funereal grandeur, displaying its sarcophagi, enriched with the mortal remains of departed worth, and calling back so powerfully the recollections of past times, that we almost believe that we are conversing with our departed friends who now sleep in their silent tombs.'

The museum was also flanked by almshouses, which were converted into galleries in 1880, and the space was further expanded with a series of rooms on the entrance side at the start of the 20th century. The building was so badly damaged by bombing during WW2 that bones from the burial chamber littered the front lawn: these were redistributed among the sarcophaghi so that each now contains something approximating a single skeleton. Even more bizarrely, Soane's vision of a seamless connection between life and death is honoured today by newly married couples who choose the tomb as a site for glowingly lit photographs.

18. Dulwich Picture Gallery & Mausoleum, Gallery Rd, SE21 7AD
www.dulwichpicturegallery.org.uk

8.5 Joseph Grimaldi (1778–1837)

There is one grave in London that you are invited to dance on: the **19 memorial to Joseph Grimaldi**, inventor of the modern clown, in Grimaldi Park on Pentonville Road in Islington. Or at least, you are invited to dance on bronze tiles laid out in the shape of coffins dedicated to Grimaldi and his theatre manager Charles Dibdin; Grimaldi himself lies a few metres away, surrounded by decorous iron railings hung with masks of tragedy and comedy. Apparently the tiles play the tune of Grimaldi's most famous number 'Hot Codlins', a participatory song about a toffee-apple seller who gets drunk on gin while at work. It is hard to stamp out anything that resembles a tune, but the temptation to try is irresistible.

Joseph Grimaldi was the son of Giuseppe Grimaldi, an actor, dancer and serial philanderer who at the age of 60 seduced his 13-year-old assistant Rebecca Brooker. After she had borne him two sons, the eldest of whom was Joseph, he moved in with her in the hope of raising an acting dynasty. A violent monster nicknamed 'Grim-All-Day', Giuseppe feared being buried alive so intensely that he left his daughter by another mistress £5 to have him decapitated after his death. As a model for the irrational behaviour and arbitrary justice meted out to the stereotypical, childlike clown, he could not have been bettered.

Joseph – who gave his name 'Joey' to thousands of his clown followers – made his stage debut at the age of three and was the family breadwinner by the time his father died six years later. At the age of twelve he appeared in one of Dibdin's pantomimes in a newly invented clown costume with the garish colours, bold geometric patterns and ruff that were to become standard issue. A decade later he designed his clown character's unsettling make-up: flat white foundation, thick black eyebrows and kohl-ringed eyes, and exaggerated red cheeks, lips and nose. He was to reprise the 'Joey' character throughout his career, most famously in *Harlequin and Mother Goose; or, The Golden Egg*, which ran for 111 performances at Covent Garden in 1806. A few years later, appearing in *Don Juan* in Cheltenham, he met Lord Byron, who said he felt 'great and unbounded satisfaction in becoming acquainted with a man of such rare and profound talents'. Grimaldi's response is not recorded.

In addition to his invention of the clown, Grimaldi was one of the first pantomime dames in an 1820 version of *Cinderella* and developed the tradition of audience participation through call-and-response catchphrases and communal singing. He retired in 1823, his ill-health exacerbated by the many injuries he had sustained in the course of his clowning, including shooting himself in the foot and dramatic plunges through rickety trapdoors. Following the deaths of his son and wife he ended his life alone, a depressed alcoholic and sad clown.

Since the 1940s Grimaldi has been commemorated through an annual memorial service (now held on the first Sunday in February at Holy Trinity Church in Hackney) attended by hundreds of performers in full clown costume. Grimaldi Park is on the site of the

former graveyard of his local church, St James's, and you can find other gravestones stacked against the walls. The coffin memorials are an art installation created in 2010 by Henry Krokatisis. It seems fitting that a pioneer of pantomime should be commemorated by an interactive monument – and as you dance, of course, he's behind you!

19. Grimaldi grave and 'coffins', Grimaldi Park, Pentonville Rd, N1 9HW

19

8.6 Burial Grounds

Bunhill Fields

20 Bunhill Fields, just south of the Old Street roundabout on City Road, has a long history as a burial ground that predates its fame as England's pre-eminent Nonconformist cemetery. The name probably derives from 'Bone Hill' in recognition of the role of this site as a dumping ground first for animal bones from the medieval Smithfield market and then in 1549 for more than a thousand cartloads of human skeletons from the charnel house of St Paul's cathedral. Previously the dead had been buried in St Paul's churchyard until their flesh rotted before their bones were moved to the charnel house, supposedly to await the Resurrection. By the mid-16th century, however, this arrangement was decried as 'Popish' and the charnel house was demolished. The 'hill' formed by the bones is still visible in the raised ground level of the cemetery today.

A century later, the 1662 Act of Uniformity, which enforced prescribed formats for Church of England services and prayers, led to what became known as the Great Ejection. More than 2,000 clergy who refused to tow the line were deprived of their posts and there was a huge rise in Nonconformist or dissenting Christians practising their religion outside the established church. Bunhill Fields – unusual in not being attached to a church with a vicar required to follow official dogma – soon became London's prime burial ground for those who advocated freedom of conscience in religious practice. Among its inhabitants are John Bunyan (d.1688), author of *The Pilgrim's Progress*; Daniel Defoe (d.1731), author of *Robinson Crusoe*; Susannah Wesley (d.1742), mother of the founder of Methodism, whose house and chapel on the other side of City Road overlook the cemetery; hymn writer Isaac Watts (d.1748); and artist and poet William Blake (d.1827). The oddest memorial, however, must be that to Dame Mary Page (d.1729, aged 56), wife of a merchant and MP, whose tomb, in the central paved area, bears the epitaph: 'In 67 months, she was tap'd 66 times, had taken away 240 gallons of water, without ever repining at her case, or ever fearing the operation.'

More than 120,000 bodies, not counting the cartloads of bones from St Paul's, were buried at Bunhill Fields in the 200 years before it was closed in the 1850s. The site seems densely packed with gravestones, but in fact each of its 2,500 monuments could be taken as representing a further 50 corpses stacked underneath. The northern section was damaged during WW2 and subsequently laid out as a small park; the main axis that runs between City Road and Bunhill Row is a popular shortcut, making Bunhill Fields one of the most densely populated cemeteries for both the living and the dead.

20. Bunhill Fields, 38 City Rd, EC1Y 1AU

IN 67 MONTHS SHE WAS TAP'D 66 TIMES
Had TAKEN AWAY 240 GALLONS OF WATER
WITHOUT EVER REPINING AT HER CASE
OR EVER FEARING THE OPERATION

Plague Pits

The Bunhill Fields site was licensed as a plague pit in 1665–66 but there is some debate over whether it was used. Some 100,000 people (perhaps as much as a quarter of London's population) were wiped out by the Great Plague, so it is hardly surprising to find plague pits – huge holes lined in quicklime to form mass graves – throughout the city. Often the only evidence is a patch of undeveloped land, as with Islington Green between Upper Street and Essex Road. Other examples include Charterhouse Square in Farringdon, Golden Square in Soho and Knightsbridge Green off the Brompton Road.

For a sense of the scale necessary to cater for so many corpses, visit the Royal Oak Court estate off the appropriately named ㉑ **Pitfield Street**, just north of Bunhill Fields. Here a large stretch of raised, uneven ground running the entire length of the estate and a smaller patch beside the children's playground are claimed to be burial grounds 'pertaining to the Black Plague of 1665–1666'. The explanatory notices from Hackney Council also warn residents to keep off the grass – though there is no indication of whether the restriction is out of respect, from fear of contamination or simply a convenient means of reinforcing a council prohibition.

Ironically, it seems probable that the irregular distribution of the blocks of flats that form the estate came not from a desire to produce people-friendly landscaping but from the difficulty of finding solid ground in which to sink foundations. So green spaces for 20th-century social tenants were laid on the bones of the poor who had lived and died in the area 300 years earlier.

21. Pitfield St N1 6EL

Cross Bones

㉒ Cross Bones in Redcross Street in Southwark was also probably a plague pit, though it is better known as a burial ground for prostitutes, nicknamed 'Winchester Geese' because their activities were permitted only under licence from the Bishop of Winchester. A tapestry of ephemeral scraps of fabric, flowers and feathers clings to the municipal metal fencing of the memorial gateway in what seems an apt metaphor for the lives of those interred behind it. Inside is a makeshift-looking shrine with a Madonna surrounded by cheap jewellery, hearts, candles, an empty gin bottle and statues of geese.

Known until the mid-17th century as the Liberty of the Clink, this area of Southwark, directly opposite the City across the Thames, was London's pleasure ground. Activities outlawed within the City walls – from taverns to theatres and bear pits to brothels – were permitted and taxed by the bishop, who also held the post of chancellor to the king. As well as the reconstructed Globe theatre, you can see a further reminder of the area's history in the ruin of the great hall of Winchester Palace – itself something of an oddity – beside Southwark Cathedral, on the corner of Clink and Stoney Streets.

While the bishop was happy to profit from allowing prostitutes to ply their trade in life, they were excluded from Christian burial in death. The area of the episcopal parkland that now constitutes Cross Bones acted as a burial ground for 'single women' from the 12th century. By the mid-1800s it contained between 15,000 and 20,000 corpses of paupers and prostitutes, piled up in dense layers; in 1853 it was closed on the orders of parliament as being 'completely overcharged with the dead'. It served briefly as a fairground during the last decade of the 19th century and was later developed with commercial buildings and warehouses.

In the late 1980s, Transport for London acquired the site to build an electricity substation for the Jubilee Line extension. During an excavation led by the Museum of London, 148 bodies were exhumed and examined including the skeleton of a teenage girl buried during the final years of the cemetery's use. It seems that she had suffered several infections of syphilis, beginning as a child – perhaps following a vile practice where syphilitic men sought sex with a virgin in the belief it would effect a cure – before being repeatedly re-infected as a teenager. Almost one third of the excavated graves were of children under a week old and the majority of adult bodies were of women.

The Cross Bones memorial gate is the site of a monthly vigil as well as an annual Halloween ritual to 'remember the outcast' led by local poet and playwright John Constable. Ribbons commemorating the lives of Southwark characters reimagined by Constable are hung on the gate along with personal tributes to more recent 'outcasts'. Following campaigns for its preservation, part of the burial ground (still owned by TfL) has now been transformed into a somewhat sanitised garden that includes a dramatic wooden entrance canopy in the form of a goose wing and a central planter shaped like an infinity symbol. Its outsider edginess may have disappeared, but no doubt the trade-off would have been welcomed by many of its desperate and impoverished inhabitants.

22. Cross Bones, Redcross Way, SE1 1TA

St Pancras Old Church & Gardens

The burial ground of **㉓ St Pancras Old Church**, in Pancras Way just north of King's Cross, also fell victim to the demands of public transport when part of it was requisitioned to make way for the Midland Railway in the 1860s. The task of supervising the exhumations and reburials was given to Arthur Blomfield, the architect responsible for rebuilding the nave of Southwark Cathedral, which in 1665 had been granted the lease of Cross Bones.

Blomfield passed the task to his apprentice Thomas Hardy, who was to become better known as the author of some of the grimmest novels in the English language. Bringing dignity and an unexpected hopefulness to a gruesome undertaking, he ordered the displaced headstones to be arranged in pairs around the base of an ash tree, radiating from the trunk like a sunburst. Over time the tree grew so its roots writhed among the stones, distorting the arrangement and literally raising the dead. Intentionally or not, the effect was of a powerful symbol of life after death or resurrection.

Hardy was to draw on the experience 20 years later for his poem *The Levelled Churchyard* (1880–81),

> O passenger, pray list and catch
> Our sighs and piteous groans,
> Half stifled in this jumbled patch
> Of wrenched memorial stones!
>
> We late-lamented, resting here,
> Are mixed to human jam,
> And each to each exclaims in fear,
> 'I know not which I am!'

What became know as The Hardy Tree fell in a storm in 2022 and has since been removed, leaving the gravestones circling a vacant space. The St Pancras graveyard is also the site of the tomb of architect John Soane, which is said to have inspired the design of the iconic red telephone box (see page 75).

23. St Pancras Old Church & Gardens, Pancras Rd, NW1 1UL

Novo Beth Chaim Jewish Cemetery

Surrounded by brash new buildings at the heart of Queen Mary University on Mile End Road in Tower Hamlets, the **24** **Novo Beth Chaim Jewish Cemetery** is a much bleaker memento mori, with none of the overblown monuments or romantic landscaping that so often mask the reality of death. An oddity in being stranded in the centre of a university campus, it seems largely ignored by the students who walk past it every day. Flat slabs marking the graves are laid out in neat lines, with rows for adults interspersed with the smaller graves of children. Wild flowers grow among the stones in spring, but in winter only a few mature trees bring any relief to the largely unornamented markers.

The nearby Velho (old) Cemetery, part of which can still be glimpsed through a fence on Mile End Place, was established in 1657 when Oliver Cromwell granted Jews the right to hold religious services and burials, leading to an influx of Sephardim fleeing the Spanish and Portuguese inquisitions. The Novo (new) Cemetery was created in 1733 and the burial ground within Queen Mary is part of its 1855 extension. When the college acquired the land in 1974, it reburied some 7,000 corpses in Brentwood in Essex but this section was preserved because of the likelihood that close relatives of the dead might still be living. At one side is a circular enclosure marking the spot where a bomb fell in WW2, with a pedestal commemorating those whose graves were destroyed.

Some 2,000 graves lie within this relatively small area, many of them bearing Hispanic names such as Da Costa, Mendoza or Pezaro. The majority of slabs have inscriptions in English and Hebrew; many are cracked or crumbling. The burial ground's bleak appearance stems both from its lack of visitors and from the Sephardic tradition of eschewing upright headstones and monuments in favour of simple stones laid flat: a reminder that in death we are all equal.

24. Novo Beth Chaim Jewish Cemetery,
    Queen Mary University, Mile End Rd, E1 4NS

8.7 Brompton Cemetery & The Magnificent Seven

The Magnificent Seven cemeteries – Kensal Green, West Norwood, Highgate, Abney Park, Nunhead, Brompton and Tower Hamlets – were built in less than a decade from 1832, the work of private companies whose shareholders hoped to make a long-term buck from burying the dead. Previously Londoners had been buried in parish churchyards, but these had become increasingly overcrowded, threatening water supplies, air quality and the stability of neighbouring buildings. To placate the clergy, who relied on burials to supplement their income, the new cemeteries paid ten shillings to local parishes for each corpse they took.

㉕ Brompton Cemetery, between Fulham Road and Old Brompton Road in Kensington & Chelsea, is an oddity among the Magnificent Seven and in Britain as a whole in being the country's only nationalised cemetery. At the time of writing, bizarrely, it comes under the jurisdiction of the Department for Culture, Media and Sport. It is managed by Royal Parks on behalf of the Crown Estate, with all revenues (and debts) going to the UK Treasury.

The mastermind behind three of the new cemeteries – Brompton, Highgate and Nunhead – was Stephen Geary (1797–1854), an architect, inventor and entrepreneur who held patents for artificial fuel and street paving and was credited with the design of London's first gin palace (he later became teetotal in regret at his role in promoting the consumption of alcohol). Geary's London Cemetery Company was already working on Highgate and Nunhead when in 1837 he was appointed as architect to the Westminster and West London

Cemetery Company, which had bought 16 hectares of land – previously the site of a market garden and brickworks – from Lord Kensington for the creation of Brompton. To Geary's surprise, shareholders voted to hold a competition for the cemetery's design, which was won by the unknown Benjamin Baud, an assistant to Jeffry Wyattville, head of the judging panel. His own designs rejected, Geary resigned.

To compensate for the flat, uninspiring site and in the hope of attracting wealthy clients, the judges had chosen a grandiose scheme. But costs soon spiralled and by 1841 builder Philip Nowell was lending the company money to enable work to continue. When the shareholders began to notice structural defects, Nowell and Baud blamed each other; the company took Nowell's side and Baud unsuccessfully sued. There was further litigation following claims that Lord Kensington had never been entitled to sell the site in the first place, as well as problems in acquiring the strip of land needed to create an entrance on Fulham Road.

Brompton attracted only 89 burials in its first year and even by the late 1840s dividends were minute. In 1850 the Metropolitan Interments Act prohibited further burials in London's congested churchyards and crypts and gave the state powers of compulsory purchase over commercially run cemeteries. A deal was struck for Brompton, though the eventual settlement of £75,000 was less than half the money shareholders claimed to have spent. Two years later the act was repealed, making Brompton the only London cemetery to have fallen into state ownership.

Anomalous in its legal status, Brompton is also anomalous in the formality of its design.

Baud likened his monumental scheme to an open-air cathedral, with a 'great west door' or northern gatehouse on Old Brompton Road opening on to a 'nave' or central avenue stretching 600 metres to the 'high altar' of the octagonal domed chapel. In front of the chapel – inspired by the piazza of St Peter's in Rome – is a 'crossing' or great circle, 92 metres in diameter and surrounded by colonnades with catacombs underneath. Built of expensive Bath stone, the structures have little ornament beyond simplified rustication intended to convey a sense of strength.

The colonnades were to have had matching bell towers, but lack of funds meant only one was built. Projected chapels modelled on the Parthenon on either side of the circle were also abandoned. Despite the grandiose plan, other economy measures make the end result less impressive than it may have looked on paper – for instance, the back of the colonnades, intended to be covered in plaques commemorating the inhabitants of the catacombs below, are not Bath stone but dingy brick.

Several of the Magnificent Seven cemeteries had catacombs, but at Brompton this proved a poor business decision, with most of the shelves still

lying empty. Interment in a catacomb has its attractions: with coffins in full view rather than buried six feet under, it counters fears of being buried alive as well as making the dead seem more accessible to mourners. Both comforts are illusory: unlike in Italian catacombs, where skulls and bones are exposed, in heavily regulated Britain the dead are hermetically sealed in standardised lead cases, soldered shut. In fact, the coffins are triple: the corpse is laid in a plain wooden box that fits snugly inside a lead casket, which in turn is placed in an ornate wooden casing. In the Brompton catacombs, disturbingly, many of the wooden outer layers have decomposed and lie in fragments on the shelves, exposing the lead beneath.

Visitors today are taken through heavy **26 catacomb metal doors** – decorated with inverted torches to signify the extinguishing of life wrapped by snakes symbolising eternity – into an earth-floored passageway (another economy measure) lined by slate shelves. In most catacombs bodies are stored at right angles to the passage, feet first, but here the coffins on one side are laid parallel to the corridor, either through a flaw in the design or another economy measure. Purchase of a **27 catacomb shelf**, like the purchase

of a plot, allowed relatives to add other family members (usually in urns) as well as decorations such as railings or plaques. Amazingly, you can also still distinguish the preserved remnants of wreaths. Against expectations, there are no cobwebs because there are no insects – though the cemetery itself, which is mown sparingly to encourage biodiversity, is home to more than 200 species of moth as well as the expected squirrels, foxes and birds.

All London's cemeteries have monuments that are extraordinary, and Brompton is no exception. For aesthetic interest, visit the tomb of shipowner and art collector **28** **Frederick Leyland,** a copper-clad chest decorated with floral swirls designed in 1892 by pre-Raphaelite painter Edward Burne-Jones; for historical interest, you can find suffragette Emmeline Pankhurst, scientist John Snow (see page 97) and composer Constant Lambert among many others. Children's author Beatrix Potter (1866–1943) lived nearby and among the graves are names such as Nutkin and Fisher that she appropriated for her characters.

The 'marble' tomb of painter **29** **Valentine Prinsep** (d.1904) is notable for exposing shoddy practices as rusting metal reinforcing bars now show through a

structure that was probably sold in Italy as solid stone. Other monuments are bizarre confections made by combining pick-and-mix elements from catalogues – even the statue of singer **30** **Blanche Macchetta** (d.1896) has a standard mass-produced body topped by a bespoke head. Sioux chief Long Wolf (d.1892), who died of pneumonia while on tour with William Cody's Wild West Show, was buried here until 1997 when his body was returned to his native South Dakota; his tombstone, decorated with a wolf he drew on his deathbed, is still in place.

West Norwood, Highgate, Abney Park, Nunhead and Tower Hamlets cemeteries all went bankrupt and are now run by local boroughs, but Kensal Green is still owned by its founder, the General Cemetery Company. Plots are still available at Brompton: the lease on a grave is 75 years, but presumably interment in the catacombs gives you eternal shelf life.

8.8 Necropolis Railway

The ㉛ **Necropolis Railway** was an innovative solution to the overcrowding of London's graveyards – a bespoke service that could transport coffins and mourners to Brookwood Cemetery in Surrey, 25 miles from the capital. The London Necropolis Company was formed in 1852, partly in response to raised demand for plots following a cholera epidemic that had killed 15,000 Londoners a couple of years earlier. Working in partnership with London & South Western Railway, the company bought up 800 hectares of land on and around Woking Common, setting aside some 200 hectares to create the first stage of the biggest burial ground in the UK.

The plan was not without its opponents. For instance, the Bishop of London, Charles Blomfield, worried about the mix of classes and religions in trains carrying the living and dead between Waterloo and Brookwood: 'It may sometimes happen that persons of opposite characters might be carried in the same conveyance,' he warned a parliamentary select committee. 'For instance, the body of some profligate spendthrift might be placed in a conveyance with the body of some respectable member of the church, which would shock the feelings of his friends.' As the railway company was also understandably worried about the reaction of commuters to sharing carriages and facilities with Necropolis customers, a completely separate service was established, running from a new station in Leake Street near Waterloo.

Blomfield's concerns were answered by offering a choice of three classes of ticket to both living and dead, with coffins travelling first class treated to the luxury of more highly decorated compartment doors. There were also separate carriages for Nonconformists and Church of England members (each with a choice of class of travel); at Brookwood, the two denominations had separate stations serving the section of the cemetery reserved for their dead.

In 1902, when Waterloo Station was extended, the terminus for the Necropolis Railway was moved to 121 Westminster Bridge Road. You can still see the outside of the building: entrance for first-class ticket holders was via the stone-clad archway, with a driveway lined with bay and palm trees; the upper storeys housed a first-class waiting room and offices. Designed to impress, the façade has elaborate terracotta dressings including a curved pediment decorated with snakes as a symbol of eternity. The station offered five separate waiting rooms – two for members of the Church of England (divided between first and second classes), two for Nonconformists, and a communal third-class space (third-class passengers were relegated to a side entrance and took stairs rather than a lift to the platforms). Other facilities included a mortuary chapel where bodies could lie in state or funeral services could be held for mourners unwilling to make the trek out to Surrey.

Confusion over rail prices is not just a modern-day phenomenon. Fares for the Necropolis route were lower than for regular trains, so golfers travelling to the nearby West Hill golf course often used the service. Despite the low prices, Brookwood was not a success, with trains running only once or twice a week by the 1930s. The death knell came when the London terminus was bombed during WW2, with only the entrance building you see today surviving. British Rail, however, continued to carry coffins until 1988.

31. Necropolis Railway Terminus,
    121 Westminster Bridge Rd, SE1 7HR

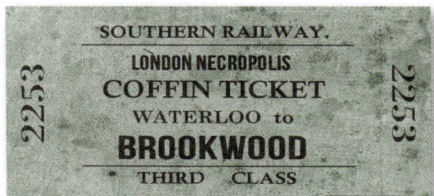

SOUTHERN RAILWAY.

LONDON NECROPOLIS

COFFIN TICKET

WATERLOO to

BROOKWOOD

THIRD CLASS

2253 2253

St Dunstan in the East, see page 279

Places of Worship

Places of Worship

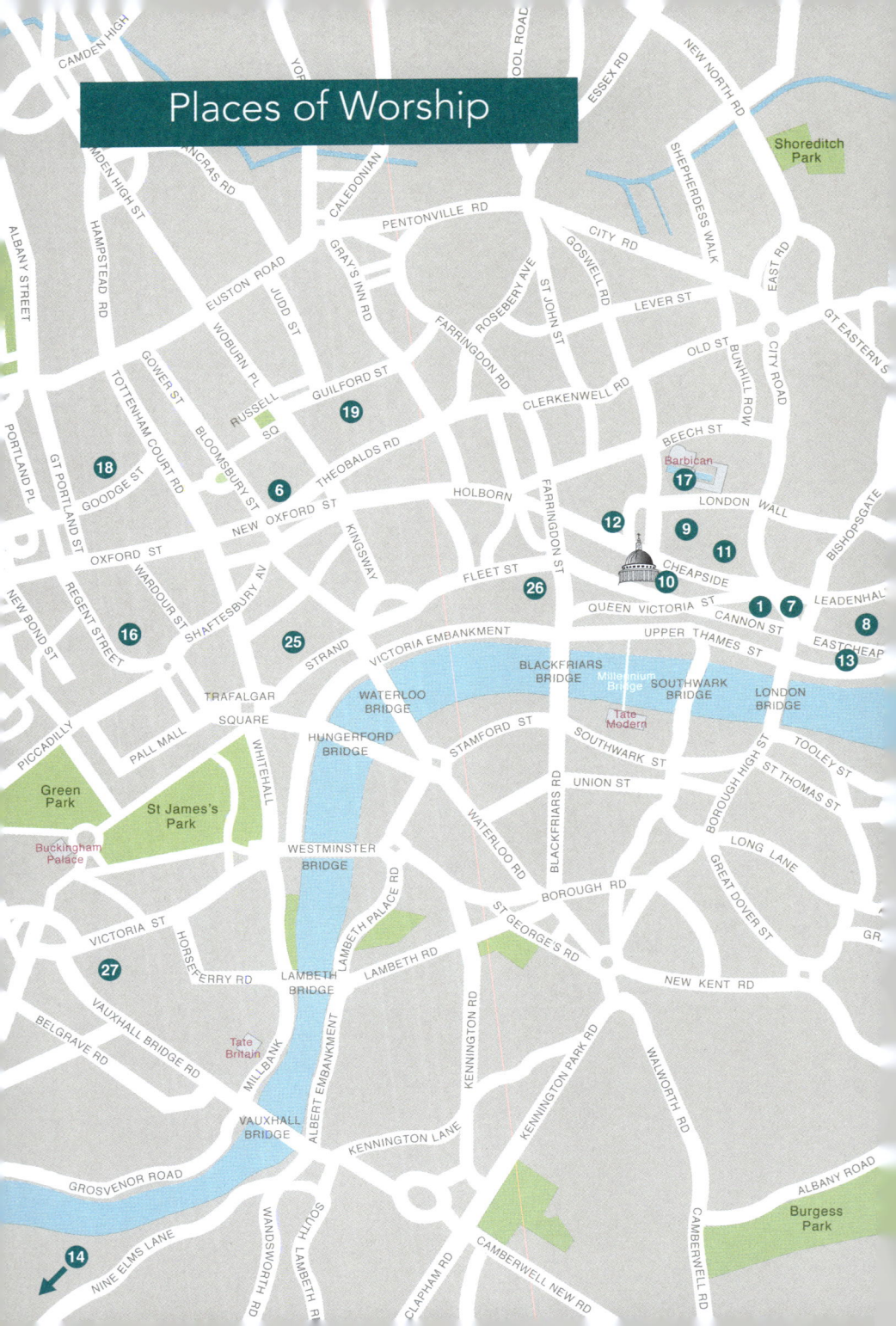

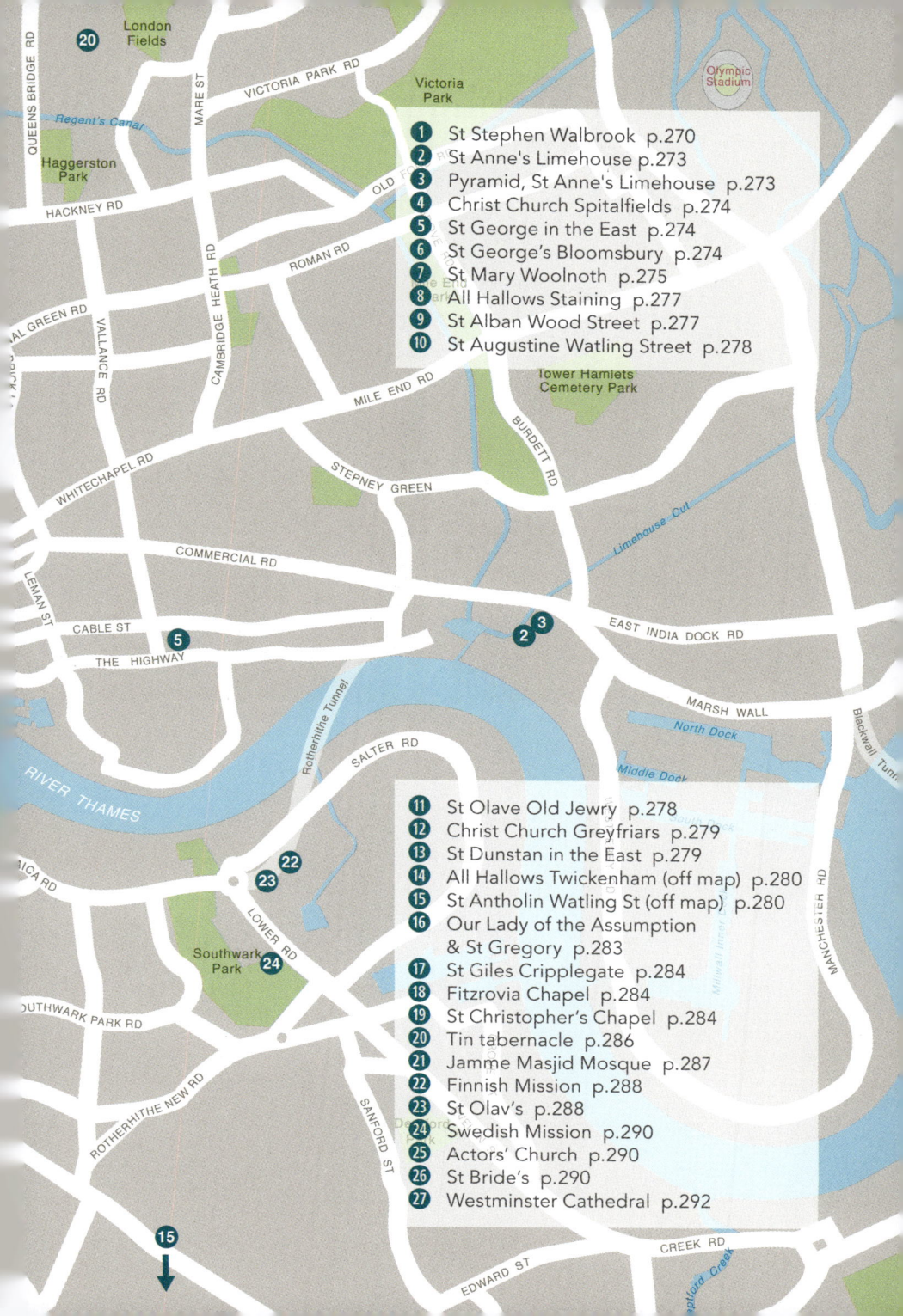

St Stephen Walbrook p.270
1. St Stephen Walbrook p.270
2. St Anne's Limehouse p.273
3. Pyramid, St Anne's Limehouse p.273
4. Christ Church Spitalfields p.274
5. St George in the East p.274
6. St George's Bloomsbury p.274
7. St Mary Woolnoth p.275
8. All Hallows Staining p.277
9. St Alban Wood Street p.277
10. St Augustine Watling Street p.278

11. St Olave Old Jewry p.278
12. Christ Church Greyfriars p.279
13. St Dunstan in the East p.279
14. All Hallows Twickenham (off map) p.280
15. St Antholin Watling St (off map) p.280
16. Our Lady of the Assumption & St Gregory p.283
17. St Giles Cripplegate p.284
18. Fitzrovia Chapel p.284
19. St Christopher's Chapel p.284
20. Tin tabernacle p.286
21. Jamme Masjid Mosque p.287
22. Finnish Mission p.288
23. St Olav's p.288
24. Swedish Mission p.290
25. Actors' Church p.290
26. St Bride's p.290
27. Westminster Cathedral p.292

9.1 St Stephen Walbrook

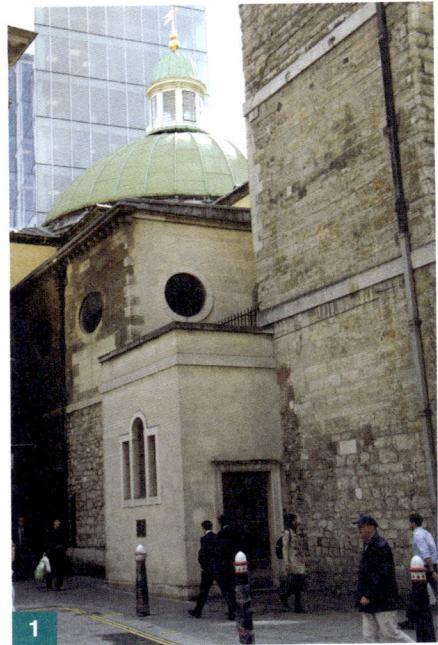

In the two decades following the Great Fire of London in 1666 Christopher Wren (1632–1723) was given the job of rebuilding more than 50 City parish churches, as well as St Paul's Cathedral. The programme, overseen by the Archbishop of Canterbury, the Bishop of London and the Lord Mayor, was to be financed by a tax on coal.

In a kind of public–private finance arrangement, any parish able to raise £500 could jump the queue and kick-start work on its church; the money, viewed as a deposit, would be repaid when enough tax revenue had accumulated. To start proceedings, parish officers would usually take the great architect out to lunch and shower him with gifts, in return for which their churches would find their way to the top of his to-do list.

The concentration of so many churches by a single architect within an area of just over a square mile makes Wren's City churches a London oddity in their own right – even if pressure of work made it impossible for him to design every detail of every new building. But one, St Stephen Walbrook, on Walbrook between Bank and Cannon Street, shows more signs of his own hand than most.

This was the only church begun in 1672, meaning the architect's attention was less divided, and it was also his own parish church, near his home of 15 Walbrook. Construction took five years and some of Wren's grander ideas were never realised, such as plans for colonnades that would lead from an imposing portico on the north front to an equestrian statue of Charles II at the end of the meat and fish market on the site now occupied by Mansion House. In 1850 the northern doorway was blocked up to keep out the stench from the market.

Originally surrounded by other buildings, the exterior of ❶ **St Stephen Walbrook** is unassuming and roughly finished; it is quite possible to walk past the entrance without noticing the vast dome that dominates the interior. Visitors enter up a steep flight of steps – necessary to accommodate the surviving crypt – into a porch before stepping into an interior flooded with light. The 19-metre-high dome, supported on eight soaring arches which are in turn supported by the columns that line the perimeter, was the first of its kind in England, allowing its architect to experiment with a form that was later to find fame at St Paul's. At St Stephen Walbrook, however, the construction method of lath and plaster facings on wooden frames allows for larger areas of glazing and a greater feeling of lightness than the masonry of St Paul's.

Nikolaus Pevsner described St Stephen Walbrook as one of the ten most important buildings in England, yet that did not stop property developer and Arts Council chair Peter Palumbo, who was also a churchwarden, from completely reconfiguring the interior by commissioning a new altar from sculptor Henry Moore. A massive, near-circular 2.5m diameter block of travertine marble with facets cut into its sides, it was carved in the early 1970s and finally installed in 1987. Its positioning – with pews arranged all around it – required a rare judgement from the Court of Ecclesiastic Causes Reserved, making the church interior an oddity in itself. As with many planning applications, approval was granted retrospectively.

The installation of the new altar took place under the incumbency of Edward

Chad Varah, vicar from 1953 until his retirement in 2003 at the age of 92. Near the entrance to the church, in a simple glass case, is an old-fashioned black telephone that commemorates his most enduring achievement – the founding of the Samaritans. Set up as a '999 for the suicidal', inspired by its founder's experience of burying a 14-year-old girl who had taken her own life because of ignorance, fear and shame at the onset of her periods, the organisation – and the phone you can see today – took its first call on 2 November 1953; Chad Varah, who also wrote and illustrated articles for children's comics like the *Eagle*, was able to use his journalist contacts to gain widespread publicity. The Samaritans – whose development he denounced towards the end of his life – has since grown to more than 200 branches with over 20,000 trained volunteers.

1. St Stephen Walbrook, EC4N 8BN

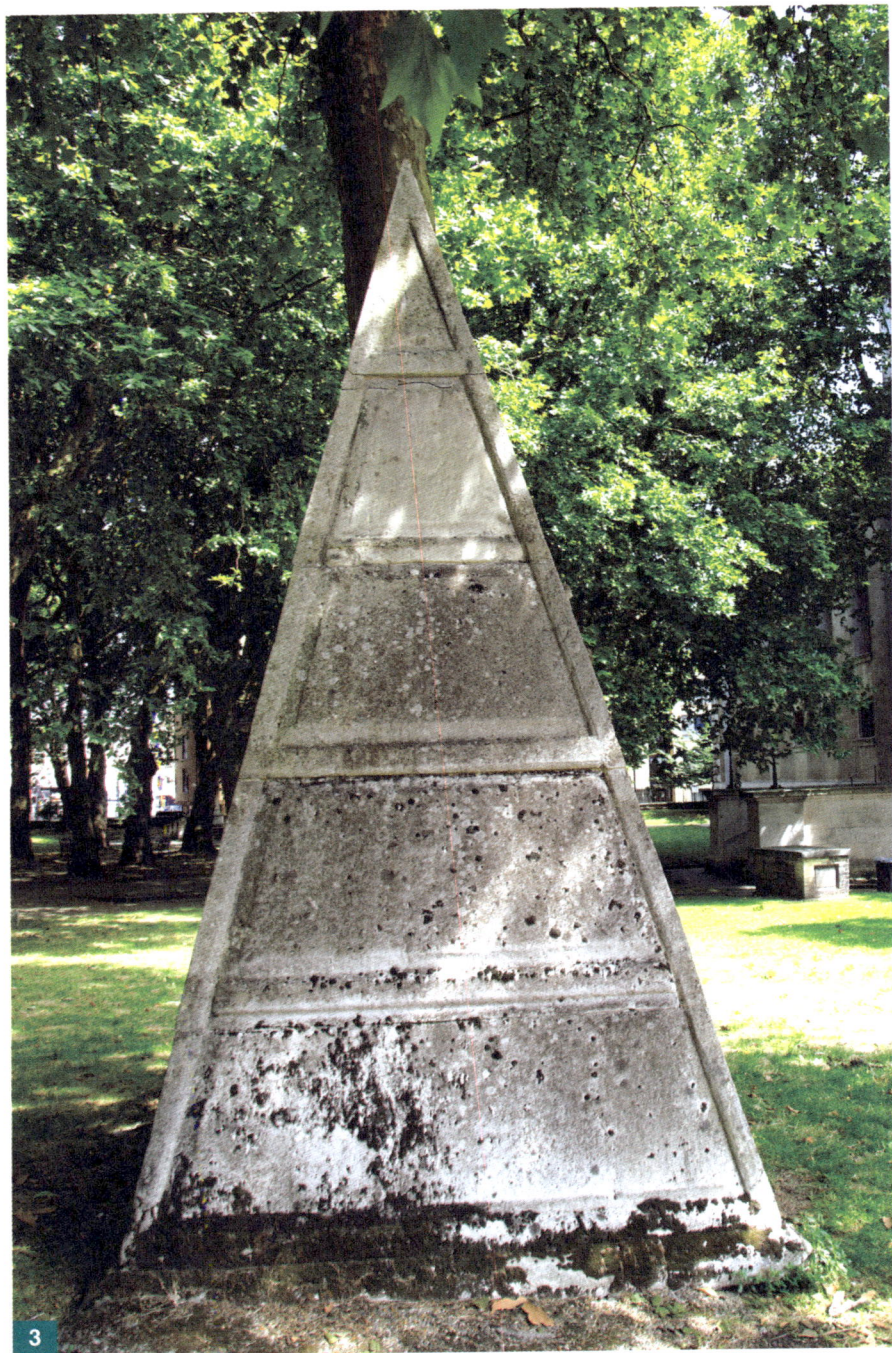

3

9.2 Churches of Nicholas Hawksmoor

Nicholas Hawksmoor (c. 1661–1736) was the great eccentric of the English Baroque – an architectural maverick who took the key elements of the classical tradition and rearranged them alongside ingredients from antiquity, the English Middle Ages and the Renaissance in ways that are always unexpected. Between 1711 and 1733 he designed six London churches and contributed to two others. Unapologetically muscular, almost brutal in appearance in comparison with their predecessors, each of these is an oddity – either as a whole, in detail, or because of subsequent alterations.

Hawksmoor won his church commissions in response to an Act of Parliament of 1710 which authorised the building of 50 new Anglican churches to counteract the increasing number of Nonconformist places of worship that had sprung up to serve London's growing population. The new buildings were to be financed through a continuation of the coal tax, instituted to help reconstruct London following the Great Fire. A commission led by the now elderly Christopher Wren was established to identify suitable land and Wren's protégé Hawksmoor was appointed as one of two surveyors. The commission was wound up after only twelve churches, known as the Queen Anne churches, were built.

Born into a Nottingham farming family, Hawksmoor joined Wren's office as a clerk at the age of 18 and worked with the master on St Paul's. Unlike his more wealthy contemporaries, he was never able to make a Grand Tour, so his knowledge of architectural precedent came from studying drawings and engravings – which may explain some of the oddity of his borrowings and their usage. While the commissioning committee for the Queen Anne churches may have expected economical, bland boxes, Hawksmoor

instead produced a series of distinctive buildings that are all recognisably his, while having a particular character of their own.

The first was St Alfege Greenwich at the southern end of Greenwich Church Street, a restoration of a building that had largely collapsed following a storm in 1710. Though the church was completed by 1714, consecration was delayed until 1718 because rebellious parishioners objected to the commissioners' insistence on installing a 'seat of distinction' for the royal family. Money was tight, which is perhaps why the interior decoration is minimal, with a plain ceiling and an east end with trompe l'oeil by James Thornhill – who was busy using similar effects in the nearby Painted Hall of the Old Royal Naval College (see page 218) – rather than elaborate carving. Lack of funds also led to the rejection of Hawksmoor's projected tower, designed to feature several of the bizarre baroque capitals carrying urns that decorate the roofscape, in favour of re-casing the relatively undamaged tower from the old church. Hawksmoor was to reuse his tower design for his next project, St Anne's Limehouse. St Alfege maximises dramatic impact through a heroic entrance front and powerfully articulated façades featuring a sequence of tall arched and smaller rectangular windows topped by exaggerated but completely non-functional keystones.

St Anne's Limehouse, Christ Church Spitalfields and St George in the East were each to take this drama and simplification to a new level, their power generated through the geometric arrangement of massive forms with a complete absence of decorative flourishes. ❷ St Anne's, at the junction of Commercial Road and Three Colt Street, also boasts the highest church clock in London: both the clock and the golden ball above it served as navigational aids for ships arriving in the docks. In the churchyard stands a mysterious lone **③ pyramid** inscribed 'The wisdom of Solomon' that may have been designed to sit between the two low towers at the rear or have been part of the original tower design – or could be an unused element from an entirely different project.

Hawksmoor was soon to go out of fashion, and the gloriously unfussy interior of his next church, **④ Christ Church Spitalfields**, at the junction of Commercial Street and Fournier Street, was refurbished in the mid-19th century to look like 'a Covent Garden opera box', according to the *Times*. An ambitious restoration programme begun in 1976, when the church had been neglected to the point of ruination, entailed the removal of a thousand bodies from the crypt as well as stabilising and strengthening the structure. Today the light and clarity of Hawksmoor's original design is fully apparent, with plain wooden panels at ground level giving way to elaborate capitals and decorated vaults as worshippers raise their eyes to heaven.

The most extraordinary Hawksmoor church today, however, is **⑤ St George in the East**, at the junction of Cannon Street Road and The Highway in Shadwell. Here you enter double doors at the west end, walk through a porch beneath the tower and find yourself not, as you might expect, in a nave lined by rows of lofty columns but in a small brick courtyard that culminates in a full-height window revealing another, smaller church within – like the start of a set of Russian dolls. St George was bombed in 1941, with the roof and interior entirely destroyed: initially a prefab – known as St George in the Ruins – was erected within the shell before the present church was built in 1964. The only hint of anything unusual from the outside is a glimpse of the new church's pitched roof through Hawksmoor's upper windows. Inside, it re-uses the apse from the original as well as the low rectangular side windows. The most glorious feature, however, is the view back towards Hawksmoor's magnificent tower through the full-height glazing.

The oddest element of **⑥ St George's Bloomsbury**, just east of Museum Street on Bloomsbury Way, is its spire, which features in Hogarth's 1751 engraving *Gin Lane*. Here a statue of George I, who died as the church was being built, stands on a steeply stepped pyramid supported by four massive heraldic beasts – two lions and two unicorns, each over 3 metres tall – above a tempietto with four pedimented porticoes. The crypt

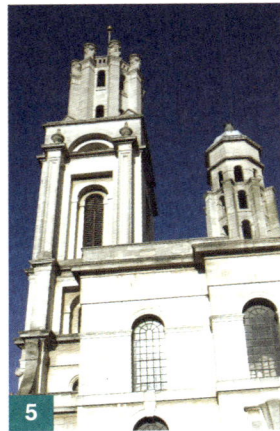

of the church now houses the Museum of Comedy. You couldn't make it up.

At the start of the 20th century the crypt of ❼ **St Mary Woolnoth** was sold to the City & South London Railway to become part of Bank Underground. Used by London's German-speaking Swiss community, the church is now supported on steel girders, with the mundane activities of the station carrying on unnoticed beneath. In the entrance lobby is a tiny coffee bar that attracts a steady stream of City workers.

The only Hawksmoor church in the City, St Mary Woolnoth gives the impression of bursting out of its small triangular site, with its eccentric entrance façade – a base with strident horizontal banding topped by twin square towers – making a flamboyant statement. Unlike Hawksmoor's other churches, it is square in plan. Though the Lombard Street façade has blind arches instead of glazing and the King William Street façade is largely masked by a screen intended to allow access to the station, the interior is flooded with light from four semi-circular windows at roof level. A memorial commemorates former rector John Newton (1725–1807), a slave trader turned abolitionist who described his conversion in the hymn 'Amazing Grace'.

St Mary Woolnoth features in T S Eliot's 1922 poem *The Waste Land* and several subsequent writers have also been attracted to the oddity of Hawksmoor's architecture. Psycho-geographer Iain Sinclair's *Lud Heat* (1975) explores mysterious cartographic connections between the six churches and puts forward the idea that this matrix attracts dark happenings including the Jack the Ripper murders; in his 1985 novel *Hawksmoor*, Peter Ackroyd used the eponymous architect as the model for a Satanist who partakes in human sacrifice in the creation of his buildings. But you don't need to theorise about evil secrets or invent mystical and murky connections to appreciate Hawksmoor's churches: their uncompromising oddness is manifest in their architecture alone.

2. St Anne's Limehouse,
   Three Colt St, E14 7HP
3. Pyramid, St Anne's Limehouse,
   Three Colt St, E14 7HP
4. Christ Church Spitalfields,
   Commercial St, E1 6LY
5. St George in the East,
   14 Cannon Street Rd, E1 0BH
6. St George's Bloomsbury,
   Bloomsbury Way, WC1A 2SA
7. St Mary Woolnoth, King William St,
   EC3V 9AN

5

6

7

13

9.3 Spires & Steeples

The City of London has several lone towers – forlorn survivors of churches that have been bombed or demolished, now standing like bemused time travellers in a forest of more recent buildings. The bombing mostly took place over the winter of 1940–41, during which London suffered some 70 devastating raids. The bulk of the demolition, however, was officially sanctioned: following a decline in population, the 1860 Union of Benefices Act legitimised the amalgamation of parishes and the destruction of under-used churches, many of them rebuilt only 200 years previously following the Great Fire of 1666.

One of the oldest survivors is **8 All Hallows Staining**, in Dunster Court off Mark Lane. The 12th-century church was largely unscathed by the Great Fire, but five years later its nave collapsed, probably because the foundations had been weakened by too many burials close to its walls. It was rebuilt in 1674, only to be demolished just over a century later when the parish was amalgamated with St Olave Hart Street, another Great Fire survivor. Surrounded by office buildings, All Hallows Staining's stand-alone tower looks distinctly old as well as odd, its walls faced in roughly dressed, rubble-like stone rather than the smooth surface of later buildings. The base dates from the 12th or 13th century, with the body of the tower built c. 1320 and the crenellations and windows added in the 18th and 19th centuries.

9 St Alban Wood Street was demolished and rebuilt in 1634, destroyed again in the Great Fire just over 30 years later, and rebuilt by Christopher Wren in Gothic style in 1685. It was badly damaged in the Blitz and the body of the church was finally razed in 1965. The elegant 28-metre-high tower now stands incongruously beside the

muscular 1960s headquarters of the City of London Police, Terry Farrell's overbearing, postmodern Alban Gate and an elegant Richard Rogers office block. Look carefully and you will see that it is now a private dwelling.

Other Wren steeples have been put to use to front new buildings. Bomb victim **10** **St Augustine Watling Street** gives drama and presence to St Paul's Cathedral School, its tower like the head of an animal with the body of the 1960s building snaking out behind it. Equally extraordinary are the remains of Wren's **11** **St Olave Old Jewry** just south of the Guildhall, demolished in 1877 apart from the tower and west wall, which were incorporated in the 1980s into a three-storey brick office building. New and old are knitted together with stone quoins and through the out-of-character casement windows you can glimpse potted plants and computers rather than marble columns or gilded mosaics.

10

12

Two Wren churches destroyed during WW2, ⑫ **Christ Church Greyfriars** on King Edward Street near St Paul's Underground and ⑬ **St Dunstan in the East** just west of the Tower of London, have been transformed into public gardens. The former uses box hedges to mark out the plan of the nave, with wooden towers, now supporting climbing plants, standing in for the columns that once held up the roof. The mix of rough-hewn walls, monumental stone pineapples that once graced the roof, and the tower itself make for an atmospheric space. The tower, as at St Alban, is a private residence: according to a sales pitch of 2008, when it was on the market for £4.5 million, it has three bedrooms distributed over ten floors, with a 360-degree open balcony at the top. From inside the garden you can catch glimpses of the ground-floor dining room while the dental practice next door is incongruously advertised on the first-floor windows.

14

14

St Dunstan was patched up rather than rebuilt by Wren following the Great Fire; a century later the walls were found to be sagging from the weight of the roof and the body of the church was completely rebuilt. Today leaves and tendrils weave through the tracery of the windows, but the drama of the building's destruction in the Blitz and the romance of its half-life as a survivor are more apparent from the blackened, ivy-encrusted exterior than from the blandly rendered inner walls.

When Wren's All Hallows Lombard Street was found to be structurally unsound in the 1930s, its tower was transported stone by stone 12 miles to the west to serve a new congregation. Designed by art deco architect Robert Atkinson, **14** **All Hallows Twickenham**, opposite Marlow Crescent on Chertsey Road, makes no attempt to integrate Wren's stone structure with its brick walls but rather maintains a distinct distance that allows both parts to

show their worth. The elaborate doorway on the otherwise unremarkable 17th-century tower has 'All Hallows Lombard Street' incised above it; inside are the beautifully carved wooden altarpiece, pews and chalice-shaped pulpit from the original church as well as several memorials to former City dwellers now languishing in obscurity in the suburbs. Most extraordinary is the oak gate that once stood outside the Lombard Street building, a memento mori carved with skulls and hourglasses and topped by macabre figures of death and time.

The top of the steeple of Wren's **15** **St Antholin Watling Street** met an even stranger fate. Brought down to earth and moved 7 miles south, it now stands in the middle of a small 1960s housing estate off Round Hill in Sydenham. Not much taller than the two-storey houses that surround it, an octagonal obelisk topped by a finial with a dragon weathervane is supported on an octagonal brick drum. Decoration is minimal – obviously the architect never imagined his work would be scrutinised at such close range.

St Antholin's was designed in 1682 to replace a predecessor destroyed in the Great Fire. Apparently the spire – praised by contemporaries and historians as 'very curious' and showing 'great powers of invention' – was the only one from Wren's 53 churches to be built entirely of stone rather than using a wooden frame with stone cladding. In 1829 the top portion was sold to printer Robert Harrild for £5, possibly because the extra weight of the solid stone threatened the entire structure with collapse. Harrild, a local churchwarden who had grown fond of Wren's spire during his daily commute to the City, transferred his prize to the grounds of his Sydenham home, Round Hill House, built four years earlier.

Harrild made his money from an invention: the composition roller, a more efficient means of inking printing presses that vastly speeded up the production of newspapers. Invention and folly have both survived – though the rest of St Antholin's was demolished in 1878 and Round Hill House in the 1960s.

8. All Hallows Staining,
   Mark Lane, EC3R 7AA
9. St Alban Wood Street, EC2V 7AF
10. St Augustine Watling Street,
    2 New Change, EC4M 9AD
11. St Olave Old Jewry,
    St Olave's Court, EC2V 8EX
12. Christ Church Greyfriars,
    King Edward St, EC1A 7BA
13. St Dunstan in the East,
    Dunstan's Hill, EC3R 5DD
14. All Hallows Twickenham,
    138 Chertsey Rd, TW1 1EW
15. St Antholin's spire, Round Hill, SE26 4RG

15

9.4 Diplomatic Immunity

16

Between the reign of Elizabeth I in the second half of the 16th century and the end of the 18th century, Roman Catholic worship was illegal in England under Acts of Parliament introduced to uphold the status of the Church of England against both Protestant Nonconformism and Catholicism. Participants were fined or imprisoned, or in the case of priests, subject to the death penalty. Unsurprisingly, there were no Catholic churches – except in private houses or on land belonging to the embassies of Catholic countries, whose priests were protected from prosecution by diplomatic immunity. **16 Our Lady of the Assumption and St Gregory** in Warwick Street, Soho, is London's only surviving embassy chapel.

Built at the back of 23–24 Golden Square, which from 1724 to 1788 was the home of the Portuguese and then Bavarian ambassadors, the chapel had a private entrance from the house as well as discreet public access for local worshippers through a narrow passage from Warwick Street. It was attacked during the anti-

Catholic Gordon Riots of 1780 and a hundred guards, sleeping on straw in the chapel and house, were sent to protect the premises. When the Bavarian ambassador left in 1788, he sold the house to the Roman Catholic Bishop of London, who immediately began to restore the now dilapidated chapel. It was hoped that if the Warwick Street façade could be made as inconspicuous as possible, the new building would pass almost unnoticed – though thick walls and fire-resistant metal doors were installed as precautionary measures.

The finished building, by architect Joseph Bonomi the Elder, who lived at 16 Golden Square, looks more like a utilitarian Nonconformist chapel than the flamboyant architectural statements associated with continental Catholicism. Built entirely in plain brick, the street elevation has three doors with arched fanlights, making the ground floor look like a small terrace of houses to the casual passer-by. Above are three blind arches, with windows on either side, topped by a plain pediment. Inside, the space is surprisingly light thanks to an unexpected series of windows above the gallery at the sides. The simple rectangle culminates in a richly decorated apse, its gilded mosaics designed by Westminster Cathedral architect John Francis Bentley (see p.293) towards the end of the 19th century.

Apart from the apse, and stars and angels added to the façade in the 1950s when the original bricks were stained red, little has been altered since the chapel's completion. The legal position may have changed, but it is still easy to imagine slipping through the doorway to an intimately scaled space where subversive acts punishable by death took place daily.

16. Our Lady of the Assumption &
St Gregory, Warwick St, W1B 5LZ

9.5 Surprising Survivors

As London has enjoyed – or suffered – successive waves of development, its religious buildings have often survived as reminders of the different layers of its history. For instance, Great Fire survivor **⓱ St Giles Cripplegate** still stands within the 1960s Barbican Estate, while other places of worship have clung on in even more surprising ways, doubling as arts venues or perhaps most bizarrely enduring conversion into a health club, as with the chapel of the former Claybury Hospital in Woodford Green.

Serving the Sick

Stranded in the newly created Pearson Square, like a fairytale princess awakened to a baffling future, the former Middlesex Hospital Chapel has made a near-miraculous recovery. Renamed **⓲ Fitzrovia Chapel** to comply with the branding of the luxury apartments that now surround it, the modest red-brick building looks more like a Nonconformist chapel from a northern industrial town than the focal point of a new London piazza.

Saved from demolition by being listed, in the early 2000s the chapel was propped up in the middle of a flattened building site while four floors of car parks were excavated around it. In fact, this was the second time the building had survived the destruction of its neighbours: designed in 1891, it did not open for another 30 years as the 18th-century hospital was demolished and rebuilt around it. Its architect John Loughborough Pearson died in 1897 and the richly decorated Italian gothic interiors, including mosaics executed by Italian craftsmen, were completed by his son Frank.

⓳ St Christopher's Chapel at Great Ormond Street near Russell Square was also saved by listing when the rest of the hospital was demolished in the 1980s. In this case, remarkably, the entire structure – originally at first-floor level – was underpinned by a huge concrete raft before being lowered to the ground and moved on greased slides to its new position. You can now find it just beyond the hospital's reception area, on the ground floor of the Viceroy Club Building.

Described by Oscar Wilde as 'the most delightful private chapel in London', St Christopher's could not be a greater contrast to the functional buildings around it. As you turn from an anonymous hospital corridor into what at first seems a very ordinary room, you suddenly notice an alabaster porch leading into a glowing, jewel-like interior – an effect not unlike climbing into a wardrobe and emerging into the magical land of Narnia. Designed in 1875 by Edward Middleton Barry, son of the architect of the Houses of Parliament, the chapel is distinctly Byzantine in feel, with every surface decorated in a bedazzling array of marble and gilding, murals and mosaics, many of them depicting children or animals. The chapel is an extremely moving place to visit – not least because of the window ledges piled with stuffed toys donated by parents of children the hospital was unable to save.

17. St Giles Cripplegate,
    Fore St, EC2Y 8DA
18. Fitzrovia Chapel,
    2 Pearson Square, W1T 3BF
19. St Christopher's Chapel,
    Great Ormond Street hospital,
    WC1N 3JH

17

18

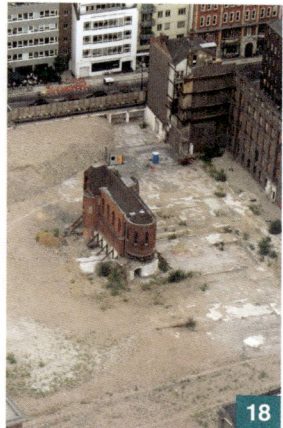

18

19

19

Tin Tabernacles

Never expected to survive for 150 years or more are the churches known as tin tabernacles – prefabricated buildings made of galvanised corrugated iron, a material invented for roofing in 1829 and adapted to produce prefabricated buildings from the 1850s. There are three remaining tin tabernacles in London – Shaftesbury Hall near Bowes Park station in Haringey, built as a chapel for railway workers in 1885 and at present a call centre for the Samaritans; the Kilburn tin tabernacle in Cambridge Avenue, built in 1863 and used as a home for the sea cadets since the 1950s, when its interior was transformed to resemble a ship; and the Sight of Eternal Life Church near the junction with Grand Union Crescent on Shrubland Road in Hackney, built in 1858 and claimed by the Hackney Society to be the oldest surviving example of an iron church in the world.

Erected in just ten weeks by Messrs Tupper and Company, a City of London firm specialising in iron-and-timber church buildings, the **20 Shrubland Road chapel** cost its original owners just £1,250. The client was a Presbyterian congregation based in Dalston, and the chapel was designed to hold up to 500 worshippers. The church was used by Sight of Eternal Life from 1971.

From the outside, the building is immediately recognisable as something special: painted white, with an undersized grey steeple topped by a wonky finial, a gothic doorway and small, symmetrically arranged lancet windows with blue-painted frames, it looks like a crinkly version of an early American clapboard chapel that has somehow found its way to suburban London. The original construction used uniform sheets of corrugated iron attached by simple rivets to a timber frame; the iron was at some point replaced by corrugated asbestos. Decoration is restricted to the

windows, with glazing in the tower and side elevations embellished with a trinity of rosettes and stylised flowers. Inside, the iron roof trusses have Gothic spandrels and there is a raised reading platform with twisted balusters.

Hackney's tin tabernacle was put up for sale at an asking price of £3 million in 2011 and was again for sale just over a decade later. Chapels like this were denigrated by A W N Pugin and other defenders of the established church as 'industrial imposters', but this one at least has survived the demolition forced on the much grander City churches as well the deluge of gentrification.

20. Tin tabernacle, 76 Shrubland Rd, E8 4NH

Jamme Masjid Mosque

The character of London's boroughs may change, but the East End has achieved a degree of continuity as the home of successive influxes of immigrants, from Huguenot silk weavers fleeing persecution in Catholic France in the 1680s, through Jews escaping Eastern Europe from the late 19th century, to Bangladeshi refugees from the war of independence in the 1970s. The building that now houses the ㉑ **Jamme Masjid Mosque** on the corner of Brick Lane and Fournier Street in Spitalfields is unique in having served the changing population's often opposed religious ideologies with little alteration to its exterior form.

A dominant and dignified presence on the street, with pedimented brick elevations, arched windows and a Serliana with stone dressings and handsome stone door surrounds, the building was designed in 1743 as a Protestant church (La Neuve Eglise) for Huguenot refugees, with a school next door. Surprisingly for a religious building, the cellars were occupied by wine merchants and brewers until the end of the 19th century. In 1809 the site was leased by the London Society for Promoting Christianity among the Jews, which provided board for Jewish children whom it hoped to convert, while in the church sermons were delivered to large congregations by a vicar who had himself converted from Judaism. A decade later the site became a Methodist chapel.

The Methodists remained in residence for almost 80 years, after which the lease and then ownership were transferred to Machzike Hadath (Upholders of the Faith), a society of Jews recently arrived from Central Europe and Russia who advocated stricter observance than most established communities. The chapel was adapted by its new owners and operated as the Spitalfields Great Synagogue until 1975. It re-opened as a mosque a year later, with the addition of a space-age minaret, and is now a focal point for East London's Muslim community. A remarkable survivor, it demonstrates in microcosm the near-miraculous way a city's fabric can be adapted to the needs of a fluctuating population.

21. Jamme Masjid Mosque, Brick Lane, E1 6QL

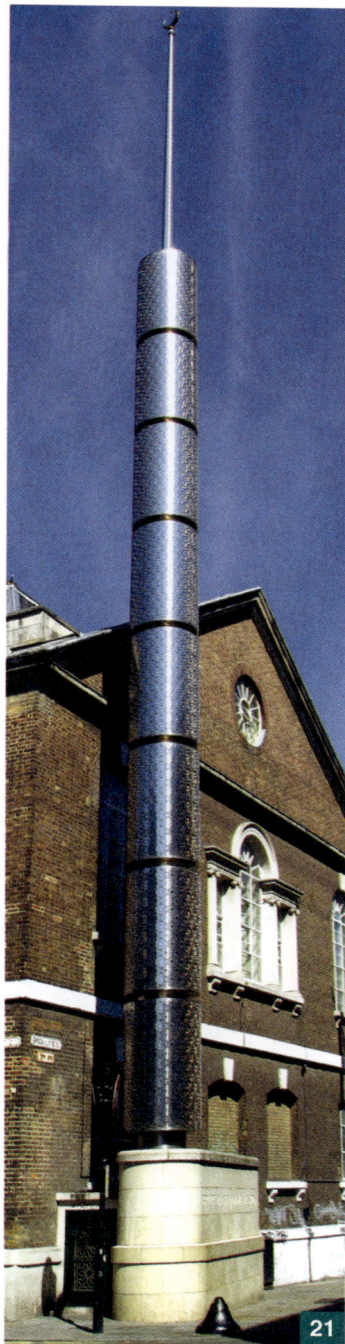

9.6 Serving the Workplace

There are religious centres catering for London's diverse communities scattered throughout the capital, their locations and histories reflecting changing demographics. Some, like the blue-domed Russian church in Chiswick, built in 1998, or Europe's largest Hindu temple, the magnificently elaborate Shri Swaminarayan Mandir in Neasden, opened in 1995, are traditional buildings reimagined for new locations. Others, like the classic 1930s Astoria cinema in Seven Sisters Road, Finsbury Park (later the Rainbow Theatre, where Jimi Hendrix first burned a guitar), or the 1914 Apollo cinema in Stoke Newington Road, now a mosque (see page 59), are leisure venues repurposed for new audiences. The examples below derive their oddity not from representing different faiths or nationalities, but as religious centres created for or adopted by different professions. All but one are still flourishing, despite the changes in working conditions since their foundation.

Within a few streets of each other, near the southern entrance to the Rotherhithe Tunnel, are three buildings created to serve Scandinavian seamen passing through the Port of London. Britain was a major importer of lumber from Scandinavia and the Baltic from the mid-17th century and the first Swedish church opened in Wapping in 1727. Over the next 150 years, as the docks expanded to become the world's largest port, Surrey Commercial Docks (now Surrey Quays) became the main point of entry for Scandinavian trade. London's docks suffered extensive damage during WW2 and Surrey Commercial Docks eventually closed in 1969. But the Finnish and Norwegian seamen's missions remain, now catering for London's landlubber Scandinavian population.

These churches have an oddity value not just as examples of Scandinavian architecture relocated to London, but by continuing to offer the social facilities and home-from-home provided for their original worshippers. The ㉒ **Finnish Mission** on Albion Street must surely be the only church in London with a sauna attached. The church itself – a rectangular room with unfussy wood detailing and an altar wall faced in slate – is divided from the café only by a sliding screen. Simple columns support a gallery housing a library, its balustrade used to air duvets from the hostel the mission still runs. From the outside, the complex could easily be mistaken for an elegant low-rise block of flats, were it not for the dramatic, skeletal bell tower that stands alongside it. Designed in 1958 by Cyril Mardall-Sjöström, the son of a Finnish architect and English opera singer who took his mother's maiden name to become the 'M' in the highly successful architectural practice YRM, the mission retains its link with the sea through a model boat suspended from the church ceiling and a rector who conducts services at sea on request.

The Norwegian Church, ㉓ **St Olav's**, further west down the same street, also looks comfortingly domestic – if you ignore the spire. Dating from 1927 and built of red brick with simple stone dressings, its most prominent reminders of home are the lettering above the elaborate door surround and the glittering Viking-ship weathervane. As with the Finnish Mission, the building's religious function is literally relegated to the background: from the porch you enter a large space for socialising with no partition between it and the narrower church behind. In the lobby are simple brass plates with long lists of individuals lost at sea along with a statue of St Olav, King of Norway from 1015 to

1028. During WW2 the church served the government in exile, and King Haakon VII used it to broadcast speeches to the Norwegian people living under Nazi rule.

Built in 1964 as a remodelling of an earlier church on the site, the ㉔ **Swedish Mission** in Lower Road closed in 2012. Again, the first point of contact is the secular part of the site, with the church and its modest tower tucked in behind. The complex serves as a showcase for post-war Swedish design, with its brick street elevation punctured by a glorious coloured glass wall and copper-clad door. It was listed at the end of 2014 and its fate at the time of writing is uncertain.

Other London churches have been adopted by, rather than created for, particular communities. Designed by Inigo Jones in 1631, St Paul's Covent Garden has long been known as the ㉕ **Actors' Church**. The plan is an oddity in itself: the imposing pedimented portico on the Covent Garden piazza is no more than a piece of theatre, sheltering only a false door behind the altar, with the church entered discreetly through the churchyard at the back. Otherwise, the building is a simple brick rectangle with a plain interior: its Puritanically inclined patron, the Earl of

Bedford, allegedly asked the architect for a church 'not much better than a barn', to which Jones replied: 'Then you shall have the handsomest barn in England.' Despite its lack of interior drama, its location means the church has been associated with the acting community since the opening of the nearby Theatre Royal in Drury Lane in 1663. Today its walls are lined with plaques to actors and dancers as diverse as Marie Lloyd, Vivien Leigh, Boris Karloff, Stanley Holloway, Robert Helpman, Ivor Novello, Don Ross ('Past King Rat') and Hattie Jacques (squeezed ignominiously behind the reception desk).

Despite the dispersal of newspaper offices to sites all over London, ㉖ **St Bride's**, tucked between two alleys just off the east end of Fleet Street, retains its place as the journalists' church. A small brass plaque at the entrance commemorates the 300th anniversary of the founding of the first daily newspaper, the *Daily Courant* in 1702, and the pews bear the names of the sponsors who paid for their installation, ranging from the *Daily Star* and *OK!* to the *Sunday Telegraph* and *Financial Times*. 'Quality' newspapers tend to have dignified gold lettering on black backgrounds while 'red tops' have shouting logos on red backgrounds. The journalists' altar, in the north aisle, is piled with framed photographs and information commemorating those who lost their lives in recent wars; alongside it is a plaque remembering 18 reporters from around the world who died covering the Iraq conflict.

Designed by Christopher Wren following the destruction of the Great Fire and badly damaged during WW2, the St Bride's interior, with its lofty vaulted ceiling and clear geometry, is a glorious example of English Baroque. One of the largest and most expensive of the Wren churches, it is probably best known architecturally for its spire, the architect's tallest steeple after St Paul's, which was added some 25 years after completion of the body of the church. Made up of four octagonal drums of diminishing size set one on top of the other, each with eight arched openings, it is said to have inspired local baker William Rich to create the first tiered wedding cake in 1703, the year after the spire's erection.

The extensive crypts – formed from the remains of six previous churches on the site – were used for burials until a cholera plague of 1854 led parliament to ban future interments in the City's overcrowded sites. Today they house an exhibition about the church's history and links with the printing industry, sponsored by news agency Reuters, as well as a dress belonging to the wife of baker William Rich. With the decline of print, might the spire – or even name – of St Bride's inspire the seemingly unstoppable wedding industry to adopt the church as its own?

22. Finnish Mission,
      33 Albion St, SE16 7HZ
23. St Olav's, 1 Albion St, SE16 7JB
24. Former Swedish Mission,
      120 Lower Rd, SE16 2UB
25. Actors' Church, Bedford St, WC2E 9ED
26. St Bride's, Fleet St, EC4Y 8AU

26

9.7 Westminster Cathedral

27 **Westminster Cathedral**, the mother church of the Catholic Church in England and Wales, is an oddity for at least three reasons: first, in re-using the walls of a former prison as its foundations; second, in borrowing the architecture of the schismatic Byzantine church for the seat of Roman Catholicism in the UK; and third, for the fact that more than 120 years after the foundation stone was laid, the interior remains largely unfinished.

The site of the cathedral was originally marshland reclaimed by the monks who owned Westminster Abbey; subsequently it was used as a market, fairground, maze and ring for bull-baiting. From 1834 it accommodated the Westminster House of Correction, a panopticon in the shape of a shamrock or ace of clubs, whose near-circular design enabled warders, God-like, to observe the cells of any of its 900 inmates from a single central position. In theory, the prisoners, knowing that they could be overseen at any time, regulated their own behaviour. The prison was demolished in 1885 and its foundations formed part of the cathedral designed a decade later by John Francis Bentley.

Approaching the building from Victoria Street, you are confronted by a gingerbread confection of banded red brick and cream Portland stone with an 83-metre-high bell tower topped by a viewing platform and arcades supporting a dome. The entrance front is a disorderly amalgam of borrowings from Byzantine and Venetian architecture reworked using the materials and colour scheme of the neighbouring London mansion blocks. A confusing array of small domes gives no clue about the interior layout; other motifs include screened windows that might be more at home in a harem and arcaded balconies supported by underpowered columns festooned with medallions depicting early archbishops. The overall effect is so unlike a traditional cathedral that UKIP supporters mistook the building for a mosque, complaining about 'liberal bias' following a BBC news report that used it as a background.

Unlike a traditional Byzantine church, the cathedral has no narthex or entrance lobby, allowing for an uninterrupted view from exterior doors to high altar. Inside, the crazy exuberance of the façade gives way to a series of profoundly gloomy caverns, with the decoration of the body of the church limited to marble cladding on the lower storey. Raise your eyes, and instead of sparkling golden domes representing the glories of heaven you see only a sequence of black holes, like a giant's empty eye sockets. The sooty brick arches seem more appropriate to an industrial building, with the full weight and scale of the structure exposed rather than camouflaged with gothic tracery or uplifting decoration. To call it odd is an understatement: it is both magnificent and deeply unsettling, as if the pretentions of religion have been stripped bare to reveal the inglorious edifice beneath.

Bentley died in 1902, a year before the exterior was finished, and left few drawings for the interior. So over the next century individual chapels were decorated piecemeal by mosaicists appointed by successive archbishops and committees, in a variety of styles that have often caused controversy. Current plans include a mosaic designed by Tom Phillips RA for the Chapel of St George and the English Martyrs that depicts the Tyburn gallows (see page 234) where St John Southwark, whose body will lie at the entrance, was executed in 1654 for his Catholic faith.

The ground floor of the cathedral is lined with over a hundred different types of marble from 24 countries including surprises such as Ireland, Norway, Chile, Brazil and the US. At times it feels as if

it could double as a marble showroom. Mounted on pillars that line the nave, the limestone low reliefs depicting the Stations of the Cross, installed between 1915 and 1918, are by sculptor and type designer Eric Gill, a convert to Catholicism whose diaries, discovered posthumously, detail extramarital affairs, incest with his daughters and sisters and bestiality. He used himself as a model for Christ. Elegantly stylised and aptly described by their creator as 'a statement without adjectives', the works caused uproar, with letters to the press describing the initial examples as 'grotesque and undevotional'. Gill's suggestion was to cover them with a sheet and wait until he had produced more.

It is worth making a trip to the top of the tower, where you can see the cathedral stretched out before you with its three green copper-clad domes and red brickwork interleaved with cream piping. Return to the extraordinary interior, contemplate the origin of the walls beneath your feet, and pray that like the Piranesi *Carceri d'invenzione* ('Imaginary Prisons') it strangely resembles, Westminster Cathedral may remain forever gloriously unfinished.

27. Westminster Cathedral,
    42 Francis St, SW1P 1QW

NO SMOKING
It is against the law to
smoke in these premises

Woolwich Ferry, see page 324

Getting Around

Map labels:

Camden Lock

Camden High

CAMDEN HIGH ST

YORK WAY

CALEDONIAN RD

PENTONVIL

FINCHLEY ROAD

PRINCE ALBERT RD

London Zoo

Regent's Park

Outer Circle

ALBANY STREET

CAMDEN HIGH ST

PANCRAS RD

GRAY'S INN RD

ABBEY ROAD

PARK RD

HAMPSTEAD RD

EUSTON ROAD

JUDD ST

THEOBALDS RD

ST JOHN'S WOOD RD

LISSON GROVE

WOBURN PL

GOWER ST

RUSSELL SQ

GUILFORD ST

EDGWARE RD

MARYLEBONE ROAD

BAKER ST

MARYLEBONE HIGH ST

PORTLAND PL

TOTTENHAM COURT RD

BLOOMSBURY ST

NEW OXFORD ST

KINGSWAY

Paddington Basin

SEYMOUR PL

GT PORTLAND ST

GOODGE ST

OXFORD ST

WARDOUR ST

SHAFTESBURY AV

SUSSEX GDNS

SEYMOUR STREET

WIGMORE ST

REGENT STREET

OXFORD ST

NEW BOND ST

BAYSWATER RD

PARK LANE

STRAND

VICTORIA EM

Hyde Park

TRAFALGAR SQUARE

WATERLOO BRIDGE

Kensington Park

PICCADILLY

Green Park

PALL MALL

WHITEHALL

HUNGERFORD BRIDGE

QUEEN'S GATE

EXHIBITION RD

BROMPTON RD

SLOANE STREET

KNIGHTSBRIDGE

St James's Park

Buckingham Palace

WESTMINSTER BRIDGE

LAMBETH PALACE RD

LAMBETH RD

PALACE RD

GROSVENOR PL

VICTORIA ST

HORSEFERRY RD

LAMBETH

ALBERT BRIDGE

Battersea Park

TOWN RD

NINE

CLAPHA

1	Lower Robert Street p.300	10	Cabmen's shelter, Russell Square p.306
2	Exit on Savoy Place p.300	11	Gants Hill Underground (off map) p.309
3	Savoy Court p.301	12	Waterloo International p.311
4	Wood-paved road p.303	13	Blackfriars p.312
5	Horse Hospital p.303	14	King William Street p.314
6	Stables Market p.303	15	Aldwych p.314
7	St Mary's Hospital p.304	16	Down Street p.314
8	Mounting block (outside the Athenaeum Club) p.304	17	Brompton Road p.316
		18	Kingsway Tramway Subway p.317
9	Drinking fountain & cattle trough p.304	19	Model of London Bridge p.318
		20	Coping stones p.319

Getting Around

11
23

London Fields

Regent's Canal

Victoria Park

Shoreditch Park

Haggerston Park

Mile End Park

35

HACKNEY RD

UPPER ST

ESSEX RD

NEW NORTH RD

SHEPHERDESS WALK

KINGSLAND

QUEEN

ROMAN RD

OLD FORD RD

GROVE RD

CITY RD

GOSWELL RD

GT JOHN ST

LEVER ST

EAST RD

CITY ROAD

GT EASTERN ST

BETHNAL GREEN RD

VALLANCE RD

CAMBRIDGE HEATH RD

9

OLD ST

BUNHILL ROW

4

BEECH ST

BRICK LANE

STEPNEY GREEN

KENWELL RD

ARTERHOUSE ST

FARRINGDON ST

Barbican

LONDON WALL

BISHOPSGATE

COMMERCIAL ST

WHITECHAPEL RD

WHITECHAPEL RD

COMMERCIAL RD

CHEAPSIDE

QUEEN VICTORIA ST

CANNON ST

LEADENHALL ST

EASTCHEAP

MANSELL ST

LEMAN ST

CABLE ST

THE HIGHWAY

37

13

UPPER THAMES ST

14

19

26 Tower of London

27

Rotherhithe Tunnel

SALTER RD

KFRIARS IDGE

Millennium Bridge

SOUTHWARK BRIDGE

LONDON BRIDGE

TOWER BRIDGE

Tate Modern

SOUTHWARK ST

21 20

TOOLEY ST

25

31

UNION ST

22 24

ST THOMAS ST

BERMONDSEY ST

TOWER BRIDGE ROAD

DRUID ST

JAMAICA RD

RIVER THAMES

LOWER RD

BLACKFRIARS RD

BOROUGH HIGH ST

LONG LANE

ABBEY ST

Southwark Park

ROUGH RD

GREAT DOVER ST

GRANGE RD

NEW KENT RD

OLD KENT RD

EVELYN ST

Deptford Park

Legend

28 29 30 32

10.1 Lower Robert Street

① **Lower Robert Street**, one of London's oddest roads, is the only survivor from a warren of underground streets and tunnels created over 250 years ago to run beneath some of the city's most exclusive homes. A single-track carriageway, flanked by narrow cobbled pavements, it twists downwards from York Buildings through a vaulted tunnel that seems hewn out of rock. It then turns sharply into a roofed passageway with storerooms on either side before emerging through a tall and graceful opening – decorated with a Greek key pattern frieze – on the western corner of **②** **Savoy Place**. A public road, complete with a City of Westminster name sign, double-yellow lines, and no-entry and height-restriction warnings, it is used by anyone who knows about it as a short-cut between the Strand and Victoria Embankment.

Lower Robert Street was part of the Adelphi district, several streets of grand neoclassical houses built between 1768 and 1774 by Robert, James and William Adam. Their new development took its name from the Greek for brothers and individual streets

included Robert Street, Adam Street and John Street, after their eldest brother who remained in Scotland while his siblings came south to seek their fortunes. Like many of today's London developers, the brothers hoped to gentrify a run-down area. Before its reclamation in the 1860s to create Victoria Embankment to accommodate Joseph Bazalgette's sewerage system (see page 33), the north bank of the Thames – previously the site of the palatial York House (see page 93) and Durham House, once the London home of the Bishop of Durham – was the largely derelict haunt of prostitutes, beggars and criminals. Perhaps only the ambitious Adams could have thought of transforming this unpropitious site, steeply sloping and prone to flooding at high tide, into one of London's most desirable residential areas.

Their plan involved the ingenious idea of building elegant new homes on top of an embankment made up of warehouses and workshops. To accommodate the gradient of the site – and in a visual echo of the sea front of Diocletian's Palace in Split, Croatia,

Original Adelphi scheme

which Robert Adam had studied – the structure stepped downwards through tiered brick arches, with each level topped by a terraced roadway. Access to the internal spaces was via a series of subterranean routes – including Lower Robert Street – running parallel to the streets above.

Unfortunately, the brothers neglected to obtain permission for the development from either the government or the freeholder until after the costly substructure was near completion; retrospective planning, including permission to reclaim land from the river, was at first refused then waved through by parliament (helped, no doubt, by Robert Adam's role as an MP) when it was realised that the new buildings would solve the problem of

tidal flooding. However, building costs exceeded expectations and soon the half-finished development looked in danger of going bust. Again parliament stepped in, authorising a lottery of 4,370 tickets each costing £50, with prizes ranging from houses within the prospective development to works of art. Perhaps unsurprisingly, the brothers bought up unsold tickets and scooped the top prize.

The Adams had hoped the government would lease the riverside warehouses but the plan fell through. The new homes above proved easier to dispose of, their desirability and celebrity cachet boosted when actor David Garrick, a friend of the architects, agreed to take the central house ahead of its completion. Another building, on John (now John Adam) Street, is still occupied by the Royal Society of Arts; running beneath it from Durham House Street is a vaulted undercroft similar to Lower Robert Street. Much of the development was razed in the 1930s to make way for the art deco Adelphi office building, but you can still see some of the original houses with their typically Adamesque features including engaged fluted columns with delicately wrought capitals, stuccoed pilasters and medallions embellished with patterns of flowers or putti, and elaborate doorcases.

Another anomalous piece of roadway is nearby ❸ **Savoy Court**, leading from the Strand past the Savoy Theatre to the Savoy Hotel. Here traffic drives on the right to enable taxis to deposit passengers outside the theatre then turn around in front of the hotel to pick up another fare on their exit. Both theatre and hotel were built by opera impresario Richard D'Oyly Carte, who lived at 4 Adelphi Terrace from 1888 to 1901.

1. Little Robert Street
    (entrance on York Buildings), WC2N 6JN
2. Exit on Savoy Place, WC2R 0BL
3. Savoy Court, WC2R 0EZ

10.2 The Age of the Horse

A more pervasive reminder of the age of the horse are London's mews – small two-storey terraces behind grand houses, often planned with stabling below and haylofts or living quarters for grooms and drivers above. Most have now been converted into bijou homes, with cobblestones and carriage entrances the only reminders of their former function. But at the ⑤ **Horse Hospital** at the corner of Herbrand Street and Colonnade in Bloomsbury you can still detect the plan of the stalls in the basement (one is fitted with a surprisingly ornate tethering ring) and see the interior ramps that allowed horses to access both lower and upper levels. Now an arts venue, the former stables and headquarters for veterinary surgeons was built in 1797 as part of the redevelopment of Russell Square by property magnate James Burton.

By 1900 there were some 50,000 horses transporting people around the capital. The clatter of horseshoes and iron wheels on stone cobbles was deafening during the day and disturbing at night, but quieter wooden blocks, introduced during the first half of the 19th century, wore out more quickly and had the additional disadvantage of smelling rank on hot days, having absorbed large quantities of urine as well as manure diluted with rainwater. (A healthy horse can produce as much as 15 litres of urine and 20 kilos of manure a day!) Australian eucalyptus – hard-wearing and unabsorbent – was the most popular wood for paving, though unsurprisingly more affluent areas used more expensive hardwood, while poorer neighbourhoods had less robust, more porous varieties.

Horses played an essential role within the early railway system, used to manoeuver freight within goods yards as well as for onward carriage by road. The site now occupied by ⑥ **Stables Market** in Camden, originally stabling for the London & Birmingham Railway, is the best-preserved example of its kind in England – though the bustle of the market makes it hard to appreciate.

Most of the wooden paving on London's streets was replaced after WW2 and used as domestic fuel, but you can still find a small section of ④ **wood-paved road** at the junction of Chequer Street and Bunhill Row near Old Street. Peer closely and you can see the beauty of the grain, though thankfully the smell is absent. You also occasionally find sections of old wooden blocks lining the covers of manholes.

Behind a long curved brick façade on the west side of Chalk Farm Road, punctuated by regular small square and semi-circular windows, lies a network of cobbled lanes connecting an extraordinarily rich collection of stables and workshops. The complex was established in the early 19th century with small single-storey buildings with haylofts above, but gradually two- and three-storey blocks including a horse hospital were added, with exterior ramps to the upper floors. By the second half of the 19th century as many as 700 horses were stabled on the site, moving cargo between canal, roads and the rail terminus at Euston. To minimise the danger of horses and trains operating on the same level, underground tunnels were created within the extensive warehouses beneath the raised tracks, with direct access to the canal via Dead Dog Basin at Camden Lock (see page 335).

You can find another complex of railway stables on the corner of South Wharf Road and London Street in Paddington, now an extremely odd part of **❼ St Mary's Hospital**. Flanking a courtyard with a separate building at its centre, the stables were opened in 1878 as a single storey before being extended upwards from 1910. Walk through the hospital entrance and you can see the curved exterior ramps and high-level walkways (now glazed) that enabled as many as 600 horses to move from space to space. The walls today are punctured by a muddle of hospital entrails – plumbing, pipework, openings and additions – but behind the windows on the upper level you can still glimpse stable doors. It is also worth peering into the glass-roofed verandahs on London Street where you can hear train announcements echoing along the tunnels that once connected stables and station.

Horses are still used in London for ceremonial duties, crowd control and East End funerals, but a unique remnant of their former ubiquity is the **❽ mounting block** outside the Athenaeum Club in Waterloo Place off Pall Mall – a pair of clumsily stacked granite stones inscribed with the words 'This horse block was erected by desire of the Duke of Wellington 1830'. The Iron Duke was prime minister at the time, living at 10 Downing Street while his own much larger home of Apsley House was being renovated. No doubt he was a frequent visitor to the club, founded six years earlier in premises designed by James

Burton's son Decimus, and perhaps had difficulty getting back on his horse after a night of socialising.

Anyone who has read Anna Sewell's 1877 novel *Black Beauty* – or watched one of the many film adaptations – knows about the cruelty meted out to animals in London's streets. So is hardly surprising that in 1867 the Metropolitan Drinking Fountain Association (see page 99) changed its name to the Metropolitan Drinking Fountain and Cattle Trough Association and began to install **❾ water troughs** for animals being driven to market as well as for the horses that provided the city's transport. Within a decade there were some 150 troughs of standard design – simple granite trays inscribed with the name of the organisation, with a fountain at one end – and even today most London boroughs retain a handful, often used as planters. For instance, in Islington there are five, including a more unusual double-length version at the junction of Central Street and City Road. The initiative no doubt improved the lives of the animals, but a readily available supply of water can have done little to help the problem of London's stinking urine-soaked wooden cobbles.

4. Wood-paved road, Chequer St, EC1Y 8PJ
5. Horse Hospital, Colonnade, WC1N 1JD
6. Stables Market, Chalk Farm Rd, NW1 8AH
7. Mint Wing, St Mary's Hospital, London St, W2 1PF
8. Mounting block, Athenaeum, 107 Pall Mall, SW1Y 5ER
9. Horse trough, City Rd, EC1V 8AB

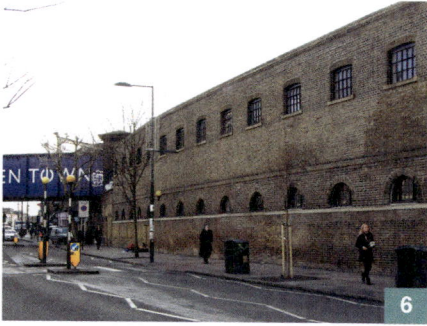

THIS HORSE-BLOCK WAS ERECTED BY DESIRE OF
THE DUKE OF WELLINGTON 1830.

METROPOLITAN DRINKING FOUNTAIN & CATTLE TROUGH ASSOCIATION.

10.3 Cabmen's Shelters

In some of the busiest streets in London you find incongruously rustic, green-painted wooden sheds – with queues of men standing outside. These are not fairytale cottages escaped from a fantasy woodland but ⑩ **cabmen's shelters**. Surprisingly, of the 60 built around London between 1875 and 1914, 13 have survived. Most still fulfil their original function of serving food and hot drinks, both to cabbies, who are allowed inside, and to passers-by, who are not.

The shelters were provided by the Cabmen's Shelter Fund, set up in 1875 by newspaper editor George Armstrong and social reformer and politician Anthony Ashley Cooper, 7th Earl of Shaftesbury (see page 192). Apparently the idea was Armstrong's. One snowy evening his servant failed to find a cab to take him to Fleet Street from his local hack stand in St John's Wood. Though there were plenty of horses and carriages, all the drivers – cold, wet and hungry – had retired to the pub, leaving their cabs in the charge of young boys who were not licensed to drive them. Like many Victorian philanthropic endeavours, Armstrong's plan to offer cabbies an alternative place of refuge had a dual aim: to keep the working classes away from the demon drink and to ensure

the philanthropists received a return that fitted their needs. Rules stipulated that all shelters had to be within six miles of Charing Cross and individual patrons tended to fund local stands – for instance, the Duke of Westminster sponsored one in Piccadilly and MPs chipped in for one at Westminster. Unsurprisingly, the first shelter to open was in Acacia Road, near Armstrong's St John's Wood home.

Originally costing £200 each, the shelters were limited to the size of a horse and four-wheeled carriage. Three panels wide by seven long, they usually have a window or door in the middle of each short side and three windows in the long sides. Overhanging eaves offer some protection to the serving hatch and the shingled or tiled roof is often topped by a slatted ventilator a bit like a dovecote. Gables and panels were sometimes pierced with decorative patterns that included the initials of the Cabmen's Shelter Fund; a metal rail around the perimeter was provided to tether horses.

Inside, the shelters could seat about a dozen cabbies on two benches behind long tables. The proprietor – often a retired cabman – was contracted to offer 'good and wholesome refreshments at moderate prices', as well as cooking food brought in by customers, who would sometimes keep their own mugs at their favourite shelter. Books and newspapers were donated by the benefactors, and gambling, drinking, swearing and political discussion were strictly forbidden, though the last of these rules, cabbies say, was largely ignored.

According to W J Gordon in *The Horse World of London* (1893), 'the cabman, as a rule, is not so much a large drinker as a large eater. At one shelter lately the great feature was boiled rabbit and pickled pork at two o'clock in the morning...' Today

the menu is more likely to feature sausage or bacon rolls or corned beef sandwiches washed down with tea or coffee. Prices are – and presumably always have been – cheaper than the high street, attracting a surprising range of customers: explorer Ernest Shackleton was a regular at the Hyde Park Corner shelter and artist John Singer Sargent frequented the one near the Ritz.

Some shelters have nicknames: Wellington Road near Lord's Cricket Ground in St John's Wood is variously known as 'the Chapel' or 'the Nursery End'; Thurloe Place in Kensington is called 'the Bell and Horns' after a local pub; Chelsea Embankment near Albert Bridge was known as 'the Pier' because of its proximity to Cadogan Pier, or 'the Kremlin' because it attracted left-wing cabmen. Many of the buildings are customised with hanging baskets or pot plants; those in upmarket Thurloe Place and Pont Street near Sloane

Street have awnings sponsored by estate agent Winkworths.

In addition to the shelters above, you can find others in Embankment Place WC2, Grosvenor Gardens SW1, Hanover Square W1, Kensington Park Road W11, Kensington Road W8, Russell Square WC1, St George's Square SW1 and Temple Place WC2, the last restored with the help of disgraced politician turned best-selling author Jeffrey Archer, according to a plaque. 'Shelters are a place to come and meet your mates, to socialise, chew the fat, grab a cup of tea and a sandwich,' says cabbie and author Bill Munro. 'Driving a taxi's a very lonely job. You meet lots of people but you never get to know them.'

10. Russell Square Cabmen's Shelter, WC1B 5EH

10.4 Charles Holden & Gants Hill Underground

11

Below a scruffy roundabout in north-east London sits a slice of Moscow. ⓫ **Gants Hill Underground** is one of the last works by Charles Holden (1875–1960), architect of some of London Underground's most distinctive stations. Holden's designs are chiefly praised for modernist exteriors that combine simple geometric shapes to effectively signal a station's presence – as at Arnos Grove in Enfield or Chiswick Park in Ealing (both Piccadilly Line, 1932 and 1933 respectively) – and ticket halls that use a limited palette of materials to stunning effect, most notably Piccadilly Circus (1928). Gants Hill (1947) has neither: its presence on the street is limited to a couple of signs at the entrances to its subways and its ticket hall is modest. Its glory is the extraordinary central concourse between the two underground platforms, the only one of its kind Holden designed and a direct tribute to the Moscow Metro on which he acted as advisor.

Holden was in many ways a Nonconformist: a Quaker, vegetarian, teetotal and a fan of the poetry of Walt Whitman, he never married his lifelong partner Margaret Macdonald, even when this became possible following the death of her abusive husband. Among his early works were two controversial collaborations with sculptor Jacob Epstein – the British Medical Association HQ (now Zimbabwe House) in 1906 (see page 194) and the tomb of Oscar Wilde in Paris six years later.

Holden's involvement with London Underground began in 1923, when assistant managing director Frank Pick – who was responsible for commissioning the network's signature typeface and logo as well as for pioneering its expansion to the suburbs – asked him to design some new stations. Pick wanted 'a new architectural idiom... for modern London' as distinctive as the network's graphics: stations that would be welcoming, brightly lit, efficient and above all instantly recognisable.

When company architect Stanley Heaps failed to fulfil the brief, Holden was asked to create seven new stations for the Northern Line extension from Clapham Common to Morden. Though the double-height entrance pavilions, featuring a glazed screen inset with a giant Underground roundel, are remarkable in their own right, it was not until the Piccadilly Line extension in the 1930s that Holden fully developed his iconic style. He was also the architect of what was until recently London Underground's headquarters at 55 Broadway, which incorporates St James's Park Underground: stepped back and rising to ten storeys, this was the capital's tallest building at the time of its completion in 1929.

Determined that their new-look Piccadilly Line extension would reflect the best of contemporary architecture, Holden and Pick made a tour of the Netherlands, Denmark and Sweden in 1930 to gather inspiration. The combination of brick and glazing Holden developed echoes contemporary Dutch housing schemes, while one of the key motifs – a double-height brick drum as at Arnos Grove – seems an adaptation of Gunnar Asplund's recently completed Stockholm Central Library. Designs for new Northern Line stations later in the decade remained unbuilt apart from East Finchley, where Holden gave prominence to Eric Aumonier's art deco sculpture *The Archer*, the only three-dimensional artwork commissioned as part of a station's original design. Gants Hill, Wanstead and Redbridge on the Central Line extension were delayed by WW2 and completed only in 1947.

Inspiration for and from the Moscow Metro flowed both ways. Soviet delegates to London were impressed by Holden's thoroughly modern redeployment of classical elements and use of high-quality materials for the circular ticket hall of Piccadilly Circus and so engaged Pick and Holden as advisors to Moscow's metro system in 1936. The Soviet capital's early stations had none of the sumptuous embellishment of later additions but instilled a sense of wonder through generous halls with widely spaced columns and high ceilings, a vast variety of marble sourced from different regions of the USSR and muted lighting that created a mood of reverence. The standard plan, as imported for Gants Hill, had an impressively proportioned, vaulted central hallway with arcades giving access to platforms on either side rather than the usual London model of platforms connected by a miserable warren of cramped tunnels and stairwells.

Holden's homage to Moscow has been described as a gesture of gratitude for the USSR's role in helping to win WW2. In this London take on the Moscow idiom, the cavernous underground hall has a barrel-vaulted ceiling with cream-coloured panels – a modern version of classical coffering – with access to the platforms on either side, also barrel-vaulted, through a screen of massive columns. Pairs of uplighters at either end of the double benches give the vault an amber glow and more lights concealed within the cornice illuminate both ceiling and floor. In Moscow, the cream-tiled walls might have been faced in marble, but nevertheless Gants Hill is still impressive. It is also worth taking a closer look at the platform clocks, on which the numbers are replaced by London Underground roundels.

In his poem celebrating the opening of the Moscow Metro *The Moscow Workers Take Possession of the Great Metro on April 27, 1935* Berthold Brecht imagines how:

The travellers rushed out and inspected
With eager, flashing eyes the finished job.
They felt the pillars
And appraised their gloss.
They tested the wall surfaces
And fingered the glass.

Take the Central Line out to Gants Hill to do the same.

11. Gants Hill Underground,
    369 Eastern Ave, IG2 6UD

10.5 Hitting the Buffers

Waterloo International

⑫ **Waterloo International**, which cost £120 million to build, opened to great fanfare in 1994 – and closed only 13 years later. The heroic project for one of the longest stations in the world – a 'gateway to Europe' catering for the 18-carriage high-speed trains that would carry some 15 million passengers a year through the new Channel Tunnel – was conceived as reprising the pioneering spirit of the large-span glass-and-iron stations engineered some 150 years earlier. Snaking for a quarter of a mile between neighbouring buildings, the new terminal consisted of a car park spanning the Underground lines above which sat an airport-like check-in level and four platforms roofed by a dramatic glass sleeve. The structure's skeleton – a mesh of blue steel tubes with the surprising delicacy of insects' legs – is expressed on the outside. Once beyond the high-tech terminus, trains would trundle through Kent before hitting full speed on the other side of the Channel.

Waterloo – not the most welcoming name for arrivals from France – was superseded by St Pancras International, built at a cost of £800 million. Initially some Eurostar trains were to stop at Stratford International – priced at a mere £210 million – on a direct route to or from destinations further north. The plan never materialised: two out of the four Stratford platforms now typically serve only eight trains an hour ranging no further than the Kent coast, the gleaming concourse lies virtually empty, and in 2016 signs marked 'Sortie' were discreetly removed. Oddly, the station name remains unchanged.

Waterloo International has suffered a similar fate: from 2017 its state-of-the-art Eurostar platforms have been pressed into service for commuter trains to Windsor and Reading.

12. Waterloo International, Waterloo Rd, SE1 8SW

Blackfriars

13

⑬ Blackfriars station – opened in 1886 by the London, Chatham and Dover Railway company (LC&DR) under the name of St Paul's – once also had international pretensions. Today it serves about 20 trains an hour running from Bedford in the north to Brighton, Sevenoaks and Sutton in the south – even if the departures wall in its main concourse gives a different impression. Here, in a series of extraordinary juxtapositions, minor Kent towns such as Deal, Herne Bay and Sittingbourne are listed alongside more romantic destinations including Baden-Baden, Geneva, Naples and Venice. Even back in the 19th century the claims were somewhat misleading: the LC&DR, of course, only ran the 80 miles or so to Dover. Here passengers could transfer to one of the company's steamships for a three-hour crossing to Calais before travelling with other rail providers to more exotic locations across the continent.

The departures wall – consisting of 54 individual sandstone blocks with gilded inscribed letters – originally formed part of the station façade. Read from left to right, the order seems random, but in

fact the destinations are alphabetically arranged down each vertical column, with a few exceptions such as Westgate-on-Sea preceding Walmer or St Petersburg tucked between Vienna and Wiesbaden. Whether the indexing errors were original or introduced as the wall was reassembled following its restoration has not been revealed.

St Paul's was also the original name of Blackfriars Bridge, built to serve the station by Henry Marc Brunel, son of Isambard Kingdom. Strangely, the new bridge was located only a few metres west of the existing Blackfriars Railway Bridge, the first to cross the Thames, which since 1864 had carried the LC&DR between Blackfriars Bridge Station on the south bank and Ludgate Hill to the north. The new St Paul's line rendered the old bridge redundant for passenger traffic – after just over 20 years of service – though it continued to be used for freight until 1964. It was eventually demolished as unsafe in the mid-1980s, leaving its piers – three rows of stone bases each supporting a cluster of four sturdy cast-iron columns with elaborate capitals – still marching across the river. Two rows remain, now red-painted, and the third has been incorporated into the spectacular state-of-the-art new Blackfriars station, with platforms spanning the river beneath a roof of some 4,000 solar panels.

Criticised for poor punctuality, shoddy rolling stock and financial mismanagement, the LC&DR merged with the South Eastern Railway in 1898. Its name lives on, however, in elaborate cast-iron cartouches made for the 1864 bridge, now mounted on the stone abutment that once marked its southern end.

13. Blackfriars Station,
     179 Queen Victoria St, EC4V 4EG

Abandoned Underground

London Underground has a surprisingly high number of disused stations across its 250 miles of track – about 40 alongside 270 stations still in operation. Some closed because routes were diverted or passenger numbers dropped away: for instance, Blake Hall, on the former Epping–Ongar branch line, had only 17 passengers a day when it was wound down in 1981. Other closures were the result of ambitious plans gone awry – for instance, the stations along the Northern Line that doubled as deep shelters during WW2 (see page 221), envisaged as part of a post-war express network, were never used for trains at all.

One of the shortest-lived stations was ⑭ **King William Street** in the City, commemorated by a plaque on the building at the corner of Monument Street. The northern terminus of London's first deep-level underground railway, it survived for only ten years from 1890 before the new service's popularity spurred plans for expansion that the site could not accommodate. North End between Hampstead and Golders Green, the deepest station on the network, never even got that far: it was abandoned just before completion when plans for a nearby housing development were shelved.

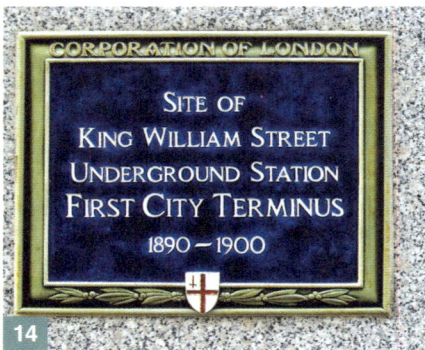

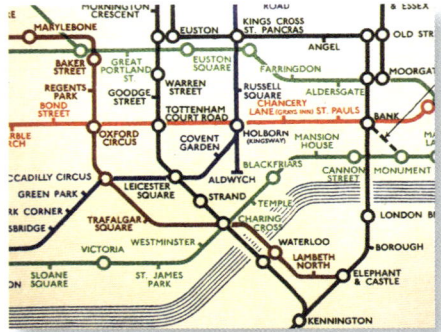

During WW2 – accessible only from passing trains – it was allegedly used to store secret archives; during the Cold War in the 1950s it became part of London Underground's civil defence preparations, with a new entrance building cunningly disguised as an electricity substation.

Both ⑮ **Aldwych** (formerly named Strand station), near the junction of Strand and Surrey Street, and Down Street, just off Piccadilly, also played a role in the defence network; they are opened for occasional Transport for London tours. Completed in 1907, the Holborn–Aldwych shuttle was reduced from two tracks to one within ten years because of lack of passengers, with the disused platforms becoming a testing ground for new designs. The spaces served as storage for some 300 paintings from the National Gallery during WW1; during WW2 the station was put out of service and used as an air-raid shelter and store for artefacts from the British Museum, including the Parthenon Marbles. It was finally closed in 1994 when replacement lifts were needed. Built on the site of the old Royal Strand Theatre, it is now used as an occasional film set and a space for art installations.

⑯ **Down Street,** also opened in 1907, was never popular; located on a side street after wealthy Mayfair residents objected to its proposed site on Piccadilly, it was within about 500 metres of both Dover Street

15

(now Green Park) and Hyde Park Corner in an area whose inhabitants had little need of public transport. Unsurprisingly, it closed within 25 years. But during WW2 it was given new life as an emergency government bunker equipped with offices, dormitories, executive bedrooms, bathrooms and kitchens. Cabinet meetings were held here until completion of the Cabinet War Rooms under the Treasury Building in Whitehall and Churchill slept here after the bombing of 10 Downing Street in October 1940. He apparently referred to it as 'the burrow' or sometimes 'the barn' because of the wind from passing trains.

Down Street also served as the wartime headquarters of the Railway Executive Committee (REC), set up to maintain the smooth running of the railways to transport troops and supplies. Senior officers could hail a train from a concealed section of platform, climbing in through the driver's cab while regular passengers assumed they were held at a red signal.

Down Street still contains remnants of its wartime telephone exchange and currently serves as an access point for emergency and maintenance crews, though Transport for London is exploring other uses.

⑰ Brompton Road on Cottage Place, opened in 1906 and closed in 1934, again because of lack of passengers, was actually purchased by the War Office in 1938 to serve as the Royal Artillery's anti-aircraft operation room and subsequently as training facilities. In 2014 the station was sold for £53 million to a Ukrainian billionaire who at the time of writing was being sought by US law enforcement agencies on charges of bribery. Aldwych, Down Street and Brompton Road, with their distinctive ox-blood tiled façades and semi-circular windows, were all designed by Leslie Green, whose 30 or so stations for the Bakerloo, Northern and Piccadilly lines from the first decade of the 20th century are as iconic as the later work of London Underground architect Charles Holden (see page 309).

17

Because London changes so rapidly, it is perhaps hardly surprising that even the best-laid plans misfire. Behind a pair of ordinary-looking doors at the bottom of the main escalators at Charing Cross are pristine, ghostly tunnels and platforms that served the Jubilee Line for just 20 years from 1979. Following the expansion of Docklands in the 1980s, the expected route for the line's extension changed, running from Green Park through to Stratford rather than from Charing Cross to Lewisham as originally anticipated. The abandoned former terminus has since been used to film the TV series *Spooks* – about a group of MI5 officers – as well as the James Bond movie *Skyfall*, in which the secret agent investigates an attack on MI6. As far as anyone knows, the station's role in international conflicts and espionage still lies within the realm of fiction.

Kingsway Tramway Subway

Running down the centre of Southampton Row, just south of Theobald's Road, is a strip of cobbles with two pairs of embedded iron tracks, sloping downwards between tiled walls to an impressive granite portal. This is the cut-and-cover 18 **Kingsway tram tunnel**, the only example of its kind in Britain, built in 1904–06 in emulation of the system in New York. A rare reminder of London's tram network, which in 1914 was the most extensive in Europe, the tunnel originally emerged at the northern end of Waterloo Bridge, a journey of around ten minutes. Tracks from Southampton Row passed through a pair of cast-iron tunnels under the Fleet sewer before rising slightly to Holborn tramway station, with stairs to the street that surfaced beside the gratings in the middle of Kingsway, just south of Holborn Underground. From there the journey was through a single rectangular tunnel to the tramway stop at Aldwych, after which the route curved sharply right, dipping through another pair of cast-iron tubes to pass under the Strand before emerging on Victoria Embankment. The tunnel remained in service until 1952.

In the mid-1960s the southern end, including the former Aldwych tram station, was converted into the Strand Underpass, taking northbound road traffic from Waterloo Bridge to Kingsway, where it surfaces between Portugal and Sardinia Streets. The northern end of the tramway tunnel is currently being used by Crossrail – which has promised to restore a listed monument no one ever sees to its original condition once work is completed.

14. King William Street plaque, EC3R 8AJ
15. Former Aldwych station,
    Surrey St, WC2R 2NS
16. Former Down Street station, W1J 7AS
17. Former Brompton Road station,
    Cottage Place, SW3 2BE
18. Kingsway Tramway Subway,
    Southampton Row, WC1B 4AP

10.6 A Tale of Two Bridges

London Bridge

One of the odd things about London Bridge is that it isn't Tower Bridge – and vice versa. The site of the city's first permanent Thames crossing, a timber bridge built by the Romans in 55CE, is now marked not by an iconic landmark but by an anonymous concrete and steel structure in place only since 1974. Even more oddly, its immediate predecessor – designed by John Rennie (who also created Southwark and Waterloo bridges) and opened in 1831 – has been standing since 1971 in Lake Havasu City, a town of some 50,000 people in Arizona, after it was bought by businessman Robert McCulloch, dismantled, carefully labelled, shipped and resurrected. McCulloch has denied rumours that he thought he was in fact buying Tower Bridge – but then he would, wouldn't he?

Between the Roman and 19th-century bridges came a crossing built in 1176 that forms the subject of the nursery rhyme 'London Bridge is falling down' – though in fact frequent bodged repairs kept it upright for over 600 years. You can see a **19** **scale model** as it might have appeared in 1400

in the church of St Magnus the Martyr in Lower Thames Street, together with a plaque as you enter the churchyard that marks the former approach to its northern end.

The bridge was begun as a penance by Henry II for the murder of his former friend, Archbishop of Canterbury Thomas Becket, after the king's imprudent cry of 'Who will rid me of this troublesome priest?' was taken as an order by overzealous knights. A grand chapel dedicated to Becket, with a river-level entrance for fishermen and ferrymen, stood at the bridge's centre. The structure took 33 years to build and inevitably overran its budget; on its completion, Henry's successor, King John, decided to lease out plots to recoup

19

the cost. A century and a half later there were 138 shops lining the roadway as well as a multi-seat public latrine overhanging the parapets and emptying into the river below. During the 1500s buildings along the sides of the bridge increased to 200, some rising to seven storeys, with jetties overhanging both river and roadway, the latter reduced to a dark tunnel. The weight of the buildings placed an impossible strain on the arches below (hence the rhyme). It soon became apparent that a new bridge was needed.

The replacement designed by Rennie also suffered from structural flaws, its foundations sinking into the soft Thames mud at a rate of about 2.5 centimetres every eight years. In 1967 the City of London came up with the unusual solution of trying to sell it and soon it had moved 5,000 miles west. Surprisingly, traces of the original remain, including the arch crossing Montague Close at its southern end, which was incorporated into the new structure, and some escaped slabs of **20** **coping stone** that now form impromptu seats on the western corner of Duke Street Hill. The granite stairs descending from the bridge to Montague Close are also part of Rennie's bridge, known as **21** **'Nancy's Steps'** because they resembled the location of the murder of Charles Dickens' 'tart with a heart' in the 1968 film *Oliver!* – though Dickens in fact used the steps not as the site of her murder but to stage the overheard conversation that gave her away.

Even more surprising are scattered remnants from the structure Rennie's bridge replaced. An elaborate **22** **royal coat of arms** installed on the new southern tollgate in 1728 has found a home above the entrance to the King's Arms pub in nearby Newcomen Street. Oddly, the arms are those used by George II at the start of his reign, but the inscription has been changed to George III and the date to 1760, marking both the tollgate's demolition and the new king's accession.

The bridge was substantially rebuilt between 1758 and 1762: not only tollgates but also shops and houses were demolished to widen the roadway, and the two central arches were replaced by a single, larger span to ease river traffic. Stone niches facing the roadway were set within the parapet: five of these have since found their way to a private housing development in Richmond in west London, to Victoria Park in east London and to the grounds of Guy's Hospital, near the bridge's southern end. The Richmond niches were moved to the grounds of Stawell House, built by a younger son of the third Earl of Dartmouth in 1839, soon after the bridge's demolition. Repurposed as a pair of 'porters' rests', they were placed at either end of a terrace walk lined with balustrading also taken from the bridge. Stawell House has since been demolished, but one of the pair still stands at the south-western edge of the gardens to the private Courtlands Estate, on the corner of Queen's Road and Sheen Road.

The two **23** **east London niches** are on the Cadogan Terrace edge of Victoria Park, while the one in Guy's – known as the Lunatick's Chair – is in the eastern courtyard of Old Guy's House, near the hospital's St Thomas Street entrance. The niches are imposing, if battered, with a baluster at each side and an ornamental boss at the pinnacle of their arches, below which you can just make out the logo of Bridge House Estates, established in 1282 to maintain London Bridge. The **24** **niche at Guy's** was purchased in 1861 at a cost of 10 guineas while those in Victoria Park were presented to Queen Victoria, who ordered their installation 'for the use of the public' in 1860. All three are lined with wooden benches, with the one at Guy's occupied to odd effect by a recent bronze statue of romantic poet John Keats, a former student at the hospital.

A plaque on the glorious colonnade that runs alongside the courtyard at Guy's commemorates philosopher Ludwig Wittgenstein, who worked incognito at the hospital as a 'drugs porter and ointment maker' in 1941–42. Removed from their original purpose and now sitting folornly in such unlikely settings, the London Bridge niches perhaps embody one of the philosopher's best-known contentions: 'I don't know why we are here, but I'm pretty sure that it is not in order to enjoy ourselves.'

Tower Bridge

Why would anyone want to disguise a pioneering feat of engineering – an inventive solution to accommodating both horse-drawn and waterborne traffic that had taken almost 20 years for the finest minds of the age to devise – as a gothic castle? It's like pretending the M25 is a country lane. Why hide a steel frame in Portland stone or try to pass off the heaviest piers in the world – supporting steel towers, high-level walkways, suspension chains holding up the bridge's outer edges as well as the bascules and lifting machinery for the revolutionary mechanism at its centre – as a simple drawbridge? The designers of Tower Bridge must have had their reasons.

Begun with the launch of a competition in 1877 and completed in 1894, **25 Tower Bridge** was not the first river crossing at the site. Tower Subway, built in 1871 as a railway tunnel, had closed after just three months when the company that ran it went bankrupt, after which it was reconfigured as a foot tunnel. At only about half the diameter of the later Greenwich and Woolwich subways (see page 325), it was described by Charles Dickens as having 'not much head-room left, and it is not advisable for any but the very briefest of Her Majesty's lieges to attempt the passage in high-heeled boots, or with a hat to which he attaches any particular value.' The toll tunnel closed to the public within five years of the opening of the free bridge and is at present used as a conduit for water mains. You can see its northern entrance, a **26 brick tower** with stone dressings built in the 1920s and encircled with the name of the London Hydraulic Power Company, at the corner of the pedestrian area at the eastern end of Lower Thames Street.

The competition for Tower Bridge was launched by mayor Henry Isaacs in the face of hostile lobbying from both ferrymen

and shipping companies. (You can find a reminder of the ferrymen in a hard stone perch where they would once wait for clients, now embedded in a wall on Bear Gardens, just east of Shakespeare's Globe on the south bank.) Among the entries was a high-level bridge by Metropolitan Board of Works chief engineer Joseph Bazalgette (see page 33) as well as the winning design from city architect Horace Jones, who also happened to be one of the judges. Jones died in 1887 and the project passed to his assistant, George Daniel Stevenson, with John Wolfe Barry, son of Houses of Parliament architect Charles Barry, as chief engineer. Stevenson was a devoted fan of the Victorian gothic style epitomised by Barry's work at Westminster – another medieval fantasy woven around a cast-iron frame, though begun over half a century earlier and designed to blend with remnants of its fire-damaged predecessor. Stevenson changed Jones' red-brick facing to Portland stone and added cast-iron parapets, decorative panelling for the walkways and gas lamp standards. The result lies somewhere between a fairytale palace – with French chateau-style roofs topped by gilded pinnacles – and a Scottish baronial castle.

Tower Bridge's high-level walkways, intended to allow pedestrians to cross even when the carriageway was raised, were little used except by prostitutes and low-lifes, in part because the speed and spectacle of lifting and lowering the roadway meant pedestrians often preferred to watch and wait. Closed in 1910, they now form part of the Tower Bridge tourist experience, complete with a partially glazed floor that creates an illusion of fragility masking strength akin to the showmanship of the bridge's exterior. From within you get a clearer idea of the extent of the fakery and disjunction between inside and outside: the lattice of girders within the towers is revealed to astonishing effect, disappearing into the

pointed roofs and semi-obscuring the fussy mullioned windows. In the first month of its operation, Tower Bridge was raised 665 times; the total today is around 15 times a month, though the excitement of watching the roadway split apart and remake itself is undiminished.

A feature of the bridge that sits oddly with its status as a symbol of London is **27 Dead Man's Hole**, a mortuary incorporated into the base of the northern pier after it was found that this was where dead bodies floating in the Thames tended to collect. You can find it by descending the steps at the bridge's north-eastern end into St Katharine's Way, then walking through the second of the two arches on your left. A metal fence seals off the wooden door that was once the mortuary entrance, with a view through to the river where it is only too easy to imagine decomposing bodies washed up by the tide. One of the welcome features of the decline in river traffic is that today only about 50 corpses a year are recovered from the Thames, rendering a mortuary – like the lifting mechanism that helped give the bridge its iconic status – largely redundant.

27

10.7 Crossing the Thames

By Ferry

The **28** **Woolwich Ferry**, which takes motor vehicles and pedestrians between New Ferry Approach in Woolwich and Pier Road in North Woolwich, is a pleasurable and uplifting mode of public transport – certainly a London oddity. Towering steel mechanisms to raise and lower gangplanks, slime-coated wooden piers emerging from the water and the sight of the two boats that operate on weekdays dancing around each other as they sweep in a wide arc across the river all inspire a child-like sense of wonder and delight.

The service was set up following a meeting of angry local residents in 1880. The Metropolitan Board of Works (later the LCC) had recently begun to purchase and allow free public access to former toll bridges such as Albert Bridge (see page 94) and Battersea Bridge in west London, and east Londoners – who were paying for the buy-up through their rates – believed that they too deserved a free means of crossing the Thames. Almost ten years later the ferry service was launched, with one boat, *Gordon*, carrying some 25,000 day-trippers on the first weekend. The

earliest boats were paddle steamers, licensed to carry 1,000 passengers and up to 20 vehicles. A second fleet was commissioned in 1930, one of which was named after former local Labour MP Will Crooks. Three diesel vessels with easier loading for vehicles were introduced in 1963 – *John Burns*, *Ernest Bevin* and *James Newman*. Journey time from bank to bank is around five minutes during which vehicle owners stay with their cars. Timetables for the ferry service can be found on the Transport for London website.

At peak times the open-air car deck is often full, but in the hull a space intended for some 500 foot passengers feels cavernously empty. As with the later Woolwich and Greenwich foot tunnels, the design is purely functional, with rows of simple slatted wooden benches arranged in an environment with no decoration or embellishment. Transport for London recently commissioned two new boats, the *Dame Vera Lynn* and *Ben Woollacott*, the latter named after a ferry worker who died in an accident in 2015.

By Foot

Walking under the Thames through the Greenwich and Woolwich foot tunnels can feel like a near-death experience: a long corridor with gleaming white walls stretches ahead, tiny figures appear in the distance, and the sound of your own footsteps booms like a heartbeat relayed through a monitor. Though the tunnels have been safely carrying cyclists and pedestrians for over a century, walking the 370 metres at Greenwich or 500 metres at Woolwich, fully conscious of some 15 metres of water sitting above you, can seem like an act of faith. It is always a relief to reach the centre point and feel the ground slowly rising towards the exit.

Both tunnels – **29 Greenwich tunnel** built between 1899 and 1902 and **30 Woolwich tunnel** a decade later – were the result of campaigning by Will Crooks, a docker who became one of the first Labour members of the London County Council (LCC) and subsequently Woolwich's Labour MP. Crooks' main aim was to give south Londoners a reliable and free way of getting to work in the docks on the north bank. It was also hoped that the new 'Workingmen's Tunnel' at Greenwich might encourage people from industrial Millwall or Cubitt Town to visit 'the more salubrious surroundings of Greenwich Park and Blackheath for recreation'. Unlike the many ornate bridges to the west, these tunnels for working-class east Londoners are starkly utilitarian, with only their entrance pavilions – on show to the public at large – dignified with decoration or architectural form. Budgets were minimal too, with the cost of each tunnel about 10 per cent of that for Tower Bridge (see page 321), completed less than a decade before Greenwich.

Both tunnels were designed by the LCC engineering department, headed until his retirement in 1901 by Alexander

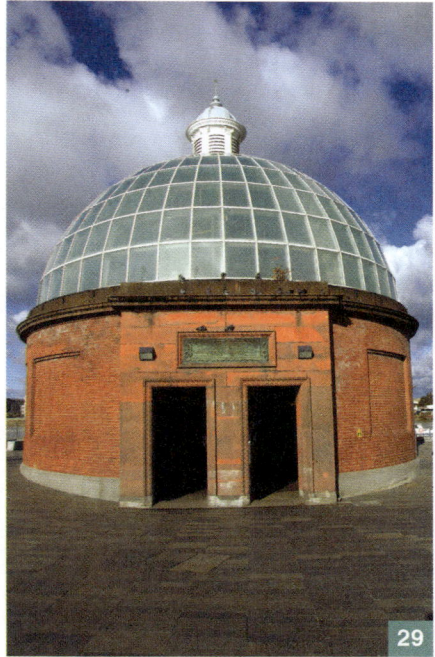

29

30

Fancy Fair Crowds in the Thames Tunnel

Binnie and subsequently by Maurice Fitzmaurice: the two men also engineered the Blackwall Tunnel, Rotherhithe Tunnel, Kingsway Tramway Subway (see page 317) and Vauxhall Bridge. Both tunnels are cast-iron tubes almost 4 metres in diameter lined with thousands of glazed white bricks. Access is via unornamented cast-iron spiral staircases circling lifts panelled in mahogany – perhaps because lift-users were assumed to be higher class. The entrances to the Greenwich tunnel, at Island Gardens in the north and beside the *Cutty Sark* in the south, are red-brick rotundas with domed glass roofs. Those at Woolwich, at Pier Road in the north and the Thames Path near the Waterfront Leisure Centre in the south, have conical copper-clad roofs with circular lanterns and decorative porches supported on cast-iron columns.

Though the footfall when the tunnels first opened was around 9,000 people a week, today it has dropped to less than half that number. As public highways, the tunnels must by law be kept open 24 hours a day; notices forbid cycling, busking, animal fouling, littering, loitering, skateboarding, skating or spitting.

If building the Greenwich and Woolwich tunnels proceeded quickly and smoothly, this was in part through lessons learned at both financial and human cost during the construction of the far more ambitious **31 Thames Tunnel** connecting Rotherhithe and Wapping. The brainchild of Marc Isambard Brunel and realised in conjunction with his son Isambard Kingdom Brunel, this was not only the first pedestrian tunnel connecting north and south London but also the first known tunnel beneath a navigable river.

Construction began in 1825 on the Rotherhithe side using what at the time was an ingenious new strategy of building a caisson: a brick tower, in this case 15 metres in diameter and almost as high, supported on a metal hoop, that gradually sank under its own weight into the mud. The same method was used to create shafts for subsequent tunnels including Greenwich and Woolwich. Excavation

for all three was by hand, with miners working behind a tunnelling shield – another Brunel invention. The Thames Tunnel proved both more costly and more difficult to realise than expected: following a flood in 1827, the Brunels staged a sumptuous underground banquet to restore confidence and raise more money from the project's backers, who included the Duke of Wellington; following an even more damaging flood in 1828, in which six men were killed and Brunel junior injured, the tunnel was bricked up for seven years. Eventually a loan was secured from the Treasury and the tunnel – which cost some six times more than Greenwich or Woolwich half a century later – was opened to pedestrians in 1843. Though it was designed to take horse-drawn carriages, there was not enough money to build the necessary ramps, a saving that eventually led to financial disaster.

Described as the eighth wonder of the world, the Thames Tunnel was at first an attraction in its own right. A marble-faced entrance hall where visitors were entertained by circus performers and magicians led via a dramatic grand staircase to two generous tunnels connected by some 50 arched openings lined with souvenir shops. In its first three months the tunnel received one million visitors (about half the population of London) but soon the novelty wore off and by the mid-1850s the run-down structure was mostly the haunt of tramps and drunks. It was incorporated into the railway and Underground systems from 1869 and since 2010 has carried the Overground line. The original entrance hall, part of the Brunel Museum on Railway Avenue in Rotherhithe, is now once again used for performances.

28. Woolwich Ferry, Pier Rd, E16 2JS
29. Greenwich Foot Tunnel,
    Island Gardens, E14 3EA
30. Woolwich Foot Tunnel, Pier Rd, E16 2JS
31. Brunel Museum,
    Railway Ave, SE16 4LF
    www.brunel-museum.org.uk

By Air

The Dangleway, or **32 IFS Cloud Cable Car**, is perhaps the most oddly named of London's transport links. Running from nowhere to nowhere – or more precisely, from Western Gateway just south of Royal Victoria DLR station to East Parkside on the Greenwich Peninsula – it is a string of cable cars installed in 2012 at the insistence of London mayor Boris Johnson in emulation of services already in place from Adelaide in Australia to Rio de Janeiro in Brazil.

Though Johnson had touted the service as a vital commuter link and vowed that no public money would be used in its construction, the reality turned out to be sadly different. With taxpayers having contributed £24 million of its £60 million total cost (more than twice the initial estimate), the cable car line typically attracts only 30,000 passengers per week – about 12 per cent of its total capacity. Saturday and Sunday are its busiest days and in a week in October a year after its opening only four 'commuters' were found to have made the one-way crossing more than five times a week.

The ten-minute journey, covering about two-thirds of a mile at a height of up to 90 metres, offers views of City Airport, the Thames Barrier and the docks. There is a certain amount of excitement – especially when the wind rocks the lightweight metal gondolas – but in comparison with the nearby east London foot tunnels and ferry, built to serve commuters of old, the IFS Cloud Cable Car offers little more than spectacle. Perhaps most extraordinary is that it ever got off the ground.

32. IFS Cloud Cable Car,
    27 Western Gateway, E16 4FA

32

Canals have traditionally shown us parts of the city not intended for general consumption – the disorderly jumble that lies behind the uniform street façades, an industrial hinterland where planners have relaxed their pretensions. In London, however, Regent's Canal has now become prime real estate, lined with businesses and apartments whose inhabitants look down, literally and sometimes figuratively, on those who cruise the waterways. A canalside view or direct access to the towpath is now a desirable extra rather than a potentially dangerous drawback.

Running for just over eight and a half miles from Paddington Basin in the west (see page 132) to Limehouse in the east, Regent's Canal was begun in 1812 to link the Grand Junction Canal, which flows north to Birmingham, with the Thames. Dropping almost 30 metres through a dozen locks, it provides a visual panorama of slices of city life, from the stuccoed Regency villas and palaces of ③③ **Little Venice** and Regent's Park, through the scruffy vintage markets of Camden Lock, to the warehouses and workshops of Shoreditch and Mile End. It is as if its trajectory traces the shift of the centre of fashionable London from west to east over the last couple of centuries. Along the way it snakes through the middle of London Zoo, past animal enclosures and the dramatically web-like 1960s ③④ **Snowdon Aviary**, where you can look at and listen to the inmates for free.

At Regent's Canal Dock (now Limehouse Basin), seaborne coal from Newcastle or Yorkshire and timber and ice from Scandinavia were once unloaded on to narrow boats and barges. City Road Basin in Islington, which used to extend under City Road almost to Old Street, was the major hub for distributing this cargo on to carts or lorries, along with raw materials brought down the Grand Junction. The ice, used by butchers, fishmongers and ice-cream manufacturers, was stored in ice wells at what is now the Canal Museum at Battlebridge Basin near King's Cross.

Surprisingly, the route and overall design of the canal were the work of John Nash, architect of the grand terraces of Park Crescent south of what is now Regent's Park and of Carlton House Terrace on the Mall. Nash, who was a director of the canal company, had been commissioned by the Prince Regent (later George IV) to produce a new masterplan for the area, and the functional canal took its place within his grandiose scheme – though fears that unruly boatmen might cause problems for more genteel residents led to a diversion across the north of Regent's Park, away from the new streets and crescents.

The immense feat of engineering took only eight years. Most difficult and costly was the three-quarter-mile ③⑤ **Islington Tunnel** between Angel and St Pancras,

though the canal also runs through two much shorter tunnels: Maida Hill, under Edgware Road, and Lisson Grove, which is straddled by a strange-looking house at its east side. Among the many bridges is ③⑥ **Macclesfield Bridge** in Regent's Park, a graceful arch supported on ten sturdy Doric cast-iron columns manufactured by Coalbrookdale, makers of the first iron bridge. In 1874 it was the site of the biggest London explosion before WW1 when a barge laden with gunpowder blew up, shattering windows a mile away and destroying the bridge. When it was rebuilt, some of the columns were replaced the wrong way round: you can see the grooves worn by towing ropes on the landward rather than the water side. Of course, all canal boats were once pulled by horses and at regular intervals you find recesses with underwater ramps that enabled animals which had fallen in to clamber back to the towpath: the one just east of Regent's Park Road has an explanatory plaque.

Other engineering landmarks include the ③⑦ **Limehouse accumulator tower** and chimney beside the DLR tracks (best viewed from Limehouse station), which was used to store water under high pressure to provide instant hydraulic power for the cranes, gates and swing bridges of the basin. Built in 1869 and in operation until the 1920s, it is a typically Victorian example of serious infrastructure disguised as castle-like folly.

Moving west, the ③⑧ **St Pancras waterpoint** at St Pancras Lock – built in 1870 to supply water for the station's steam locomotives – is the only example in England of a water tower designed as a building rather than a tank on stilts. Its ornate polychrome brickwork was intended to complement the gothic elaboration of the station; more recently it was sliced into three parts and moved 700 metres up the road to make way for the extended platforms needed for the Eurostar service.

Contrary to appearances, the ㊴ **Pirate Castle** at Camden Lock, spanning the canal with a castellated bridge, is not a relic of Victorian engineering in fancy dress but a centre for canoeing and kayaking designed in 1977 by the modernist Richard Seifert, architect of the National Westminster Tower (see page 112) and Centre Point. Just beside it is the entrance to the disued Dead Dog Basin, an underground wharf that forms part of an impressive system of tunnels used to store equipment and to stable horses working on the railways (see page 303).

From 1845 there were several aborted attempts to convert Regent's Canal into a railway and in the late 1960s there were plans to fill it in to create a new road. Nationalised since 1948, it is now run by the Canal & River Trust charity and has shed its industrial past to become a place of recreation as well as a wildlife corridor within some of the capital's most densely populated areas. Walk along the towpath and you can see herons perched on the roofs of moored boats, coots bringing up families on precarious nests of twigs and plastic, swans and ducks competing for clumps of weed, cormorants drying their feathers between dives and humans fishing for perch and pike. Towpaths that even 20 years ago were no-go areas are now lined by bars and cafés and cyclists and joggers fight for pre-eminence (pedestrians have priority, though it may not always seem the case). New buildings exploit rather than ignore their canalside setting.

But perhaps the oddest thing about the new-look canal is that boat-dwelling has become a way of life not only for those who work its waters or for self-confessed eccentrics who enjoy the idea of having no fixed abode. London canal boats today are homes to architects and engineers, teachers and lawyers, dancers and musicians, writers and office workers shut out of the inflated land-based property market. Boats range from the fully fitted, with dishwashers, baths and underfloor heating, to more primitive affairs with rudimentary washing facilities and living areas warmed solely by woodburners. A few owners have permanent moorings at basins such as Limehouse, Kingsland, Eagle Wharf, Wenlock, Battlebridge or St Pancras, which supply electricity, water and sometimes showers and toilets. Many of these have no public access, but the stretch of ㊵ **towpath east of Lisson Grove Tunnel** has well-established moorings, allowing you to walk (but not cycle) among residents' exotic planting, open-air toolsheds and outdoor

sitting rooms. Most canal-dwellers, however, move every one or two weeks in compliance with Canal & River Trust rules, tying up where they can to fill their water tanks and relying on their own generators and rooftop solar cells for power.

A surprising number of services have grown up for both boat dwellers and Londoners who use the canals for pleasure. Boat owners can take advantage of the expected toilet pump-outs and fuel deliveries as well as docks for maintenance. But a floating bookshop, cinema, ice-cream parlour, sandwich barge, combined bar and vodka distillery and even a village hall also cruise Regent's Canal, moving around as necessary. Permanently moored boats include the 41 **Feng Shang Princess** Chinese restaurant at the Cumberland Basin near Regent's Park Road and the Puppet Theatre Barge at Little Venice. There is even a floating church – St Peter's Barge – in West India Quay (not actually part of the canal system, but an oddity too good to omit).

As when Regent's Canal was first built, there are still prejudices against boat owners, regarded by some as unregulated, uncivilised nomads who increase noise and air pollution and take advantage of local-council services without contributing by paying taxes. Yet boat-ownership is on the increase – with craft on Regent's Canal often double or triple moored – and the 3,000 or so people who live on London's canals form a friendly, alternative community the size of a small town.

33. Little Venice, W2 6NE
34. Snowdon Aviary, London Zoo, NW1 4RY
35. Islington Tunnel entrance, N1 8AP
36. Macclesfield Bridge, NW8 7PU
37. Limehouse accumulator tower, E14 7JB
38. St Pancras waterpoint, N1C 4PN
39. Pirate Castle, NW1 7EA
40. Lisson Grove moorings, N8 8RZ
41. Feng Shang Princess, NW1 7SS

Word on the Water – the London Bookbarge

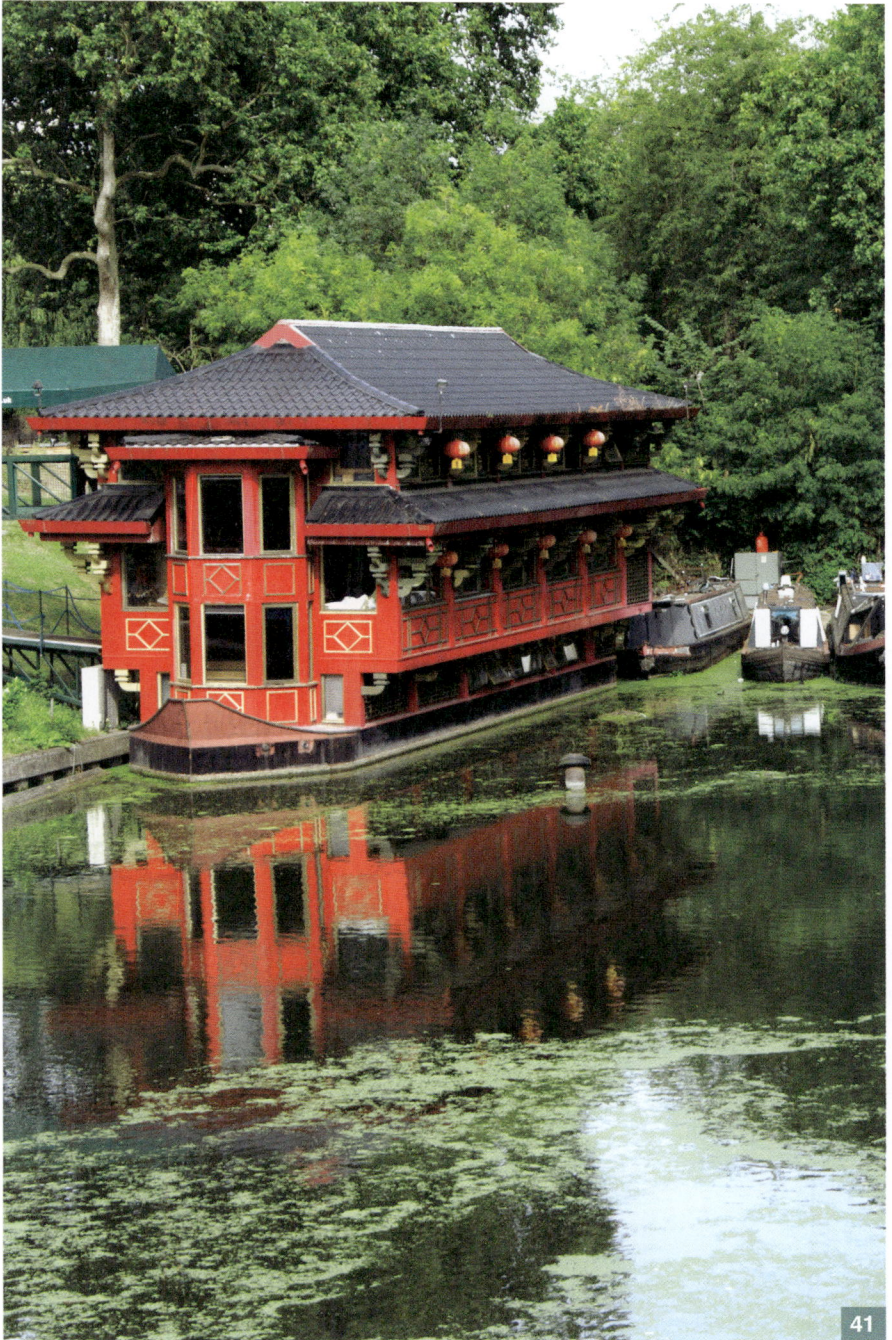

Index

S

T

U

V

W

XYZ

Oceanides, see page 187

Image Credits

About us:

Based in London, Metro is a small independent publishing company with a reputation for producing well-researched and beautifully-designed guides.

London's Hidden Walks Series

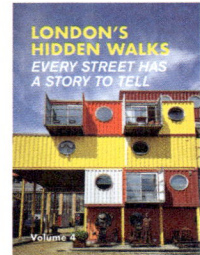

LONDON'S HIDDEN WALKS
THE LONDON WE KNOW IS JUST THE SURFACE!
Volume 1

LONDON'S HIDDEN WALKS
EXPLORE LONDON AND DISCOVER HOW 2000 YEARS OF HISTORY HAVE SHAPED THIS CITY
Volume 2

LONDON'S HIDDEN WALKS
WALK, EXPLORE, DISCOVER...
Volume 3

LONDON'S HIDDEN WALKS
EVERY STREET HAS A STORY TO TELL
Volume 4

A wonderful way to explore this sometimes secretive city." Robert Elms, BBC London 94.9FM

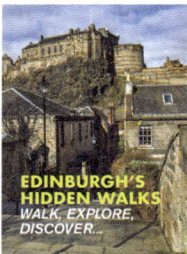

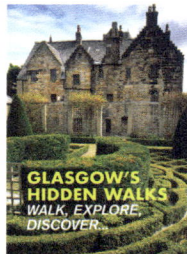

EDINBURGH'S HIDDEN WALKS
WALK, EXPLORE, DISCOVER...

GLASGOW'S HIDDEN WALKS
WALK, EXPLORE, DISCOVER...

To find out more about Metro and order our guides, take a look at our website:

www.metropublications.com

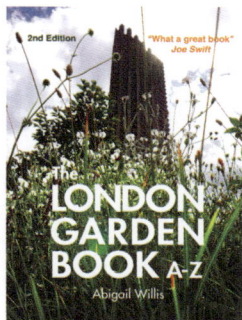

2nd Edition

"What a great book"
Joe Swift

The
LONDON
GARDEN
BOOK A-Z

Abigail Willis

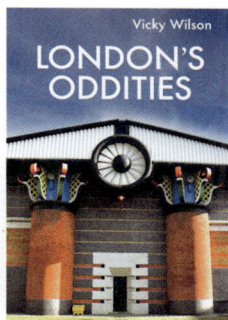

Vicky Wilson

LONDON'S
ODDITIES

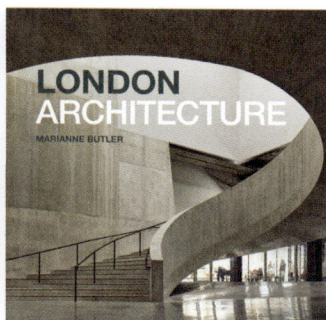

LONDON
ARCHITECTURE

MARIANNE BUTLER

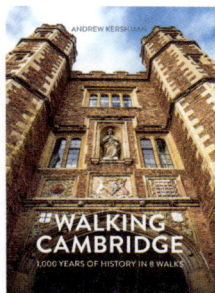

ANDREW KERSHMAN

WALKING
CAMBRIDGE

1,000 YEARS OF HISTORY IN 8 WALKS

ANDREW KERSHMAN

WALKING
BRIGHTON
& HOVE

500 YEARS OF HISTORY IN 8 WALKS

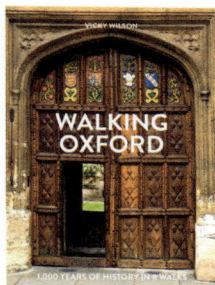

VICKY WILSON

WALKING
OXFORD

1,000 YEARS OF HISTORY IN 8 WALKS

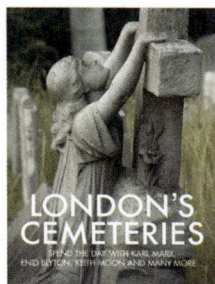

LONDON'S
CEMETERIES

SPEND THE DAY WITH KARL MARX,
ENID BLYTON, KEITH MOON AND MANY MORE

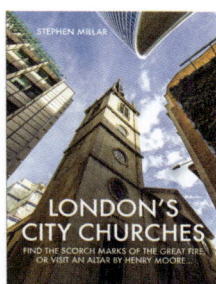

STEPHEN MILLAR

LONDON'S
CITY CHURCHES

FIND THE SCORCH MARKS OF THE GREAT FIRE
OR VISIT AN ALTAR BY HENRY MOORE

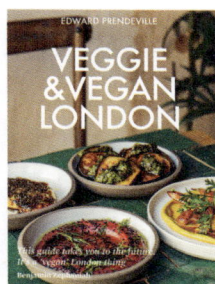

EDWARD PRENDEVILLE

VEGGIE
&VEGAN
LONDON

This guide takes you to the finest
in a 'vegan' London thing
Benjamin Zephaniah

LONDON'S
HOUSES

FROM WORKHOUSE
TO ROYAL PALACE,
COME IN, CLOSE THE
DOOR AND STEP
BACK IN TIME...

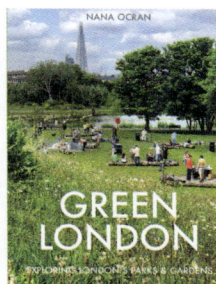

NANA OCRAN

GREEN
LONDON

EXPLORING LONDON'S PARKS & GARDENS

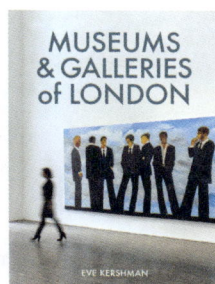

MUSEUMS
& GALLERIES
of LONDON

EVE KERSHMAN